MARC 21 :
CATALOGING FORMAT FOR 21ST CENTURY

R.S. Aswal

Ess Ess Publications

4837/24, Ansari Road, Darya Ganj,
New Delhi-110002
✆ : 23260807
Fax : 23274173
E-mail: essess@del3.vsnl.net.in
url:http://www.essessbooks.com

First Published 2004

ISBN : 81-7000-384-9

Price : Rs. 1200/-

Published by :

Ess Ess Publications

4837/24, Ansari Road, Darya Ganj,
New Delhi - 110 002
Phone : 23260807
Fax : 23274173
E-mail : essess@del3.vsnl.net.in
url: http://www.essessbooks.com

Laser Typesetting:

Mukesh Graphics

L-2/8, DDA Market,
Mangolepuri, New Delhi
Ph. : 27924405

Contents

MARC 21 :
CATALOGING FORMAT FOR 21ST CENTURY

Preface

MARC 21, ISO 2709 communication format is the name of harmonized CAN/MARC and USMARC format, it is designed to facilitate the exchange of bibliographic and related information. It is an International exchange format, and supports the revised Anglo American Cataloguing Rules (AACR-2, 2nd ed., 2002 revision). In this format a proper place is provided for each of the bibliographic information, if a bibliographic record has been marked correctly and saved in a computer data file, computer programs can then be written to search for and retrieve certain types of information within a specific fields, and also to display lists of items meeting the search criteria. Computer can read and interpret the data or information traditionally shown on a catalog card as Author, Title, Subject Heading, and Publishers etc.

ANSI Z39.5 is one of the sets of standards produced to facilitate the interconnection of computer systems. The standards specify formats and procedures governing the exchange of messages between a client and server, enabling the user to search remote databases, identify records which meet specified criteria, and to retrieve some or all of the identified records.

This book consists the MARC 21 concise format for Bibliographic, Authority and Holding Data ...

The Marc 21 Format for Bibliographic Data is designed to be a carrier for bibliographic information about printed and manuscript textual materials, computer files, maps, music, visual materials, missed materials and continuing resources (Prior to 2002, continuing resources were referred to as serials.) Bibliographic data commonly includes titles, name, subjects, notes, publications data, and information about the physical description of an item.

The Marc 21 Format for Authority Data is designed to be a carrier for information concerning the authorized forms of names and subjects to be used as access points in MARC records, the forms of these names, subjects and subdivisions to be used as references to the authorized forms, and the interrelationships among these forms. A name may be used as a main, added, subject added, or series added access entry.

The Marc 21 Format for Holding Data is designed to be a carrier for holding information for three types of bibliographic items that are identified by a code in Leader Position as, Leader/06, code x for Single-part item, Leader/06, code v for Multipart item and Leader/06, code y for Serial item.

Acknowledgements

I wish to express my sincere thanks to Mr. Shankar Singh, Manager, PFC, New Delhi and Mr. K. Santha, Country Manager, VTLS Software Pvt. Ltd., Noida who have given proper guidance and valuable suggestions. My special thanks to my publishers M/s. Ess Ess Publications for their friendly cooperation and untiring efforts in bringing out this book in excellent form.

Readers' views, comments, criticism and suggestions are most welcome.

R.S. Aswal

M.A., M.Lib.I.Sc., PGDCA, PGDM

9/603, Vasundhara
Ghaziabad
Uttar Pradesh
E-mail : rs_aswal@hotmail.com
rajendra_vtls@yahoo.com

1

WHAT IS MARC AND WHY IS IT NECESSARY?

1. WHAT IS MARC?

MARC is a *Machine Readable Cataloging*. The Machine Readable Cataloging format was designed by the Library of Congress in order to allow libraries to convert their card catalogs into a digital format. The advantages of having computerized card catalogs were soon realized, and now all sorts of libraries around the world to provide computerized access to their collections are using MARC. MARC data in transmission format is optimized for processing by computers, so it's not very readable for the normal human.

What is a Machine Readable Cataloging?

Machine-readable: *"Machine-readable"* means that one particular type of machine, a computer, can read and interpret the data in the *cataloging record*.

Cataloging record: *"Cataloging record,"* means a record or the information traditionally shown on a catalog card. The record includes Author, Title, Subject heading, Publisher, etc.

2. WHY IS A MARC RECORD NECESSARY?

Why can't a computer read bibliographical information on a catalog card? The information from a catalog card cannot simply be typed into a computer to produce an automated catalog. The computer needs a means of interpreting the information found on a cataloging record. The MARC record contains a guide to its data, or little "signposts," before each piece of bibliographic information

The place provided for each of these pieces of bibliographic information (author, title, call number, etc.) is called a "field." The records in simpler computer files sometimes have a fixed number of fields, and each field contains a fixed number of characters.

However, to allow proper cataloging of books and other library items, the best file structure allows for records with an unlimited number of fields and unlimited field lengths. This flexibility is necessary because not all titles are the same length. Some books are part of a series, requiring a field for that information, while others have no series statement. And audiovisual items have much longer physical descriptions.

Data *"signposts:"* The computer must have assistance if it is to read and interpret the bibliographic record. If a bibliographic record has been marked correctly and saved in a computer data file, computer programs can then be written to punctuate and format the information correctly for printing a set of catalog cards, or for displaying the information on a computer screen. Programs can be written to search for and retrieve certain types of information within specific fields, and also to display lists of items meeting the search criteria.

Why one standard?

You could devise your own method of organizing the bibliographic information, but you would be isolating your library, limiting its options, and creating much more work for yourself. Using the MARC standard, prevents duplication of work and allows libraries to better share bibliographic resources. Choosing to use MARC enables libraries to acquire cataloging data that is predictable and reliable. If a library were to develop a "home-grown" system that did not use MARC records, it would not be taking advantage of an industry-wide standard whose primary purpose is to foster communication of information.

Using the MARC standard also enables libraries to make use of commercially available library automation systems to manage library operations. Many systems are available for libraries of all sizes and are designed to work with the MARC format. Systems are maintained and improved by the vendor so that libraries can benefit from the latest advances in computer technology. The MARC standard also allows libraries to replace one system with another with the assurance that their data will still be compatible.

3. WHAT IS ELECTRONIC ENCODING:

In the age of online catalogs the content of catalog records must use some kind of electronic encoding scheme in order to be machine-manipulability for searching and display. Encoding allows each part of a record to be set off from every other part. Then computer programs can be written so that each part will be displayed in a certain position according to the wishes of the Programmer. Encoding also allows for access to a catalog record through the creation of search programs that provide for the searching of certain parts of a record (e.g., the author, the title, a subject, etc.)

MARC record must consist of variable length fields with content designators; the record should have a record label, a directory, data field separators and record separators. Within these constraints different implementations of the standard have used different numbered tags and different sub field codes to identify the same type of bibliographic data.

The standard allows for optional indicators to appear after the tag and these are used in many MARC formats to qualify the tag. Within the text of a record, embedded sub field identifiers can be used to further identify data elements. ISO 2709 allows for fixed length data as part of the record label and this is used to store codes relating to material type, language, dates and so on.

4. HOW BIBLIOGRAPHIC INFORMATION SEARCH AND RETRIEVAL

Search and retrieval of bibliographic information over the Internet is particularly designed to accommodate the search and retrieval of MARC records. The protocol can be used to pass searches of MARC fields from a Z39.50 client to a Z39.50 server fronting databases of MARC records; and retrieved records can be returned in MARC format. The Z39.50 protocol uses attributes to identify how the server in a search should treat search terms. The bib-1 attribute set is defined in the standard and within that set the 'Use Attributes' were designed to map onto bibliographic records such as MARC. The bib-1 Use Attribute set does not contain any location or other non-bibliographic data so it is not possible to search on these fields. The protocol does allow for delivery of MARC records in full or abridged versions. There is no attempt in the standard to identify whether records searched or delivered are in the US or UK or other MARC formats. This can cause problems for interoperability in, for example, author personal name searches where the name is stored differently in UK MARC and US; similarly because the 'flavor' of MARC format is not identified it is not easy for the client to vary the display depending on the MARC format of the retrieved records. The standard allows for delivery of holdings information in OPAC records. At present the electronic address (and other non-bibliographic information) is not part of the bib-1 attribute set and is not searchable, however it would be displayed in a retrieved MARC record.

The majority of library automation systems allow for input and retrieval in MARC format, even if the records are stored internally in another format. Any changes in MARC, particularly regarding the display of the 856 fields, will need to be reflected in OPAC software.

5. PROCESSING AND GENERATING MARC WITH PEARL

One thing that would be very useful for the metadata handling communities would be some freely available tool for processing and generating MARC records. Whilst any general-purpose computer language could be used to handle MARC records, the approach this work has taken is to start working on a MARC processing module for Pearl. The reason for this is partly because Pearl offers some nice modularization features and data structures that make producing an Application Programming Interface (API) relatively painless. It is also widely used in the web, library systems and metadata communities for building Common Gateway Interface scripts, OPAC support tools and metadata handling systems

An alpha release of the Pearl module discussed here is available online and interested parties are encouraged to download it and have a play. It's still in a pretty raw state; at the moment it only knows how to read and write BLCMPMARC (the MARC format that we use at Loughborough University) and exports just two subroutines into the program that uses it. These subroutines are Read Marc Record and Write Marc Record and as their names suggest they are used to read and write MARC records.

The Read Marc Record subroutine currently takes a single argument that is the file handle of an input stream to read the MARC record in from. The first thing that this routine does is read the Leader in by reading in the first 24 bytes from the current file pointerposition. It then calls another routine that reads in the directory entries and then loads in the actual field themselves. The information from both the Leader and the fields is then loaded into a Pearl 5 style complex hashed data structure.

6. MARC DEFINITION AND EXPLANATION

"MARC, Machine-Readable Cataloging format is a set of standardized data structures used to describe bibliographic materials that facilitates cooperative cataloging and data exchange in bibliographic information systems." MARC is one standardized set of metadata. It is a structural standard that cannot be duplicated. It is a mature standard, very well accepted internationally, and operates as a protocol for communication of bibliographic data. It is being continuously updated and revised in response to the new and developing technology that must be cataloged. The national library of each country interprets MARC. Until MARC 21, US MARC, Canadian MARC, UK MARC, etc. existed. In the United States, the Library of Congress interprets the rules.

Currently, the USMARC encoding system holds the position of being the one used for bibliographic records in the majority of the world's online catalogs. The remainder of this chapter contains an introduction to this system. Unique information appears at the beginning of the MARC record. Preceding the main bibliographic record parts — which are known to all librarians because of their presence on catalog cards — the MARC record contains some less familiar information. Automated cataloging systems usually provide default data or prompts to help a cataloger input this information.

7. ORIGINATED OF MARC RECORD

MARC (Machine Readable Catalogue Format) originated in the 1960s as a means of exchanging library catalogue records. MARC was a response to the need for a standardized format for co-operating libraries to exchange and share catalogue records. It also met the requirements of national bibliographies for a format for their printed bibliographies, and it was used by bibliographic agencies for their supply of records to libraries. As library systems became computerized, MARC was used in library automation software as the basic for manipulating library records for display and indexing.

Since the mid-1960s an encoding system called MARC, has been used to create electronic catalog records. An excellent history of its development may be found in Deborah Byrne's MARC Manual.1 Other encoding systems have been developed recently in response to the desire to make catalog records available on the Web. SGML (Standard Generalized Markup Language) is an international standard for document markup. It is a set of rules for designing markup languages that describe the structure of a document. The markup languages thus designed are SGML applications called DTDs (Document Type Definitions). DTDs often used for bibliographic data include TEI (Text Encoding Initiative), HTML (Hypertext Markup Language), and EAD (Encoded Archival Description). A DTD for MARC records has been developed, and at this writing is in experimental stages. XML (Extensible Markup Language), a subset of SGML that adds some features that solves earlier problems with SGML and HTML. It is gaining in use.

8. FORMAT OF A MARC RECORD

As the original MARC records were developed in the 1960's and the basic layout of the record has remained largely unchanged since then, the format of a MARC record owes a lot to the state of computer technology at that time. MARC is a binary format designed for writing to magnetic tape. It contains enough information to allow machines with what we would now consider to be very small memories to load just the parts of a MARC record that they are interested in whilst skipping over the rest. It was also designed with some of the popular computer languages of the time in mind, with a fixed length record header that would be easy to read into the data structures available. Structurally therefore MARC is quite simple; the complexity is derived from the fact that it can carry a wide variety of information in precise and detailed formats (such as AACR2 rules).

The basic layout of a MARC record is to first have a 24-byte leader, then a variable number of *directory* entries and then a variable number of variable sized *fields*. The fields are sometimes split into variable *control field* and variable *data fields*. The layout of a whole MARC record is thus:

```
+--------+-----------+-------------------------+----------------------+
| Leader | Directory | Variable Control Fields | Variable Data Fields|
+--------+-----------+-------------------------+----------------------+
```

The leader is designed to provide basic information about the size of the whole MARC record, the size of some of the data structures in the directory and data fields and the some very basic information about type of work that the MARC record is describing.

Leader: The leader is the first 24 characters of the record. Each position has an assigned meaning, but much of the information in the leader is for computer use. MARC record creation and editing programs usually provide a window or prompts to assist the cataloger in filling in any leader data elements that require input.

Directory: MARC records are called "tagged" records. Before it becomes a tagged record, a MARC record (in what is called the MARC communications format), looks very different — like one long run-on sentence. In the communications format, tags do not precede the fields. However, immediately following the leader is a block of data called a directory. This directory tells what tags are in the record and where they are placed (by a count of the characters to the position where each field begins). The directory is constructed (by computer) from the bibliographic record, based on the cataloging information, and, if any of the cataloging information is altered, can be reconstructed in the same way.

Variable control field: The 008 field is referred to as Fixed-Length Data Elements, or Fixed Field Codes. Its 40 characters contain important information, but in an abbreviated form. Although it is not yet used to its fullest in online catalog systems, this field can be used to identify and retrieve records matching specific criteria.

For example, there is a code in this field to indicate whether a book is large-print, a code to identify the country of publication, a code to identify juvenile materials, a code to indicate the language of the text, and so on.

Variable Data Fields:

Data in the record is contained in fields identified by a three-digit tag. Fields containing data with a similar function is organized into groups identified by the first number in the tag:

9. STANDARDIZATIONS AND EASE OF CREATION

The proliferation of MARC formats was possible because the 'MARC standard' ISO 2709 Format for bibliographic information interchange on magnetic tape only governs record structure or encoding, it does not prescribe the content of the record within that structure. The record content of different MARC formats is defined in 'de facto' standards, usually controlled by national libraries; these take the form of cataloguing manuals outlining the formats and offering guidelines for their use.

There is a move towards convergence of MARC formats: English-speaking countries are converging to USMARC; European countries are looking to UNIMARC to map divergent MARC formats. Convergence of other national MARC formats with USMARC mean that developments within USMARC are becoming increasingly influential. The critical mass of libraries using this format mean that it is possible for projects such as Interact to find interested participants. The large numbers of USMARC users could be used as leverage with library automation system vendors for inclusion of format changes to be applied in OPACs, although this is an outstanding problem for Interact participants.

The creation of high quality MARC records requires training and experience in the use of cataloguing rules. Although the input of data to a record can be automated, the cataloguer needs to view the resource in some detail, and then interpret cataloguing rules before

Formatting the required information correctly in the MARC record. Within libraries specialist staff is assigned to cataloguing, they are often familiar with only one national format and indeed often specialize by material type (e.g. by subject area or format).

10. CONCLUSION

Shared cataloging information — shared bibliographic records — has been a reality for a number of years. Many librarians have chosen to maximize limited resources by acquiring cataloging data rather than creating it themselves. For almost a century they have been able to order sets of catalog cards for their new books from the Library of Congress, or, more recently, from book jobbers.

Others typed their own cards, using the Cataloging in Publication (CIP) data found on the verso of the title page of many books. Librarians also adapted the partial or full cataloging records printed in library journals or in bibliographies.

Once computers became available, it was no longer necessary for librarians everywhere to constantly "reinvent the wheel." Why should hundreds of catalogers each use valuable time to compose nearly identical cataloging records for the same item when one cataloger could do it and share the record that had been created? Why should hundreds of typists retype that same record on cards when a computer could be programmed to print them?

After the MARC record was developed, libraries shared in the benefits of machine-readable cataloging whether they had an online system or not. The cards, purchased from the Library of Congress or from a jobber, were computer-printed from bibliographic records based on Library of Congress MARC files.

Colleges and universities with large library budgets joined bibliographic utilities such as OCLC, WLN, RLIN, and A-G Canada. For an on-going fee plus communication costs, their technical service departments went online with the utilities' powerful mainframe computers. These ventures allowed those libraries to use and contribute MARC records. Catalog cards could be ordered, and a printer could be hooked up to the system to receive data over the phone lines and print book labels.

Now we are in an exciting age when powerful, inexpensive computers are available for the management of library operations in all types and sizes of libraries. Computer software programs allow an individual library to have its own self-contained circulation system or online public access catalog. These programs often can read, store, and print MARC records. Today's computers use hard disks and floppy disks for storage of information rather than the tape drives used by mainframe computers. For computers, data is commonly sent and received on floppy disks. From the floppy disks, bibliographic records are uploaded to the stationary hard disk.

As library automation technology changes and as cataloging needs change, the MARC 21 formats and related MARC 21 documentation are changing also. Although the Library of Congress originally developed the MARC format and the MARC 21 format documentation is maintained and published there, the Library does not make changes or revisions unilaterally.

More recently, specifications have been developed also for the distribution of MARC records via file transfer (FTP). The diskette and FTP distribution specifications first appeared in the 1994 edition of MARC 21 specifications.

2

TYPES OF MARC FORMAT AND THEIR DESIGNATION

1. COMMON COMMUNICATION FORMAT (CCF)

CCF was developed by Unesco/UNISIST and is being implemented primarily in developing countries where MARC does not have such a strong. This format has been used for exporting the data from MATA DATA format or other MARC format.

2. USMARC

USMARC - The USMARC formats are (American) standards for the representation and communication of bibliographic and related information in machine-readable form. Formats are defined for five types of data: bibliographic, holdings, authority, classification, and community information.

Environment of use

The record structure of USMARC, as for all MARC formats, adheres to ISO 2709: 1981. This appears also as a national standard in the US, ANSI Z39.2.

The content of the USMARC record is not governed by an international standard, but by a cataloguing manual produced by the Library of Congress. The Library of Congress and additions issue the USMARC manual and the Library of Congress on the advice of the US MARC ADVISORY GROUP controls amendments. This Group is made up of MARBI (The American Library

Association's Machine-Readable Bibliographic Information Committee) and representatives from the US National Libraries. the National Library of Canada, the National Library of Australia, large bibliographic utilities (OCLC and RLIN), special library associations and library system vendors. The Library of Congress regularly publish discussion documents and proposals for comment which are considered at the twice yearly MARC Advisory Group meetings and, if agreed, are published occasionally as updates to the MARC format.

Constituency of use

Traditionally the library community in the US has used USMARC. Over recent years the national libraries of Canada and Australia have also adopted USMARC rather than maintaining separate formats. In addition the British Library have agreed on a timescale for a convergence programmed with USMARC (see UKMARC section for details). Within the US the dominant bibliographic utility, OCLC, uses USMARC with some added variants. Widespread use of USMARC in the US enables sharing of cataloguing effort between the majority of academic and public libraries.

Over the last five years the USMARC community has been considering and adopting changes to the format to allow for cataloguing of electronic networked resources. At the start this was seen as an extension of the work done in the 1980s to describe computer files. The formats had become increasingly inadequate as a means of describing networked resources, which needed to include details of access methods and addresses. After considerable debate within the USMARC community a new field, 856, has been adopted for the location of electronic resources. The Library of Congress has issued guidelines for its use. Changes for describing online services are still under consideration.

The Interact project has been instrumental in progressing format development in this area. This is a project, which started in July 1995 for cataloguing Internet resources, and the timescale has recently been extended. It is led by OCLC with partial funding from the US Department of Education. The project involves participation of 200 libraries more than 60% of which are academic libraries; almost all active participants being in the US.

The Interact project has catalogued a total of approximately 6000 resources to date. This relatively small number (as a comparison during a similar period OCLC's Net First database added 50,000 records, and WebCrawler global search services many millions) reflects the co-operating libraries selection criteria. Libraries select only those resources they wish to integrate with their MARC library catalogues, and they select resources only if they are of sufficient quality and stability to warrant the effort of cataloguing. The project is by no means an attempt to 'catalogue the Internet'. There has been extended a discussion on the Interact mailing list on their criteria for selection of material. Many libraries intend to include in their catalogue only locally available resources i.e. those electronic resources held on a local server which are 'owned' or 'managed' by their own institution.

Standardizations

The encoding of USMARC adheres to ISO 2709 in the same way as other MARC formats. The specific USMARC format is governed by a 'de facto' standard in the form of the USMARC manual produced by the Library of Congress. There is no move to formalize this as an international standard.

Encoding & Designation

USMARC is an implementation of ISO 2709. USMARC records are written in the extended ASCII character set. The records consist of the leader, the directory and the data content fields. The leader consists of fixed fields containing coded data defining parameters for the processing of the record (such as the length of the directory entry), the directory contains entries listing the tag, starting location and length of each field in the record. The data content of the record is continued in fields of two types: variable control fields (fixed fields) and variable data fields.

USMARC formats are defined for three data types: bibliographic, holdings and authority records. This report will deal with the bibliographic record only. The USMARC Format for Bibliographic Data is designed for the description of different forms of bibliographic material: books, archives and manuscripts, computer files, maps, music, visual materials, serials. At one stage separate formats existed for each material type, but these have now been integrated.

Data in the record is contained in fields identified by a three-digit tag. Fields containing data with a similar function is organized into groups identified by the first number in the tag:

* 0XX control numbers, provenance
* 1XX main entry
* 2XX titles and related information
* 3XX physical description
* 4XX series statements
* 5XX notes
* 6XX subject access
* 7XX added entries; linking fields
* 8XX series added entries
* 9XX reserved for local fields

The remaining numbers in the tags indicate further sub-division of content, and in general parallel content designation is preserved across the groups e.g.

* X00 personal author
* X10 corporate name
* X11 meeting name
* X30 uniform title

Further content designation is identified by a two-character indicator following the tag, and by a two character sub-field markers. Within this scheme the digit 9 is used to indicate a local implementation. Most fields, and some sub-fields can be repeated.

The 0XX fields in the USMARC record contain fixed length data for information such as material type, date of publication, form, and language.

Basic descriptive elements

The MARC record is highly developed for bibliographic and bibliographic-like data.

USMARC developed in the context of library cataloguing. It therefore deals with the various bibliographic data elements in a detailed way. However it is important to note that the content of fields is governed by cataloguing rules. USMARC is designed to provide a formatted display of 'a catalogue card' giving a description of the resource as well as to provide access for the purposes of information retrieval. The Anglo American Cataloguing Rules, and the ISBD govern the rules for the content within fields. So the content of the 1XX and 7XX tag ranges are defined in terms of the cataloguing concepts main and added entries and, depending on their relationship with the work, an author might appear in one or the other ranges. Similarly an author could be defined as a personal author, corporate author or meeting name and this will affect the indicator value.

In addition USMARC format has implications for the authority control of the data content. Normally the data in fields 1XX, 4XX, 6XX, 7XX, 8XX will be subject to authority control.

In order to integrate cataloguing, of network resources into existing legacy USMARC databases, it is necessary to create bibliographic data elements according to AACR2. As the Interact project has discovered, this requires further extension of the cataloguing rules and extended guidelines if it is to be done in a standardized way.

Although library-cataloguing data is still by far the most predominant use for USMARC, there are possibilities for use as a 'vehicle' for metadata created to other standards such as GILS or Dublin Core. MARBI Discussion to raises some of the problems in such attempts, and in particular looks at the problem of defining a generic author field in USMARC.

Specific 6XX tags are used for different controlled subject heading schemes e.g. Library of Congress subject headings, Mesh etc.

Uniform Resource Locator

The 856 fields have been approved for URL. This field is designed to contain location and access information to make a connection, locate and retrieve an electronic document. Guidelines for the use of the 856 fields have been issued by MARBI. This field may be repeated, and more than one access method may be used.

The 856 fields is a structured field with sub fields describing method of access, and it can be repeated to allow for different access methods. The 856 indicator details the mode of access over the network (e-mail, FTP, Telnet, dial up) or if none of these (e.g. HTTP, gopher, wais, prospero) then the mode can be defined in a sub field. Within the 856-field description of access methods, other than those taken from the indicator, follow the controlled vocabulary for Internet media types (also known as MIME types).

Resource format and technical characteristics

Non-bibliographic data is unstructured and tends to be placed in notes fields. The MARBI Discussion presented a preliminary list of data elements to describe network information resources. This is developed in MARBI Discussion Paper No 54 (Providing Access to Online Information Resources). These papers map the required data elements onto USMARC fields and sub fields. For example there are proposals for:

* Type of resource 256$a File characteristics
* Frequency of update 310$a Current frequency
* Other providers of a database 582$a Related Computer File Note
* The Interact project has also involved discussion on its mailing list of the use of various other fields in this context. For example:
* Detailed contents e.g. list of web links 505 $a Contents note

Ability to represent relationships between objects

USMARC uses tagged links to indicate relationships between

parts of a collected work. Tags can also be used to specify other relationships e.g. continued as; replaced by.

Although format integration should be completed by spring 1996, the future may hold some interesting developments. In November 1994, Sarah E. Thomas of the Library of Congress announced that representatives of the British Library, the Library of Congress, and the National Library of Canada met to discuss the future alignment of CAN/MARC, UKMARC, and USMARC into a common MARC format. It is envisioned that a unified MARC format would assist:

* catalogers - by facilitating timely record sharing;
* collection development - by providing earlier and more accurate access to the Bibliographic records representing recently published works;
* reference librarians - by enabling enhanced international cross-catalog searching;
* Library systems vendors - by creating one unified format to support instead of three;
* MARC format developers - by establishing a solid unified foundation on which to propose augmentation.

While USMARC and CAN/MARC specifications are very close already, a number of differences have been identified, especially in coding of fixed fields. Greater variations exist between USMARC and UKMARC, although the similarity of the cataloging traditions should assist with format alignment. The original group from the three national libraries plan on meeting in December 1995 to reevaluate the timetable and to chart the path for the introduction of more detailed proposals in 1996.

The implementation of the current round of format integration has been slow and frustrating at times. In fact, since it affects only a small number of cataloging records, some librarians have questioned the value of the implementation. However, the standardization present with USMARC format integration offers many long-range benefits in terms of format unity, system maintenance, training of new catalogers, more precise searching by material type increased flexibility in description, and more concise documentation Time will tell if format integration is the ultimate answer to the question of how to best

3. UKMARC

The UKMARC format is the standard developed, managed and promoted by the British Library and applied by the Library in its bibliographic products and services and by many UK libraries in their bibliographic processing operations. (UKMARC Web Page, British Library National Bibliographic Service (NBS), 1999)

There are many similarities in the structure and content of USMARC and UKMARC. However the differences are significant and sufficient to make high quality conversion between the two formats complex. In addition the use of variants in the UK (e.g.. BLCMP and SLSMARC) and the minor differences in the US (USMARC and OCLCMARC) means high quality conversion between particular datasets need apply additional algorithms. UKMARC and USMARC are set to converge: the impact of this is not yet clear.

Given the planned changes to UKMARC, this review will give only a brief overview.

Documentation

In the UK the national standard appears as BS 4748: 1982. (*Specification for format for bibliographic information interchange on magnetic tape*. London: British Standards Institution). The *UKMARC Manual* (2nd ed. 1980) is published by the British Library and consists of a loose-leaf publication with several updates. The British Library National Bibliographic Service (NBS) is responsible for the UKMARC format. There are less complex procedures for agreeing amendments than for USMARC. The British Library (BL) introduced consultation procedures in 1992 whereby BL's proposals initially go for comment to the Book Industry Commission (BIC) Bibliographic Standards Working Party Technical Subgroup. The Subgroup is made up of UK representatives of the different library sectors, book suppliers, bibliographic utilities that are also library system vendors, as well as the NBS. This is followed by a period of public consultation with proposals included in the BL *Interface NBS Technical Bulletin*. After a period for comment the proposals may be adopted according to the final decision of the BL.

Constituency of use

Within the UK the majority of libraries have used UKMARC. In recent years some academic and national research libraries have moved to USMARC.

Comments

The 856 fields have not yet been incorporated into UKMARC. At present there is an outstanding proposal from the British Library to adopt the USMARC 856 field as part of the convergence between UK and USMARC. This proposal will be considered in 1996 as part of the consultation procedure outlined above. Discussion of the detailed implications of convergence are now starting, particularly on the UKMARC e-mail list. As yet there has been little significant discussion regarding the more specific issue of cataloguing Internet resources using UKMARC.

Implementations

LINK, the emergent replacement to BUBL, and the associated Catriona project are planning to catalogue electronic resources using UKMARC. The few other UK libraries who are investigating cataloguing electronic resources tend to be using USMARC.

There are many similarities in the structure and content of USMARC and UKMARC. However the differences are significant and sufficient to make high quality conversion between the two formats complex. In addition the use of variants in the UK (e.g.. BLCMP and SLSMARC) and the minor differences in the US (USMARC and OCLCMARC) means high quality conversion between particular datasets need apply additional algorithms. UKMARC and USMARC are set to converge: the impact of this is not yet clear. Given the planned changes to UKMARC, this review will give only a brief overview.

ENVIRONMENT OF USE

In the UK the national standard appears as BS 4748: 1982 (*Specification for format for bibliographic information interchange on magnetic tape* London: British Standards Institution) The *UKMARC Manual* (2nd ed. 1980) is published by the British Library and consists of a loose-leaf publication with several updates. The British Library National Bibliographic Service (NBS) is responsible for the UKMARC format. There are less complex procedures for agreeing amendments than for USMARC. The British Library (BL) introduced consultation procedures in 1992 whereby BL's proposals initially go for comment to the Book Industry Commission (BIC) Bibliographic Standards Working Party Technical Subgroup. The Subgroup is made up of UK representatives of the different library sectors, book suppliers, bibliographic utilities that are also library system vendors, as well as the NBS. This is followed by a period of public consultation with proposals included in the BL *Interface NBS Technical Bulletin*. After a period for comment the proposals may be adopted according to the final decision of the BL.

Within the UK the majority of libraries have used UKMARC In recent years some academic and national research libraries have moved to USMARC.

4. CANMARC

Can MARC - The Canadian MARC Communication Formats serve as the common standard for the exchange of machine-readable authority, bibliographic, classification, and holdings data in Canada. (Introduction to CAN/MARC, National Library of Canada, 1998)

Note: Can MARC and USMARC have been harmonized into MARC21. However, continued support for these record types has been provided to ensure backwards compatibility. US marc should be used when the user specifically desires MARC21.

Introduction

CANMARC also uses the |w sub field code, but has authorized different values for the sub field. These values **must** be converted to USMARC format, when deriving an authority record from the NLC authorities database.

Each 4XX or 5XX field will have a control sub field |**w** to provide control information at the field level. This sub field is fixed in length at *five* characters and is not repeatable. The fill character may be used in the sub field |**w** when the institution creating the record chooses not to encode a given position in the sub field.

Conversion

CANMARC contains five characters where the USMARC coding contains four. Because there is no equivalent in USMARC for the CANMARC doe 5 (Byt3 4), it has been stripped out of the records received from the National Library of Canada.

A certain amount of machine translation has been performed on this sub field. However, since a certain amount of judgement must be exercised in translating this information, some work will still have to be done at the time an authority record is derived into the Queen's database.

Codes which are given a *different* meaning in CANMARC than they are in USMARC are indicated with a *. The USMARC version, if there is one, will be given in brackets following the CANMARC explanation. Codes, which are given in addition to the ones used in USMARC, are indicated with **.

Because of the restrictions of Code 2 (Byte 1), all NLC records contain a |w sub field in *all* of the 4XX or 5XX fields. In many cases it will be possible to delete the sub field entirely. Moreover, NLC uses all positions of the sub field in every case (i.e. every |w sub field is four positions long, after conversion). When editing an NLC record, it may be possible to shorten the |w sub field, in the cases where it is still needed.

5. UNIMARC

UniMARC - The primary purpose of UniMARC is to facilitate the international exchange of bibliographic data in machine-readable form between national bibliographic agencies. UNIMARC may also be used as a model for the development of new machine-readable bibliographic formats. (IFLA Universal Bibliographic Control and International MARC Core Programme (UBCIM), 1994)

Environment of use

UNIMARC conforms to the ISO 2709 standard and to ISBD standards. UNIMARC: (the Universal MARC Format) was developed and published in 1977.

The latest edition of the UNIMARC Manual (2nd edition) was published in 1994.

A draft version of the UNIMARC Guideline 3 for Computer Files was issued in June 1995. These guidelines result from meetings of the IFLA Permanent UNIMARC Committee and the requirements of the International Standard Bibliographic Description for Computer Files, ISBD (CF). A new draft of this Guideline is expected in July 1996. (The changes in the draft of the 2nd ed. of ISBD (CF), now being circulated for comment, will be applied to UNIMARC).

Constituency of use

The proliferation of national formats and the difficulty that resulted for the exchange of data was the main reason for the creation of an international MARC format which would accept, in principle, records created in any MARC format and act as a common format in terms of conversion. Since 1977 several national libraries have undertaken projects to convert from an existing national format to UNIMARC or have adapted UNIMARC for their national format needs. It covers monographs, serials, and cartographic materials, music, sound recordings, graphics, projected and video material, with provisional fields for computer files.

Ease of creation

UNIMARC was first developed as an exchange format and offers several options for description, so that records created on the basis of different cataloguing rules can all be included.

Standardizations

The Permanent UNIMARC Committee (PUC), under the

auspices of the IFLA Universal Bibliographic Control and International MARC (UBCIM) Programme, supervises the format. Changes will be made only through the Permanent UNIMARC Committee. The content is described in the UNIMARC Manual (latest ed. 1994).

Although the PUC tries to maintain the standard, libraries implement the format in different ways, e.g. linking (4XX) can be used or not. In particular French libraries work with a variety of interpretations of the format.

Designation

Data in the records is contained in fields identified by a three-digit tag. Fields containing data with a similar function is organized into groups identified by the first number in the tag. UNIMARC consists of the following nine blocks:

- 0XX Identification block
- 1XX Coded information block
- 2XX Descriptive information block
- 3XX Notes block
- 4XX Linking entry block
- 5XX Related title block
- 6XX Subject analysis block
- 7XX Intellectual responsibility block
- 8XX International use block
- 9XX National use block

Basic descriptive elements

UNIMARC deals with all the necessary bibliographic data. The following will concentrate on the adaptation of the format to enable input of data pertaining to online resources. The probable need for additional fields or content designators and for redefinition of existing fields in the near future is acknowledged. Those should be brought to the attention of the IFLA UBCIM Programme Office. Fields of which the use for computer files is specified include:

- Title (field 200): Title as it appears on container, box, opening screen, formal title screen, first display of information, header of the file etc.
- Parallel title (field 510): Title in another language appearing on the computer file.
- Author(s) (fields 200$f $g and/or 700, 701, 710, 711): Authors, programmers of the computer files as listed on the computer file.
- Author affiliation(s) (fields 700$p, 701$p, 710$p, 711$p): Institutional affiliations of the authors, programmers at the time the computer files were written or programmed.
- Edition statement (field 205): Any word or phrase indicating that the information was available previously in a different form.
- Publication, distribution (field 210).
- Physical description of the computer file (fields 215, 230): To be omitted for remotely accessed computer files, because there is no physical item.
- Accompanying materials (fields 215, 307): User handbooks.
- Series (fields 225, 410).
- Availability information (fields 345, 010, 011): Price units, stock number, agency for ordering a copy of the computer files.

Apart from the above-mentioned fields, some of the (extra) information should be put in different fields of the Note block (3XX). This concerns the following data:

- Type of computer file (field 336)
- Technical details of computer file (field 337)
- Notes pertaining to title and statement of responsibility (field 304)
- Notes pertaining to edition: (Licensed by...) (field 305)
- Notes pertaining to publication, distribution (Shareware, etc.) (Field 306)

- Notes pertaining to series (field 308)
- Notes pertaining to availability (field 310)
- Contents notes
- Users/Intended audience note

The 1XX block provides fields for:

- Coded data
- Qualifying data
- Language of computer file
- Target audience
- Publication date
- Country of publication or production
- Coded data relating to computer files: program, representational, textual.

Subject description

The 6XX Subject analysis block is used for subject data constructed according to various systems, both verbal and notational (e.g. UDC, DDC, Library of Congress Classification).

Uniform Resource Locator

In Guideline 3 no special field is provided yet for information pertaining to location. USMARC 856 is being examined to see if it can be adopted for UNIMARC.

Resource format and technical characteristics

Field 135 is the provisional Coded Data Field for Computer Files. For type of computer file and technical details fields 336 and 337 in the Notes block are defined.

- In field 135, a one-character code indicates the type of data file:
- a = numeric
- b = computer program(s)
- c = representational (pictorial or graphic information)

- d = text
- u = unknown
- v = combination
- z = other
- Type of computer file (field 336): contains information characterizing the type of computer file. In addition to a general descriptor (e.g. text, computer program, numeric), more specific information, such as the form or genre of textual material (e.g. biography, dictionaries, indexes) may be recorded in this field.

  Technical details note (field 337): This field is used to record technical information about a computer file, such as the presence or absence of certain kinds of codes or the physical characteristics of the file (e.g. recording densities, parity, or blocking factors). For software, data such as the software programming language, the number of source program statements, computer requirements (e.g. computer manufacturer and model, operating system, or memory requirements), and peripheral requirements (e.g. number of tape drives, number of disk or drum units, number of terminals, or other peripheral devices, support software or related equipment) can be recorded.

Host administrative details

No fields are specified for information pertaining to the host. USMARC practice may be adopted for UNIMARC.

Administrative metadata

There are no fields for record review date and creation date.

Provenance/source

Availability information is included in fields 345 (Acquisition information note), 010 (ISBN), 011 (ISSN). Further notes pertaining to availability go in field 310 (Notes pertaining to binding and availability).

Terms of availability/copyright

The relevant USMARC fields are being examined for this purpose.

Field 801 (Originating Source), sub field $g, contains an abbreviation for the cataloguing code used for bibliographic description and access. The Manual gives a list of the accepted codes in an appendix. Other codes may be registered with the IFLA UBCIM Programme.

Encoding

For data interchange in UNIMARC, ISO character set standards should be used.

Multi-lingual issues

Character positions 26-29 and 30-33 of field 100 sub field $a are used to designate the default and additional graphic character sets used in the record. Sets approved for use with UNIMARC are:

- ISO 646 (IRV), Basic Latin set
- ISO 5426-1980, Extended Latin set
- ISO Registration #37, Basic Cyrillic set
- ISO DIS 5427, Extended Cyrillic set
- ISO 5428-1980, Greek set
- ISO 6438-1983, African coded character set

Ability to represent relationships between objects

The 4XX block is reserved for making tagged links to indicate relationship between objects.

Fullness

UNIMARC is a more concise version of the MARC format and compared with USMARC offers less richness of data, e.g. in description of materials.

The Guideline for Computer Files seem to have been formulated with offline products in minds i.e. CD-ROMS, diskettes.

No special fields such as URLs are specified for metadata specific for networked resources. In a table showing the data elements prescribed by ISBD (CF) and their corresponding UNIMARC locations, 'Access points: Technical details access' is referred to blocks 6XX and 7XX. The Guidelines are still being developed to be better suited for online materials as well.

Implementations

In International Cataloguing and Bibliographic Control (vol. 24, no 4, oct/dec 1995), a quarterly published by the IFLA/UBCIM programme, an overview is given of international UNIMARC Users and Experts. This list is the result of a questionnaire sent out in 1993 and updated in 1995. 35 of the total of 62 institutions that had replied indicated that they were currently using the UNIMARC format. Thirty of those institutions are located in European countries, the other five in the USA (Library of Congress), China (National Library), India (National Library), Japan (National Diet Library), South Africa (The State Library)

Central and East European countries especially seem to be interested in formats that guarantee easy access to international communities and in recent years there has been a growing interest in UNIMARC.

The need for easy exchange of information is recognized within the MARC communities. There is a programme for the harmonization of the national MARC formats of Canada (CANMARC), the UK (UKMARC) and the United States (USMARC). Also, the British Library and the Library of Congress are committed to the development of UNIMARC. The Commission of the European Communities funded Use MARCON (User Controlled Generic MARC Converter) project aims to develop a toolbox capable of converting bibliographic records from any MARC format into any other MARC format through a central conversion format.

6. DUBLIN CORE META DATA

Background

The Dublin core is a proposed minimal set of data elements for describing network-accessible materials. It was initially proposed at a workshop held in March 1995 at Dublin, Ohio. Workshop participants included librarians and archivists, researchers, computer and information scientists, software developers, publishers, and members of Internet Engineering Task Force (IETF) working groups. Their intent was to suggest a minimal set of data elements that might be provided by the creators or publishers of digital objects and included in, or linked to, the objects themselves.

Metadata included with digital materials has significant potential as a source of information about those materials. Such metadata can be used as the basis for designing an information storage and retrieval system. Alternative, the metadata can be imported into existing data structures (such as USMARC bibliographic records) and used by existing information storage and retrieval systems.

The specific interest of the Committee on Cataloging: Description and Access is in the use of metadata as a source of information for standard descriptive cataloging records that conform to the *Anglo-American Cataloguing Rules*. As various metadata standards have been emerging in recent years, the Committee began to take a formal interest. The first result of that interest was a position paper by Sherry Kelley and Brad Eden, which looked at one particularly relevant metadata standard, the specifications for a file header for electronic texts encoded according to the Text Encoding Initiative.

Following a recommendation in the position paper, the Committee appointed a Task Force on the Relationship of the TEI Header and the Cataloging Rules. Quickly realizing that the TEI Header was but one metadata scheme among many, the Committee expanded the Task Force's charge to include other metadata schemes. The Task Force has been re-named Task Force on Metadata and the Cataloging Rules. Part of the Task Force's charge is to investigate "the proposed Dublin Metadata Core Element Set and evaluate [e] its use as a source of information for cataloging." This Web page is intended to serve as the focus for that investigation and evaluation.

An Invitation

The best way to investigate and evaluate the usefulness of Dublin Core metadata as a source of cataloging information is to work through some examples. The process that will be followed is outlined below. Briefly, it involves selecting an HTML document, filling in a template with the appropriate metadata, then putting that same data into a USMARC record work form, and commenting on the results.

3

MARC 21 Formats: FOR THE 21st CENTURY

1. INTRODUCTION

The MARC 21 formats are standards for the representation and communication of bibliographic and related information in machine-readable form. A MARC record involves three elements: the record structure, the content designation, and the data content of the record. The structure of MARC records is an implementation of national and international standards, e.g., Information Interchange Format (ANSI Z39.2) and Format for Information Exchange (ISO 2709). Content designation, the codes and conventions established to identify explicitly and characterize further the data elements within a record and to support the manipulation of those data, is defined in the MARC 21 formats. The content of most data elements is defined by standards outside the formats, e.g., Anglo-American Cataloguing Rules, Library of Congress Subject Headings, and National Library of Medicine Classification. The content of other data elements, e.g., coded data section 9 below), is defined in the MARC 21 formats. A MARC 21 format is a set of codes and content designators defined for encoding machine-readable records. Formats are defined for five types of data: bibliographic, holdings, authority, classification, and community information.

MARC 21 Format for Bibliographic Data contains format specifications for encoding data elements needed to describe, retrieve, and control various forms of bibliographic material. It is an integrated format defined for the identification and description of different forms of bibliographic material. MARC 21 specifications are defined for books, serials, computer files, maps, music, visual materials, and mixed material. With the full integration of the previously discrete bibliographic formats, consistent definition and usage are maintained for different forms of material.

MARC 21 Format for Holdings Data contains format specifications for encoding data elements pertinent to holdings and location data for all forms of material.

MARC 21 Format for Authority Data contains format specifications for encoding data elements that identify or control the content and content designation of those portions of a bibliographic record that may be subject to authority control.

MARC 21 Format for Classification Data contains format specifications for encoding data elements related to classification numbers and the captions associated with them. Classification records are used for the maintenance and development of classification schemes.

MARC 21 Format for Community Information provides format specifications for records containing information about events, programs, services, etc. so that this information can be integrated into the same public access catalogs as data in other record types.

1. WHAT IS MARC 21?

MARC 21 is the new name of the harmonized CAN/MARC and USMARC formats.

From 1994-1997, the Library of Congress and the National Library of Canada worked with their user communities, through their MARC committees, to reconcile format differences. In Canada, the Canadian Committee on MARC represents the user community on MARC format issues. MARC 21 is the result of the activity undertaken to align CAN/MARC and USMARC. It represents the continuation of the CAN/MARC and USMARC formats in a single edition with a new name, The MARC 21 Formats.

2. BACKGROUND AND PRINCIPLES

As library automation technology changes and as cataloging needs change, the MARC 21 formats and related MARC 21 documentation are changing also. Although the Library of Congress originally developed the MARC format and the MARC 21 format documentation is maintained and published there, the Library does not make changes or revisions unilaterally.

Two groups, which are responsible for reviewing and revising MARC 21 format documentation, are MARBI and the MARC Advisory Committee. The Machine-Readable Bibliographic Information (MARBI) Committee is a committee of the American Library Association (ALA) and is composed of three representatives from each of the three function-oriented divisions of ALA: ALCTS (technical services function); LITA (automation); and RUSA (reference). ALA tries to assure that all types of expertise are represented on MARBI. The MARC Advisory Committee is composed of representatives from the national libraries, the bibliographic utilities, vendor groups, and other library and scholarly associations. MARBI meets in conjunction with the MARC Advisory Committee at each ALA conference (annual and mid-winter). The major activity of the Committee is the review of discussion papers and proposals submitted by or through the Library of Congress for changes or additions to existing MARC formats, or the development of new MARC format support in emerging areas.

In 1987, the Library of Congress issued the first edition of the document MARC 21 Specifications for Record Structure, Character Sets, and Exchange Media to aid libraries and other organizations that create or acquire MARC 21 records. Subsequent editions were published in 1990, 1994, and 2000. This document provides technical information on the structure of MARC records, the character sets used in MARC records, and the format for distribution media for MARC 21 records. It is intended for the use of personnel involved in the design and maintenance of systems for the exchange and processing of MARC records.

With the proliferation of computer systems in libraries, it became apparent that a standard was also needed for the exchange of MARC records on floppy diskette. Working closely with representatives from book and data vendors and library automation systems vendors, MARBI and the Advisory Committee recommended proposals which resulted in the necessary changes and additions to the MARC 21 format to fully specify record transfer using diskettes.

More recently, specifications have been developed also for the distribution of MARC records via file transfer (FTP). The diskette and FTP distribution specifications first appeared in the 1994 edition of MARC 21 specifications.

Librarians, vendors — anyone at all — who distributes cataloging data, should be able to provide standard MARC 21 cataloging in standard format. Library automation systems vendors should be able to design their systems to correctly receive and process standard MARC records. Individual librarians using computers to manage their libraries are the direct beneficiaries of all this MARC 21 standards work.

November 1996, American Library Association's ALCTS/LITA/RUSA Machine-Readable Bibliographic information Committee in conjunction with Network Development and MARC Standards Office Library of Congress. The following statement of background and principles for content designation in the MARC 21 formats was approved by the American Library Association's ALCTS/LITA/RUSA Machine-Readable Bibliographic Information Committee (MARBI), in consultation with representatives from United States and Canadian national libraries and designated bibliographic networks. The statement includes the principles under which the MARC 21 formats were developed and constitutes a set of working principles for the ongoing process of format development. This document will be revised as necessary.

In January 1998, the National Library of Canada issued an update to the CAN/MARC bibliographic format, which included all of the changes resulting from harmonization with USMARC. In June 1998, a document listing changes to the CAN/MARC authority format resulting from alignment with USMARC was posted on the National Library of Canada Web site. The format specifications in the MARC 21 publication have, therefore, already been made available to users of existing CAN/MARC documentation.

The first format was published for bibliographic data. It was released in the summer of 1999 in English and French followed by the authority, holdings and classification formats. The National Library of Canada and the Library of Congress has acted as co-publishers of the English versions of the formats; the National Library of Canada has published the French versions of the formats.

The National Library of Canada has implemented the specifications in the MARC 21 bibliographic and authority formats in two phases. The first phase of implementation was implemented in January 1999. The second phase was implemented in late 1999.

On December 1, 2002, OCLC will begin implementation of the changes in MARC 21 needed to support the revised rules in Anglo-American Cataloguing Rules (AACR2, 2nd ed., 2002 revision, chapter 12). Chapter 12 encompasses all continuing resources.

Rules for integrating resources both in print (loose-leaves) and electronic format (updating databases and web sites) have also been added to this chapter. These rules were added to accommodate the seriality aspects of both serials and integrating resources.

4. ROLE OF LIBRARY OF CONGRESS:

The Library of Congress in consultation with various user communities maintains the MARC 21 formats. Through maintenance and revision, content designation is added to and existing content designation is made obsolete or deleted from formats. Content designation is made obsolete when it is found to be no longer appropriate or when the data element involved is no longer needed. An obsolete content designator may continue to appear in records created prior to the date it was made obsolete. Obsolete content designators are not used in new records. A deleted content designator is one that had been reserved in MARC 21 but had not been defined or one that had been defined but it is known with near certainty that it had not been used. The principles stated in this document have developed over time. The formats contain exceptions to the principles due to early format development decisions. While many exceptions have been made obsolete, others remain because of the need to maintain upward compatibility of the formats in current development.

The MARC 21 formats are communication formats, primarily designed to provide specifications for the exchange of bibliographic and related information between systems. They are widely used in a variety of exchange and processing environments. As communication formats, they do not mandate internal storage or display formats to be used by individual systems. It particularly the bibliographic and authority formats, were initially developed to enable the **Library of Congress** to communicate its catalog records to other institutions. The formats have had a close relationship to the needs and practices of North American libraries with universal collections. They reflect both the various cataloging codes applied in the library community and the requirements of the archives community. The MARC 21 formats were designed to facilitate the exchange of bibliographic and related information. An attempt has been made to preserve compatibility with other national and international formats, e.g., UKMARC and UNIMARC. National agencies in the United States and Canada (Library of Congress, National Agricultural Library, National Library of Medicine, United States Government Printing Office, and National Library of Canada) are given special emphasis and consideration in the formats because they serve as sources of authoritative cataloging and as agencies responsible for certain data elements. The institutions responsible for the content, content designation, and transcription accuracy of bibliographic and authority data within a MARC record are identified at the record level in field 008/39 (Fixed-Length Data Elements—Cataloging source) and in field 040 (Cataloging Source). This responsibility may be evaluated in terms of the following rule.

Unmodified records—The institution identified as the cataloging institution (field 040$a) is considered responsible for data content in the record except for agency-assigned data (see section 2.5.2.1. below). The institution identified as the transcribing institution (field 040$c) is considered responsible for content designation and transcription accuracy for all data.

Modified records—Institutions identified as cataloging or modifying institutions (field 040$a, $d) are considered collectively responsible for data content in the record except for agency-assigned and authoritative-agency data (see section 2.5.2. below). Institutions identified as transcribing or modifying institutions (field 040$c, $d) are considered collectively responsible for content designation and transcription accuracy.

Certain data elements are defined in the MARC 21 formats as being exclusively assigned by particular agencies, e.g., International Standard Serial Number (field 022), Library of Congress Control Number (field 010). The content of such agency-assigned elements is always the responsibility of the agency. Certain data elements have been defined in the MARC 21 formats in relation to one or more authoritative agencies that maintain the lists or rules upon which the data is based, e.g., Library of Congress Call Number (field 050), National Library of Medicine Call Number (field 060). Where it is possible for other agencies to create similar or identical content for these data elements, content designation may be provided to distinguish between content actually assigned by the authoritative agency and that assigned by other agencies. In the former case, responsibility for content rests with the authoritative agency. In the latter case, the Responsible Parties Rule applies, and no further identification of the assigning agency is provided. The MARC 21 bibliographic format provides content designation only for data that are applicable to all copies of the bibliographic entity described. Information which applies only to some copies (or even to a single copy) of a title may be of interest beyond the institutions holding such copies. The MARC 21 formats provide limited content designation for the encoding of this information and for identifying the holding institution, e.g., sub field $5 in the 700-740 added entry fields in the bibliographic format. 2.6.2. Information that does not apply to all copies of a title, and is not of interest to other institutions, is coded in local fields. For instance, the 59X block is reserved for local notes in the bibliographic format.

Although a MARC record is usually autonomous, data elements are provided that contains information used to link related records. These linkages may be implicit, through identical access points in each record, or explicit, through a linking entry field. The 76X-78X linking entry fields in the bibliographic format may contain either selected data elements that identify the related item or a control number that identifies the related record. In addition, an explicit code in the leader identifies a record that is linked to another record through a control number.

5. STRUCTURAL FEATURES

The MARC 21 formats are an implementation of the Information Interchange Format (ANSI Z39.2). The formats also incorporate other relevant ANSI standards. All information in a MARC record is stored in character form. MARC communications records are coded in Extended ASCII, as defined in the MARC 21 Specifications for Record Structure, Character Sets, and Exchange Media. The length of each variable field can be determined either from the length-of-field portion of the directory entry or from the occurrence of the field terminator character [1E(16), 8-bit]. The length of a record can be determined either from the logical record length element in Leader/00-04 or from the occurrence of the record terminator character [1D(16)_, 8-bit]. The location of each variable field is explicitly stated in the starting character position element in its directory entry.

6. CONTENT DESIGNATION

The goal of content designation is to identify and characterize the data elements that comprise a MARC record with sufficient precision to support manipulation of the data for a variety of functions. MARC content designation is designed to support functions that include. Display—the formatting of data for screen display, for printing on 3x5 cards or in book catalogs, for production of COM catalogs, or for other visual presentation of the data. Information retrieval—the identification, categorization, and retrieval of any identifiable data element in a record. Some fields serve multiple functions. For example, field 245 (Title Statement) serves both as the bibliographic transcription of the title and the statement of responsibility and as an access point for the title. The MARC 21 formats provide for display constants. A display constant is a term, phrase, and/or spacing or punctuation convention that may be system generated under prescribed circumstances to make a visual presentation of data in a record more meaningful to a user. Such display constants are not carried in the data, but may be supplied for display by the processing system. For example, sub field $x in Series Statement field 490 (and in some other fields) implies the display constant ISSN; also, the combination of tag 780 (Preceding Entry) and second indicator value 2 implies the display constant Supersedes. The MARC 21 formats support the sorting of data only to a limited extent. In general, sorting must be accomplished through the application of external algorithms to the data.

7. ORGANIZATION OF THE RECORD

A MARC record consists of three main sections: the leader, the directory, and the variable fields. The leader consists of data elements that contain coded values and are identified by relative character position. Data elements in the leader define parameters for processing the record. The leader is fixed in length (24 characters) and occurs at the beginning of each MARC record. The directory contains the tag, starting location, and length of each field within the record. Directory entries for variable control fields appear first, in ascending tag order. Entries for variable data fields follow, arranged in ascending order according to the first character of the tag. The order of the fields in the record does not necessarily correspond to the order of directory entries. Duplicate tags are distinguished only by location of the respective fields within the record. The length of the directory entry is defined in the entry map elements in Leader/ 20-23. In the MARC 21 formats, the length of a directory entry is 12 characters. The directory ends with a field terminator character.

The data content of a record is divided into variable fields. The MARC 21 formats distinguish two types of variable fields: variable control fields and variable data fields. Control and data fields are distinguished only by structure. The term fixed fields is occasionally used in MARC 21 documentation, referring either to control fields generally or to specific coded-data fields, e.g., 007

(Physical Description Fixed Field) or 008 (Fixed-Length Data Elements).

8. VARIABLE FIELDS AND TAGS

The data in a MARC record is organized into fields, each identified by a three-character tag. According to ANSI Z39.2, the tag must consist of alphabetic or numeric ASCII graphic characters, i.e., decimal integers 0-9 or letters A-Z (uppercase or lowercase, but not both). The MARC 21 formats have used only numeric tags. The tag is stored in the directory entry for the field, not in the field itself. Variable fields are grouped into blocks according to the first character of the tag, which identifies the function of the data within a record, e.g., main entry, added entry, subject entry. The remainder of the tag identifies the type of information in the field, e.g., personal name, corporate name, or title.

Further content designation (indicators and sub field codes) for data elements subject to authority control are defined consistently across the bibliographic and authority formats. These guidelines apply only to the main range of fields in each block, not to secondary ranges, e.g., the linking entry fields 760-787 in the bibliographic format. Within fields subject to authority control, data elements may exist which are not subject to authority control and which may vary from record to record containing the same heading, e.g., sub field $e, Relater term. In fields not subject to authority control, each tag is defined independently. Parallel meanings have been preserved whenever possible. Principles have been established to assist in determining when a separate field should be defined for note data and when the data should be included in a general note field. In the MARC 21 bibliographic format, a specific 5XX note field is defined when at least one of the following is true. Categorical indexing or retrieval is required on the data defined for the note. The note is used for structured access purposes but does not have the nature of a controlled access point. Special manipulation of that specific category of data is a routine requirement. Such manipulation includes special print/display formatting or selection/ suppression from display or printed product. Specialized structuring of information for reasons other than those given in (a) or (b), e.g., to support particular standards of data content when they cannot be supported in existing fields. In the MARC 21 authority format, the specifications for notes are covered in the following two conditions. A specific note field is needed when special manipulation of that specific category of data is a routine requirement. Such manipulation includes special print/display formatting or selection/ suppression from display or printed product.

Multiple notes are generally not established to accommodate the same type of information for different types of authorities. Notes are thus not differentiated by or limited to subject, name, or series if the same information applies to more than one type.

Certain tags have been reserved for local implementation. The MARC 21 formats specify no structure or meaning for local fields. Communication of local fields between systems is governed by mutual agreements on the content and content designation of the fields communicated. The 9XX block is reserved for local implementation. In general, any tag containing the character 9 is reserved for local implementation within the block structure

The historical development of the MARC 21 formats has left one exception to this general principle: field 490 (Series Statement) in the bibliographic format. There are several obsolete fields with tags containing the character 9. Theoretically, all fields, except field 001 (Control Number), 003 (Control Number Identifier) and field 005 (Date and Time of Latest Transaction), may be repeated. The nature of the data, however, often precludes repetition. For example, a bibliographic record may contain only one field 245 (Title Statement) and an authority record may contain only one 1XX-heading field. The repeatability/no repeatability of each field is defined in the MARC 21 formats.

9. VARIABLE CONTROL FIELDS

The 00X fields in the MARC 21 formats are variable control fields. Variable control fields consist of data and a field terminator. They contain neither indicators nor sub field codes.

Variable control fields contain either a single data element or a series of fixed-length data elements identified by relative character position.

10. VARIABLE DATA FIELDS

All fields except 00X are variable data fields. Four levels of content designation are provided for variable data fields in ANSI Z39.2: A three-character tag, stored in the directory entry. Indicators stored at the beginning of each variable data field, the number of indicators being reflected in Leader/10 (Indicator count). Sub field codes preceding each data element, the length of the code being reflected in Leader/11 (Sub field code count). A field terminator following the last data element in the field.

11. INDICATORS

Indicators contain values conveying information that interprets or supplements the data found in the field. The MARC 21 formats specify two indicator positions at the beginning of each variable data field. Indicators are defined independently for each field. Parallel meanings are preserved whenever possible. Indicator values are interpreted independently; meaning is not ascribed to the two indicators taken together. Indicators may be any lowercase alphabetic or numeric character or a blank (#). Numeric values are defined first. A blank (#) is used in an undefined indicator position or to mean information not provided in a defined indicator position. The blank may have specific meaning when necessary for upward compatibility. The value 9 is reserved for local implementation.

12. SUB FIELD CODES

Sub field codes identify data elements within a field that require (or might require) separate manipulation. Sub field codes in the MARC 21 formats consist of two characters—a delimiter [1F(16), 8-bit], followed by a data element identifier. A data element identifier may be any lowercase alphabetic or numeric character. Numeric identifiers are defined for parametric data used to process the field, or coded data needed to interpret the field. (Note that not all numeric identifiers defined in the past have followed this specification.) Alphabetic identifiers are defined for the separate elements that constitute the data content of the field. The character 9 and the following graphic symbols are reserved for local definition as data element identifiers: " # $ % & ' () * + ' -. /: < = >? Sub field codes are defined independently for each field. Parallel meanings are preserved whenever possible. Sub field codes are defined for purposes of identification, not arrangement. The order of sub fields is specified by content standards, e.g., cataloging rules. In some cases, however, such specifications may be incorporated in the MARC 21 format documentation. Theoretically, all data elements may be repeated. The nature of the data, however, often precludes repetition. The repeatability/no repeatability of each sub field code is defined in the MARC 21 formats.

13. CODED DATA

In addition to content designation, the MARC 21 formats include specifications for the content of certain data elements, particularly those that provide for the representation of data by coded values. Coded values consist of fixed-length character strings. Individual elements within a coded-data field or sub field are identified by relative character position. Although coded data occur most frequently in the leader, directory, and variable control fields, any field or sub field may be defined for coded-data elements.

Certain common values have been defined whenever applicable:

— Undefined (element not defined)

N — Not applicable (element is not applicable to the item)

U — Unknown (record creator was unable to determine value)

Z — Other (value other than those defined for the element)

| — Fill character (record creator has chosen not to provide information)

Historical exceptions do occur in the formats. In particular, the blank (#) often has been defined as not applicable or has been assigned a specific meaning. Standards and Other Documents Related to MARC 21 Formats.

14. INFORMATION INTERCHANGE FORMAT: ANSI Z 39.5

With the advancement of technology and explosion of digital information in the last decade, the importance of having interoperable information retrieval networks, to find and exchange *quality* information electronically, has become paramount. Exacerbating the problem, online services accessible on the Internet and World Wide Web (WWW) have made it possible to access information in ways not possible before. To facilitate information retrieval across the diverse collections of data resources now available, a non-proprietary standards-based communications protocol for information retrieval, which is independent of database and computer environment, is essential. Z39.50 is such a standard.

What is Z39.50?

ANSI/NISO Z39.50-1995 (ISO 23950) is one of a set of standards produced to facilitate the interconnection of computer systems. The standard specifies formats and procedures governing the exchange of messages between a client and server, enabling the user to search remote databases, identify records which meet specified criteria, and to retrieve some or all of the identified records and is concerned, in particular, with the search and retrieval of information in databases.

How does Z39.50 work?

Z39.50 recognizes that information retrieval consists of two primary components-selection of information based upon some criteria and retrieval of that information, and it provides a common language for both activities. Z39.50 standardizes the manner in which the client and the server communicate and interoperate even when there are differences between computer systems, search engines, and databases.

As an information user, consumer, or provider, you need tools to keep up with the explosive growth of networked information An essential tool is ANSI/NISO Z39.50, an open standard for information retrieval. Z39.50 is a computer-to-computer communications protocol designed to support searching and retrieval of information-full-text documents, bibliographic data, images, multimedia-in a distributed network environment Based on a client/server architecture and operating over the Internet, the Z39.50 protocol is supporting an increasing number of applications - fulfilling the searching demands of the emerging information age.

In practice, most implementers begin with a simple baseline implementation using one of the available Z39.50 toolkits, verify interoperability against other applications, and then incrementally expand in functionality with additional Z39.50 features.

A baseline implementation of Z39.50 is described in the conformance section of the Standard. Minimal conformance requirements are the Init, Search and Present Services and the Type-1 query. These services provide the ability to negotiate initialization, perform a search on a database, create a result set of database records that match the query, and retrieve one or more records from the result set.

To demonstrate a such a baseline implementation examples of pseudo-application protocol data units with accompanying explanation are detailed below. For simplicity, only mandatory components are listed. (Note, the examples do not address data communications nor implementation tools)

15. FORMAT FOR INFORMATION INTERCHANGE: ISO 2709

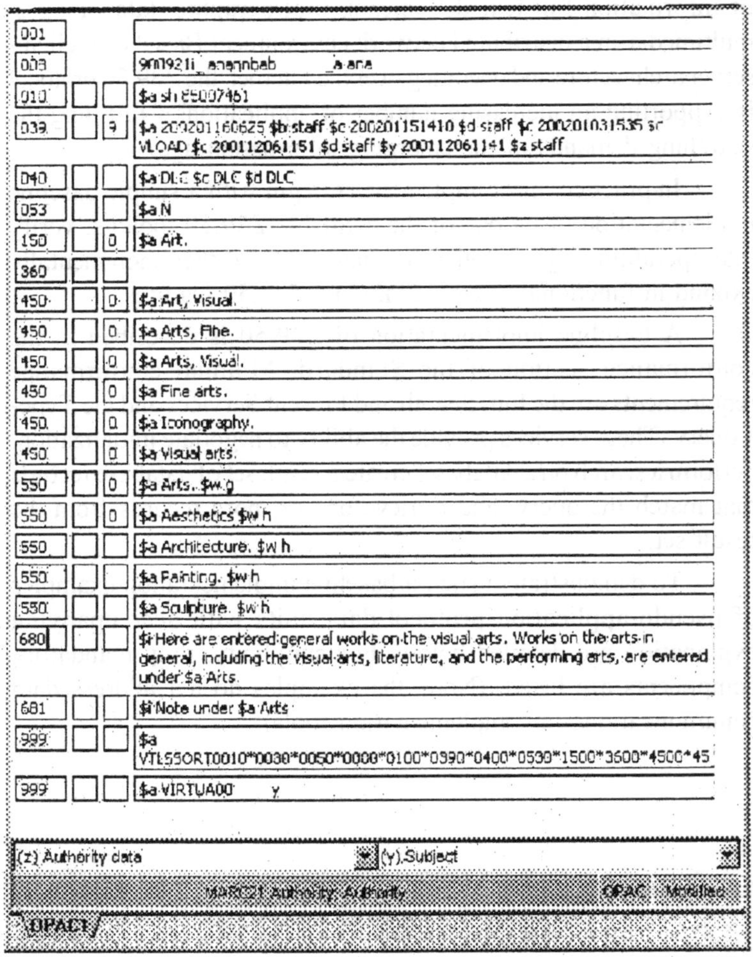

Development, approval, and maintenance

Developed and maintained by the International Organization for Standardization, TC 46: Information and Documentation. The first version was published in 1973 and a second in 1981.

Scope and structure

ISO 2709 is the international exchange format and was derived substantially from the original MARC format developed by the Library of Congress. It is more abstract than the USMARC format. however, since its intent is to provide a universally acceptable standard to which MARC formats from every country worldwide could conform.

Haggler notes, "it regulates only the essential structural features of MARC as a variable-field format and is not even limited to bibliographic records."

Like ANSI Z39.2, contains instructions for creating an information interchange format.

MARC 21 communications format: The block of data below is what the programmer sees when he looks at the contents of a MARC file. The tags do not appear before the fields, but a directory to the data tells which tags should be used and where each field starts (in other words, where each tag belongs).

01041cam 2200265 a 4500001002000000003000040002000
500170002400800410004101000240008202000250010602000
44001310400018001750500024001930820018002171000003
200235245008700267246003600354250001200390260003700
40230000290043950000420046852002200051065000330073
0 6 5 0 0 0 1 2 0 0 7 6 3 ^ # # # 8 9 0 4 8 2 3 0 # / A C /
r91^DLC^19911106082
810.9^891101s1990####maua###j######000#0#eng##^##$
a###89048230#/AC/r91^##$a0316107514: c12.95^##$a
0316107506 (pbk.): c5.95 ($6.95 Can.)^##$aDLC$cD
LC$dDLC^00$aGV943.25$b.B74 1990^00$a005.334/
2$220^
10$aThomas, Sean J., $d1970-^10$aComputer Science:
$bTechnolozy/$cSean J. Thomas.^##$a2nd ed.^##$aNew
York :$bLittle, Brown,$cc19
90.^##$a227 p. :$bill. ;$c19 cm.^\

Cracking the code, or, Interpreting the directory. Usually, only the computer programmer and the computer come into contact with the record in MARC 21 communications format, but it is interesting to understand how the directory works.

The first 24 positions are the leader. In this example the leader fills approximately 1/3 of the first line and ends with "4500." Immediately following the leader, the directory begins. Tags have been underlined in this example. Each individual tag directory is 12 characters long. The first tag is 001. Following each tag, the next four positions show the length of the field. The data in the 001 field (control number) in this record is 20 characters long. The next 5 positions tell the starting point for this field within the data string that follows the directory. The 001 field begins at the 00000 position (the first position is position 0). The next tag is 003, which is 4 characters long and begins at the 20th position (the length of the previous position — 20 — added to its starting spot — 00000 — equals 20). The next tag is 005. It is 17 characters long and begins at the 24th spot (4 + 20 = 24).

This directory tells us:

Tag	Length	Starts at	Tag	Length	Starts at
001	0020	00000	100	0032	00235
003	0004	00020	245	0087	00267
005	0017	00024	246	0036	00354
008	0041	00041	250	0012	00390
010	0024	00082	260	0037	00402
020	0025	00106	300	0029	00439
020	0044	00131	500	0042	00468
040	0018	00175	520	0220	00510
050	0024	00193	650	0033	00730
082	0018	00217	650	0012	00763

Field terminators (displayed as a ^ in this example) mark the end of the directory and the end of each field that follows. Notice that the sum of the 2nd and 3rd column in any row equals the number in the 3rd column in the next row. The starting point of one field plus its length equals the starting position of the next field.

This can be verified by counting the character positions within the data, remember that spaces count, as do the field terminators (^). (Two character positions are always reserved for indicators at the beginning of a field.) A record terminator (displayed as a \ in this example) ends each bibliographic record.

Tagged display: Most data editing screens are called "tagged displays" because they show the MARC 21 tags, inserted where they belong, as directed by the directory. A computer program has been written to do this tagging.

The example below, a sample data entry screen, is tagged.

16. SAMPLE LOCAL SYSTEM RECORD

If a librarian uploaded this record into a library automation system the data entry screen might look like this. The descriptors in the left-hand column are not stored in a MARC record. They are part of the software program's screen display. Most systems are designed so that records can be edited to add additional fields containing local information.

Leader	01041cam 2200265 a 4500
Control No.	001 ###89048230
Control No.	ID 003 DLC
DTLT	005 19911106082810.9
Fixed Data	008 891101s1990 maua j 001 0 eng
LCCN	010 ## $a ###89048230
ISBN	020 ## $a 0316107514 :
	$c $12.95
ISBN	020 ## $a 0316107506 (pbk.) :
	$c $5.95 ($6.95 Can.)
Cat. Source	040 ## $a DLC
	$c DLC
	$d DLC

LC Call No.	050 00 $a GV943.25
	$b .B74 !990
Dewey No.	005 00 $a 796.334/2
	$2 20
ME:Pers Name	100 1# $a Tomas, Sean, J.,
	$d 1970-
Title	245 10 $a Computer Science:
	$b Technolozy /
	$cBy Sean J. Thomas.
Edition	250 ## $a 2nd ed.
Publication	260 ## $a New York:
	$b Little, Brown,
	$c c1990.
Phys Desc	300 ## $a 227 p. :
	$b ill.;
	$c 19 cm.

Formatted displays: The type of screens OPAC patrons use are formatted, since MARC tags would be meaningless to the general public. Within each particular OPAC program is a routine that formats each record in the way the designers thought would best serve the public using the online catalog. A similar transformation takes place if catalog cards are printed from a MARC record, as illustrated in the 3rd example.

Sample of a brief record display as seen by a patron:

TITLE : Computer Science: Technolozy / By Sean J. Thomas.

AUTHOR : Thomas Sean J.

PUBLISHED : Little, Brown, c1990.

MATERIAL : 227 p.

Book vs. non-book: Audiovisual materials are cataloged following many of the same rules as for books (from AACR2) and tagged using many of the same MARC 21 content designators (from the MARC 21 Format for Bibliographic Data) The differences from book tagging could be summarized as follows

The 06 position of the Leader is changed to reflect the type of media.

An optional 007 tag may be added. It contains fixed-length data elements similar to those in the 008 field but related to the physical format of the item.

Definitions for data in the 008 tag in positions 18-34 change for different types of media.

Because of the number of people equally involved in the preparation of an audiovisual item, AACR2 rules often dictate a title main entry. In other words, there is often no 1XX tag.

In the 245 field, the medium or General Material Designation (GMD) follows the title proper in sub field $h. It is enclosed in brackets. Terms which may be used as GMDs are listed in AACR2 chapter 1, rule 1.1C1.

The data most different from book data is the physical description (300 tag), as it changes to physically describe the audiovisual material. Rules and examples for each media type are shown in chapters 2-11 of AACR2.

The 300 tag often contains a sub field $e for describing accompanying material such as a teacher's guide or transparency masters.

A few special tags are used to accommodate the rules for cataloging different types of materials.

In the notes area, in addition to some special tags, tag 500 is used liberally for additional cataloging information.

Remember: For complete details about the 007, 008, and any special tags used with audiovisual materials, see the MARC 21 Format for Bibliographic Data.

17. CONCLUSION

In these pages you've learned what the acronym MARC means. You've seen why a standard format for identifying elements of bibliographic data became necessary and why it is still important. You've learned to define and identify the three types of MARC content designators: tags, subfield codes, and indicators. Most important, with this knowledge you can understand the questions that should concern you when considering the purchase of bibliographic data or of a library automation system.

To build on this basic introduction to the topic. additional reading on the subject or courses in online cataloging can be beneficial. Further readings are suggested in the bibliography MARC may appear difficult at first, but with knowledge and use, it will begin to make sense. As you become more familiar with MARC, the simpler it will become.

4

SAMPLE FORMAT OF MARC 21 WITH EXAMPLE

1. MARC 21 COMPUTER FILE EXAMPLE

This example can be identified as a record for a computer file by code m in Leader/06. The record illustrates the use of two special fields for computer files: field 538 (System Details Note), and field 753 (System Details Access to Computer Files).

LDR *****cmm##22*****#a#4500

001 <control number>

003 <control number identifier>

005 19920401095900.0

008 870206s1985####miu########da#######eng##

040##$a<organization code>$c<organization code>

1001#$aAshwell, Jonathan D.

24510$aBookends extended$h[computer file] :$bthe reference management system.

250##$aV2.08.

260##$aBirmingham, Mich. :$bSensible Software.$cc1985.

300##$a2 computer disks ;$c3 1/2-5 1/4 in. +$e1 manual (107 p. ; 23 cm.)

500##$aCopyright and manual by Jonathan D. Ashwell.

500##$aContents of disks are identical.

520##$aDesigned to save, retrieve, and format references, and to print bibliographies.

538##$aSystem requirements: Apple IIe with 80 column card or Apple

IIc:128K; ProDOS; printer.

7102#$aSensible Software, Inc.

753##$aApple IIe.

753##$aApple IIc.

2. MARC 21 Monographic Component Part Example

This example can be identified as a record for printed language material by code a in Leader/06, and further as a monographic component part by code a in Leader/07. The record illustrates the use of linking entry field 773 (Host Item Entry).

LDR *****caa##22*****#a#4500

001 <control number>

003 <control number identifier>

005 19920504100110.5

008 860504s1977####mnua##########000#0#eng#d

040##$a<organization code>$c<organization code>

043##$an-us—

1001#$aNelson, Charles W.$q(Charles Winfred),$d1945-

24510$aStyle theory of architecture in Minnesota /$cCharles W. Nelson.

300##$ap. 24-34, 36-37, 40-41 :$bill. ;$c29 cm.

500##$aTitle from caption.

7730#$7nnas$tArchitecture Minnesota$gv. 3, no. 4 (July-Aug. 1977)

$w(OCoLC)2253666

3. MARC 21 Reference and Subdivision Record Example

This is an example of a reference and subdivision record. The heading in the 1XX is not used as a 4XX in any established heading record. The 1XX heading is an unestablished heading, but it may be used as a subject subdivision. The 260 Complex See Reference field gives specific instructions on the use of the subdivision. The 780 linking entry field provides information about the use of the 1XX heading as a subject subdivision.

LDR *****nz###22*****n##4500

001 <control number>

003 <control number identifier>

005 19860328161425.8

008 860328nn#gnznnbbba###########n#ann#####u

010##$aex#99037700#

040##$a<organization code>$c<organization code>$fsubject heading/thesaurus

conventions code>

150##$aDisciples

260##$isubdivision$aDisciples$iunder names of individual persons

780#7$xDisciples$2<source code>

4. BOOK EXAMPLE MARC 21 BIBLIOGRAPHIC FORMAT

Full Level Record - Book

This example can be identified as a record for printed language material by code a in Leader/06, and further as a monograph by code m in Leader/07. The record contains the basic bibliographic information fields (fields 100, 245, 260, and 300), as well as additional fields (e.g., fields 020 (International Standard Book Number), 050 (Library of Congress Call Number), 082 (Dewey Decimal Classification Number), 246 (Varying Form of Title), 500 (General Note), and 650 (Subject Added Entry Topical Term)).

LDR *****nam##22*****#a#4500

001 <control number>

003 <control number identifier>

005 19920331092212.7

007 ta

008 820305s1991####nyu###########001#0#eng##

020##$a0845348116 :$c$29.95 (£19.50 U.K.)

020##$a0845348205 (pbk.)

040##$a<organization code>$c<organization code>

05014$aPN1992.8.S4$bT47 1991

08204$a791.45/75/0973$219

1001#$aTerrace, Vincent,$d1948-

24510$aFifty years of television :$ba guide to series and pilots,

1937-1988 /$cVincent Terrace.

2461#$a50 years of television

260##$aNew York :$bCornwall Books,$cc1991.

300##$a864 p. ;$c24 cm.

500##$aIncludes index.

650#0$aTelevision pilot programs$zUnited States$vCatalogs.

650#0$aTelevision serials$zUnited States$vCatalogs.

5. MAP EXAMPLE MARC 21 BIBLIOGRAPHIC FORMAT

Full Level Record - Map

This example can be identified as a record for a printed map by code e in Leader/06, and more specifically as a globe by code d in field 007/00. This record illustrates the use of several fields related to cartographic material: field 034 (Coded Cartographic Mathematical Data) and field 255 (Cartographic Mathematical Data), as well as field 052 (Geographic Classification Code).

LDR *****cem##22*****#a#4500

001 <control number>

003 <control number identifier>

005 19920506101053.0

007 dc#cen

008 850203c19841980dk#g######d#####1###eng##

0341#aab41849600$dW1800000$eE1800000$fN0900000$gS0900000

040##$a<organization code>$c<organization code>

052##$a3170

1001#$aHarig, Karl-F.

24510$aReader's Digest world antique spot globe / $ccartography by Karl-F.

Harig.

24614$aReader's Digest world antique spot globe : encyclopedic handbook.

255##$aScale 1:41,849,600$c(W 180° —E 180° /N 90° — S 90°).

260##$a[Copenhagen] Denmark :$bScan-Globe,$cc1984, c1980.

300##$a1 globe :$bcol., plastic, mounted on plastic base ;$c31 cm. in diam.

500##$aRelief shown by spot heights.

500##$aCover title of accompanying text: Reader's Digest world antique spot globe :encyclopedic handbook.

500##$aGlobe lights up from inside by means of detachable electric cord and interior lightbulb.

500##$aWhen the globe is lit, any place on earth can be pinpointed if the latitude and longitude are known. When these two facts are given, it is possible to adjust the two scales to the given figures of latitude and longitude. It causes a pinpoint of light to indicate where the place lies.

500##$aAccompanied by text and index: Spot globe 2000 edited by Steen B. Bocher and Henrik B. Hoffmeyer. 17th ed., 1983. 168 p. : ill., maps; 15 x 21 cm.

650#0$aGlobes.

7001#$aBocher, Steen Bugge,$d1906-

7001#$aHoffmeyer, Henrik B.

7102#$aReader's Digest Association.

7102#$aScan-Globe A/S.

73001$aSpot globe 2000.

6. MULTISCRIPT RECORDS

MARC 21 Concise Bibliographic: Multiscript Records

This section describes and illustrates models for recording data in multiple scripts in MARC records. One script may be considered the primary script of the data content of the record, even though other scripts are also used for data content. (Note: ASCII is used for the structural elements of the record, and most coded data are also specified within the ASCII range of characters.) The general models for multiscript data that are followed with MARC 21 are described below.

Information for Translators and Other Users

Items highlighted in red indicate changes made after the 2001 edition of the MARC 21 Concise Formats was published and are included in the 2002 printed edition of the MARC 21 Concise Formats.

Items highlighted in green indicate changes made to the online format only. These changes will be corrected in the 2003 printed edition of the MARC 21 Concise Formats (Available late 2003).

MULTISCRIPT RECORD MODELS

Model A: Vernacular and transliteration.

The regular fields may contain data in different scripts and in the vernacular or transliterated the data. Fields 880 are used when data needs to be duplicated to express it in both the original vernacular script and transliterated into one or more scripts. There may be unlinked 880 fields.

Model B: Simple multiscript records.

All data is contained in regular fields and script varies

depending on the requirements of the data. Repeatability specifications of all fields should be followed. Although the Model B record may contain transliterated data, Model A is preferred if the same data is recorded in both the original vernacular script and transliteration. Field 880 is not used.

Model A data in the regular fields is linked to the data in 880 fields by a subfield $6 that occurs in both of the associated fields. Specifications for field 880 are under that field; description of subfield $6 is in the Control Subfields section; specifications for character sets and repertoires for scripts are found in MARC 21 Specifications for Record Structure, Character Sets, and Exchange Media.

Example Conventions

Although the data in the following records are taken from actual bibliographic items, these records are included for illustration only and are not necessarily usable for bibliographic purposes. The creator of the bibliographic data is not specified in these sample records. Escape sequences are not included in the example records.

MODEL A - VERNACULAR AND TRANSLITERATION

The following example of a multiscript record follows Model A. In this example the language of cataloging is English language (Latin script) and the language of the bibliographic item is Russian (Cyrillic script). The cataloging agency provides transliteration of some Cyrillic script data into the Latin script; notes, subjects, etc. are in English; and prefers to use Latin script in the regular fields.

040	##$a***$beng$c***
100	#16880-01$aZhavoronkov, N. M.$q(Nikolai Mikhailovich)
245	10$6880-02$aOkhrana okhotnich'ikh zhivotnykh v SSSR / $cN.M. Zhavoronkov.
250	##$6880-03$aIzd. 2-e, perer.
260	##$6880-04$aMoskva : $bLesnaià promyshlennost'.,$c1982.

300	##$a167, [1] p., [16] leaves of plates. : $bcol. ill. :$c19 cm.
500	##$aBibliography: p. 167-[168].
650	#0$aAnimals$zSoviet Union.
880	1#$6100-01/(N$a[Name in Cyrillic]$q([Name in Cyrillic])
880	10$6245-02/(N$a[Title in Cyrillic] /$c[Title in Cyrillic]
880	##$6250-03/(N$a[Edition statement in Cyrillic].
880	##$6260-04/(N$a[Place of publication in Cyrillic] : $b[Name of publisher in Cyrillic],$c1982.

The following example of a multiscript record follows Model A. In this example the language of cataloging is English language (Latin script) and the language of the bibliographic item is Hebrew (Hebrew script). The cataloging agency prefers to use the Latin script in the regular fields.

The directionality of the Hebrew text in the examples is right-to-left within each subfield, but the subfields themselves have been recorded left-to-right. The actual input of all the data is in logical order (first-to-last), parts of which may be displayed in various directions depending upon the script and the display interface.

040	##$a**beng$c**
100	1#$6880-01$aZilbershtain, Yitshak ben David Yosef.
245	10$6880-02$aTorat ha-yoledet /$cne'erakh 'a. y. Yitshak ben David Yosef Zilvershtain, Mosheh ben Yosef Rotshild.
246	14$6880-03$aSefer Torat ha-yoledet
250	##$6880-04$aMahad. 2. 'im hosafot.
260	##$6880-05$aBene-Berak : $bMekhor "Halakhah u-refu'ah",$c747 [1986 or 1987]
300	##$a469 p. ;$c23 cm.

504	##$aIncludes bibliographical references and index.
650	#0$aChildbirth$xReligious aspects$xJudaism.
650	#0$aSabbath (Jewish law)
650	#0$aFasts and feast$xJudaism.
700	1#$6880-06$aRotshild, Mosheh ben Yosef.
880	1#$6100-01/(2/r$a[Name in Hebrew]
880	10$6245-02/(2/r$a[Title in Hebrew]/ $c[Statement of responsibility in Hebrew]
880	14$6246-03/(2/r$a[Title proper in Hebrew]
880	##$6250-04/(2/r$a[Edition statement in Hebrew]
880	##$6260-05/(2/r$a[Place of publication in Hebrew] :$b[Name of publisher in Hebrew],$c747 [1986 or 1987].
880	1#$6700-06/(2/r$a[Name in Hebrew]

The last example of a multiscript record also follows Model A. In this example the language of cataloging and the bibliographic item is Arabic (Arabic script).

The cataloging agency prefers to use Arabic in the regular fields. The directionality of the Arabic text in the example is right-to-left within each subfield, but the subfields themselves have been recorded left-to-right. The actual input of all the data is in logical order (first-to-last), parts of which may be displayed in various directions depending upon the script and the display interface.

040	##$a**$bara$c**
100	1#$6880-01$a[Name in Arabic]
245	10$6880-02$a[Title in Arabic] /$c[Statement of responsibility in Arabic]
250	##$6880-03$a[Edition statement in Arabic]
260	##$6880-04$a[Place of publication in Arabic] :$b[Name of publisher in Arabic],$c1997.
300	##$a[Physical description in Arabic] ;$c[Dimensions in Arabic]

504	##$a[Note in Arabic]
650	#0$6880-05$a[Topical term as entry element in Arabic]$x[General subdivision in Arabic]
880	1#$6100-01/(B/$a Tunji,Muhammad.
880	10$6245-02/(B/$aJamaliyat al-lughah al-'Arabiyah/$cMuhammad al-Tunji.
880	##$6250-03/(B/$a al-Tab'ah 1.
880	##$6260-04/(B/$a Bayrut :$bDar al-Fikr al-'Arabi,$c1997.
880	#0$6650-05/(B/$aLughah al-'Arabiyah$xMunawwa'at.

MODEL B - SIMPLE MULTISCRIPT RECORDS

This example is a multiscript record that follows Model B. In this example the language of cataloging is English (Latin script), thus the notes, subjects, etc. are in English. The bibliographic item is a mixed Russian language (Cyrillic script) and Arabic language (Arabic script) text.

040	##$a***$beng$c***
041	1#$arus$aara
066	##$b(N$c(B$c(3
100	1#$aRuzhkov, V. I.$q (Viktor Ivanovich)
245	00$a[Title in Cyrillic] :$b[Remainder of title in Cyrillic] /$c[Statement of responsibility in Cyrillic]
246	31$a[Title proper in Arabic]
260	##$a[Place of publication in Cyrillic] :$b[Name of publisher in Cyrillic],$c1988.
300	##$a [Extent in Cyrillic] ;$c [Dimensions in Cyrillic].
650	#0$aTechnology$vDictionaries$xRussian.
650	#0$aRussian language$vDictionaries$xArabic.
700	1#$aTkhorzhevskii, L. L.$q(Lev L'vovich)

700	1#$aShagal'. V. E.$q(Vladimir Eduardovich)
700	1#$aMunir. Dawud Sulayman

This example is a multiscript record that follows Model B. In this example the language of cataloging is Russian (Cyrillic script) and the bibliographic item is mixed Russian language (Cyrillic script) and English language (Latin script) text

040	##$a***$brus$c***
041	1#$arus$aeng
066	##$b(N$c(B
245	00$a[Title in Cyrillic]$b Who is who in oil and gas industry of the CIS /$c[[Statement of responsibility in Cyrillic]]
246	31$aWho is who in oil and gas industry of the CIS
260	##$a [Place of publication in Cyrillic] :$b[Name of publisher in Cyrillic],$c1992.
300	##$a [Extent in Cyrillic] ;$c [Dimensions in Cyrillic].
546	##$a[Note in Cyrillic]
650	#0$a[Topical term in Cyrillic]$z[Geographic subdivision in Cyrillic]$v[Form subdivision in Cyrillic]
700	1#$a[Personal name in Cyrillic]$q[(Fuller form of name in Cyrillic)]

7. MARC 21 UNTRACED REFERENCE RECORD EXAMPLE MARC 21 AUTHORITY FORMAT

Full Level Record

Untraced Reference Record

The 1XX heading in an untraced name reference record (like this one from a meeting name) is not traced in a 4XX field in any established heading record. The name in this example did not qualify as a legitimate cross reference to the heading for the conference.

Similar records are often needed from a particle of personal names (e.g. De la ...) or initial parts of corporate names (e.g., Royal ...) that would otherwise never qualify as cross references alone.

The coding of the 008 field must be done with care. Many common codes change for reference records, particularly character positions 14, 15, 16, and 29. General Explanatory Reference records for names may not contain 4XX and 5XX fields. Explanatory notes are given in the 666 field.

LDR *****nz###22*****n##4500

001 <control number>

003 <control number identifier>

005 19790519201750.0

008 790519nn#bcnnnbbbn##########n#ann#####u

010##$aex#79373119#

040##$a<organization code>$c<organization code>

1112#$aPuebla

666##$aName used to refer to the 3rd Conferencia General del Episcopado Latinoamericano, held in Puebla, Mexico in 1979. Since this particular conference has come to be so well known books often refer to it simply as "Puebla", "Puebla '79", or "Puebla conference".

8. MULTILINGUAL THESAURUS RECORD EXAMPLE MARC 21

Authority Format

Full Level Record

Multilingual Thesaurus Record

This example shows equivalent established heading records for a corporate name in two languages in a multilingual catalog. Multilingual catalogs usually require establishment of equivalent headings in more than one language. Each record includes a 7XX field with linking entry to the equivalent heading in a different language When 4XX and 5XX fields are needed, the language of the tracings matches the language of the 1XX field.

English language authority record:

LDR *****czbbb2200157nbb4500

001 <control number>

003 <control number identifier>

005 19990128082638.0

008 880607nneacnnnaaa#n##########a#ana######

016##$a0060L1837E#

040##$a<organization code>$c<organization code>

1102#$aBank of Montreal.$bPublic Affairs Dept.

71025$aBanque de Montréal.$bService des affaires publiques $0

(CaOONL)0060L1837F#

670##$aSchwarze, T.L. Learning strategies for Minding my own business,

1995:$b t.p.(Bank of Montreal, Public Affairs Dept.)

9. **FRENCH LANGUAGE RECORD:**

LDR *****czbbb2200157nbb4500

001 <control number>

003 <control number identifier>

005 19990128082638.0

008 880607nneacnnnaaa#n##########a#ana######

016##$a0060L1837F#

040##$a<organization code>$c<organization code>

1102#$aBanque de Montréal.$bService des affaires publiques

670##$aSchwarze, T.L. Learning strategies for Minding my own business,

1995:$bp. de t.(Banque de Montréal, Service des affaires publiques)

71025$aBank of Montreal.$bPublic Affairs Dept.$0(CaOONL)0060L1837E#

10. SERIAL EXAMPLE MARC 21 BIBLIOGRAPHIC FORMAT

Full Level Record - Serial

This example can be identified as a record for language material by code a in Leader/06, and further as a serial by code s in Leader/ 07. This record illustrates the use of several fields related to serial material: field 022 (International Standard Serial Number), field 042 (Authentication Code), field 210 (Abbreviated Title), field 222 (Key Title), field 246 (Varying Form of Title), field 310 (Current Publication Frequency), field 362 (Dates of Publication and/or Sequential Designation), and field 780 (Preceding Entry).

LDR *****cas##22*****#a#4500

001 <control number>

003 <control number identifier>

005 19920716101553.0

008 791031c19789999dcuar1########0###a0eng#d

010##$a###85649389#$zsc#80000109#

0220#$a0273-1967

035##$a(OCoLC)5629434

040##$a<organization code>$c<organization code>$d <organization code>

042##alcansdp

043##$an-us—

05000$aSK361$b.U63a

08200$a639.9/2/0973$219

2100#$aAnnu. wildl. fish. rep.

222#0$aAnnual wildlife and fisheries report

24500$aAnnual wildlife and fisheries report /$cUnited States Department of Agriculture, Forest Service, Wildlife and Fisheries.

24614$aWildlife and fish habitat management in the Forest Service

260##$a[Washington, D.C.] :$bWildlife and Fisheries.

300##$av. :$bill. ;$c28 cm.

310##$aAnnual

3621#$aBegan with vol. for 1978.

500##$aDescription based on: 1983.

650#0$aWildlife management$zUnited States$v Statistics $vPeriodicals.

650#0$aWildlife management$zUnited States$vPeriodicals.

650 #0$aWildlife habitat improvement$zUnited States$vStatistics$vPeriodicals.

650#0$aWildlife habitat improvement$zUnited States$vPeriodicals.

7101#$aUnited States.$bForest Service.$bWildlife and Fisheries Staff.

78000$aUnited States. Forest Service. Division of Wildlife Management.

$tAnnual wildlife report$x0099-068X$w(OCoLC)2242070$w(DLC)75644790

850##$a<organization code>$a<organization code>$a<organization code>

11. TOPICAL TERM HEADING EXAMPLE MARC 21 AUTHORITY

Format

Full Level Record

Established Heading Record - Topical Term

Established heading records for topical terms typically include several 4XX and 5XX fields. The tracing fields are justified by numerous 670 fields. Sources in which no information was found are recorded in a single 675 field, each identified by subfield $a The 675 field is not repeatable.

In this record, 008/06 is coded i to indicate that the heading can be geographically subdivided by the indirect method. The descriptive cataloging rules code in 008/10 is n, because this character position is not applicable to the formulation of topical term headings.

LDR *****nz###22*****n##4500

001 <control number>

003 <control number identifier>

005 19860808072450.5

008 860719in#anannbabn###########a#ana#####u

010##$aex#86004405#

040##$a<organization code>$c<organization code>

150##$aOptical disks

450##$aDiscs, Optical

450##$aDisks, Optical

450##$aOptical discs

450##$aLaser discs

450##$aLaser disks

450##$aLaserdiscs

450##$aLaserdisks

550##wgaOptical storage devices

670##$aWork cat.: McQueen, J. Videodisc and optical digital disk technologies and their applications in libraries, 1986.

670##$aWeb. 3$b(disk or disc)

670##$aLibrary Literature$b(Laser discs x Optical discs)

670##$aMcGraw-Hill dict. sci. tech.$b(optical disk - a type of video disk storage device consisting of a pressed disk with a spiral groove at the bottom of which are submicrometer-sized depressions that are sensed by a laser beam.)

670##$aLCIB thes.$b(Optical disks, see Optical storage devices)

670##$aPrice, J. "The optical disk pilot program at the Library of Congress." Videodisc and optical disk: v. 4, Nov.-Dec. 1984: p. 424-432.

670##$aO'Neill, S. "Optical disk technology." LC science tracer bullet TB 84-6.

670##$aBPI$b(Optical disks, see Optical storage devices)

670##$aRandom House$b(Optical disk; Optical disc, also called Laser disk)

670##$aHennepin$b(Optical discs x Laser discs)

675##$aNCC thes. comput. terms;$aNASA;$aIAD.$aNCC thes. comput. terms;$aBDNE2

5

UNIMARC TO MARC 21 CONVERSION SPECIFICATIONS

INTRODUCTION: NATIONAL LIBRARY, INDIA MOVING TO MARC 21

An extensive consultation by the National Library, INDIA in 2003, expressed its preference for a move from UNIMARC, the national cataloguing format, to the MARC 21 bibliographic format.

In order to support the consistent and accurate mapping of UNIMARC data to MARC 21, the National Library, INDIA has prepared conversion tables covering all UNIMARC fields and content designation, including all fields used in records created for the Indian National Bibliography. It covers various types of materials including language material (books), notated music (scores), cartographic materials (map), projected and video material, sound recordings, computer media and three-dimensional artifacts (realia). The specifications cover the conversion of items at four biiliographic levels: analytic, collection, monograph, and serial. The team of VTLS India headed by Mr. Shanta Kumar has given the useful direction in this project.

National Library, India is using a unique US based Intregreated Library Software System in fully MARC 21 based software 'VIRTUA'.

UNIMARC TO MARC 21 CONVERSION CHARTS

IN SEQUENCE BY UNIMARC FIELD)
(RECORD LABEL, DIRECTORY, 001, 100-135)

Indian UniMARC to MARC 21 Mapping

MONOGRAPHS *and* SERIALS COMBINED

MARC 21	Indian UniMARC	NOTES
Leader/06 - Type of Record Code a: language materials Code t: manuscripts	Record Label - Type of Record Code a Code b	
Leader/07 - Bibliographic level Code a: analytic Code m: monograph/Item Code s: serial Code c: collection	Record Label - Bibliography level Code a Code m Code s Code c	
Leader/18: Descriptive Cataloging Form Code i: ISBD Code ƀ: non-ISBD Code i: ISBD	Descriptive Cataloging Form Code ƀ Code n Code i: partial/incomplete ISBD	*MARC 21 no longer uses the partial ISBD value. It has been obsolete since 1987. Use code i*
008/00-05 - Date Entered on File Pattern: yymmdd	100/00-07 - Date Entered on File Pattern: yyyymmdd	

Example: 671005	Example: 19671005	
008/06: Type of date/ Publication Status Code c: serial item currently published Code d: serial no longer being published Code u: serial item status unknown Code s: single known date Code r: reprint/reissue date and original date Code q: date of publication uncertain Code m: multiple dates Code t: publication date and copyright date Code p: date of distribution/ release/ issue Code e: detailed date	100/08 - Type of Publication Date Code a Code b Code c Code d Code e Code f Code g Code h Code i Code j	
008/07-10: Date 1 Pattern: yyyy	100/9-12: Publication Date 1 Pattern: yyyy	
008/11-14: Date 2 Pattern: yyyy	100/13-16:Publication Date 2 Pattern: yyyy	
008/22: Target Audience *Monographs only* Code j: juvenile, general Code a: preschool, ages 0-5 Code b: primary, ages 5-10 Code c: children, ages 9-14 Code d: secondary (young adult) Code f: specialized, adult Code g: general, adult Code l: no attempt to code	100/17-19: Target Audience Code a Code b Code c Code d Code e Code k Code m Code u	
008/28: Government Publication	100/20 - Government Publication	

Code f: federal/national Code s: state, provincial, territorial, dependent Code l: county/department Code l: local Code c: multilocal Code i: international intergovernmental Code z: other Code o: Government publication - level undetermined Code u: unknown Code ƀ: Not a government publication Code z: other government level	Code a Code b Code c Code d Code e Code f Code g Code h Code u Code y Code z	
008/38: Modified Record Code ƀ: Not modified Code s: Modified, shortened	100/21 - Modified Record Code Code 0 Code 1	
040: Cataloging Source Subfield ‡b: Language of cataloging (*See note*)	100/22-24: Language of Cataloging Codes: Three letter language codes from the *MARC Code List for Languages*	*Field 040 subfield should also contain subfield ‡a (MARC code or name of the organization that created the record) and subfield ‡c (MARC code or name of the organization that transcribed the record into machine readable form).* Example: 040 ƀƀ‡aCaQQLLA‡bfre ‡cCaOONL
Transliteration Code	100/25: Transliteration Code	

There is no Transliteration Code equivalent in MARC 21	Code a: ISO transliteration scheme Code b: other Code c: multiple trans- literations: ISO or other schemes Code y: no transliteration scheme used	*MARC 21 dropped this information because it proved to not be useful since particular scheme (s) could be indicated.*
<u>066: Character Sets</u> Code (B: Basic Latin Code (N: Basic Cyrillic Code (J: Extended Latin Code (Q: Extended Cyrillic Code (S: Greek Code (2: Hebrew Code (2: Hebrew	<u>100/26-29: Character Set</u> Code 01 Code 02 Code 03 Code 04 Code 05 Code 08 Code 09	<u>Format</u>: 066 ƀƀ‡a<code for character set> <u>Example</u>: 066 ƀƀ‡a(N
<u>Leader/09: Character Coding Scheme</u> Code a: Unicode	<u>100/26-29: Character Set</u> Code 50: ISO 10646 Level 3 (Unicode)	
<u>066: Character Sets</u> Subfield ‡c: Alternate G0 or G1 character set Code (B: Basic Latin Code (N: Basic Cyrillic Code (J: Extended Latin Code (Q: Extended Cyrillic Code (S: Greek Code (2: Hebrew Code (2: Hebrew	<u>100/30-33: Additional Character Sets</u> Code 01 Code 02 Code 03 Code 04 Code 05 Code 08 Code 09	<u>Format</u> 066 ƀƀ‡c<code for character set>
<u>008/33: Script of title</u> *(serials only)* Code a: Latin Code b: Extended Latin Code c: Cyrillic Code d: Japanese Code d: Japanese Code d: Japanese	<u>100/34-35: Script of Title</u> Code ba Code ca Code da: Japanese - script unspecified Code db: Japanese - kanji Code dc: Japanese - kana	

Code e: Chinese Code f: Arabic Code g: Greek Code h: Hebrew Code i: Thai Code j: Devanagari Code k: Korean Code l: Tamil Code z: Other Code z: Other Code z: Other	Code ea Code fa Code ga Code ha Code ia Code ja Code ka Code la Code ma: Georgian Code mb: Armenian Code zz: Other	
<u>001 - Control Number</u> Indicators Not applicable Subfields Not applicable <u>Example</u> 001 ƀƀƀ861043856ƀ	<u>001 - Record Identifier</u> Indicators Not applicable Subfields Not applicable <u>Example</u> 001 ƀƀƀ861043856ƀ	
<u>020 - ISBN</u> Indicators <u>First</u> - Undefined <u>Second</u> - Undefined Subfields ‡a - ISBN number ‡c - Terms of availability <u>Example</u> 020 ƀƀ‡a0-246-11007-4 ‡c£2.95	<u>010 - ISBN</u> Indicators <u>First</u> - Undefined <u>Second</u> - Undefined Subfields ‡a ‡d <u>Example</u> 010 ƀƀ‡a0-246-11007-4 ‡d£2.95	
<u>022 - ISSN</u> Indicators <u>First</u> ƀ - No level specified *(See notes)* 0 - Serial of international	<u>011 - ISSN</u> Indicators <u>First</u> - Undefined	First Indicator: *<u>Recommendation</u>: Use ƀ for all records*

interest 1 - Serial not of international interest Second - Undefined Subfields ‡a - ISSN Number *(See notes)* Examples 022 bb‡a0260-7743	Second - Undefined Subfields ‡a - ISSN Number ‡d - Terms of availability and/or price Example 011 bb‡a0260-7743	Subfields: *Subfield ‡d (Terms of availability) in UniMARC maps to MARC 21 Field 037 (Source of acquisition) subfield ‡c (Terms of availability). See below*
037 - Source of Acquisition Indicators First - Undefined Second - Undefined Subfields ‡c - Terms of availability Example *(See notes)* 037 bb‡aPB-363547‡c$4.00	011 - ISSN Indicators First - Undefined Second - Undefined Subfields ‡d Example 011 bb‡a0260-7743‡d$4.00	Subfields: *Subfield ‡a in field 037 indicates the stock number.*
041 - Language Code Indicators First 0 - Item not a translation/does not include a translation 1 - Item is a translation of the original work/contains a translation 1 - Item is a translation of the original work/contains a translation Second - Undefined Subfields	101 - Language of the Item Indicators First 0 1 2 - Item contains translations other than translated summaries Second - Undefined Subfields ‡a	*If only one language applies, use 008/35-37. If multiple languages need to be indicated, place the principle language in 008/35-37 (for primary retrieval) and repeat that language with all others in field 041.*

‡a - Language of the item ‡h - Language of the translation <u>Example</u> 008/35-37 fre 041 1ƀ‡afre‡heng	‡b <u>Example</u> 101 1ƀ‡afre‡beng	
<u>245 - Title and Statement of Responsibility</u> Indicators <u>First</u> 0 - No added entry/not significant 1 - Added entry/significant <u>Second</u> 0-9 - Number of nonfiling characters *(See note)* Subfields ‡a - Title *(See Notes)* ‡b - Remainder of title ‡c - Statement of responsibility ‡c - Statement of responsibility ‡n - Number of part ‡p - Name of part <u>Example</u> 245 00‡aOklahoma‡bCarousel ; South Pacific.	<u>200 -Title and Statement of Responsibility</u> Indicators <u>First</u> 0 1 <u>Second</u> ƀ - Undefined Subfields ‡a ‡d - Parallel title ‡e ‡f ‡g ‡h ‡I <u>Example:</u> 200 0ƀ‡aOklahoma‡eCarousel ; South Pacific.	Indicator: *The second indicator in MARC 21 specifies the number of characters in an article, especially, "the" at the beginning of title. If these articles are dropped according to Indian input rules, this indicator is always "0"* Subfield: *Subfield ‡d (Parallel title) in UniMARC maps to MARC 21 Field 246 (Varying Form of Title) subfield ‡a (Title proper/short title)*
<u>246 - Varying Form of Title</u> Indicators <u>First</u> 0 - Note, no added entry 1 - Note, added entry 2 - No note, no added entry 3 - No note, added entry	<u>200 -Title and Statement of Responsibility</u> Indicators <u>First</u> 0 1 <u>Second</u>	*There are other indicators and subfields in field 246 of MARC 21.*

Second 1 - Parallel title *(See note)* Subfields ‡a - Title 246 31‡aArchives for meteorology, geophysics, and bioclimatology.	ƀ - Undefined Subfields ‡d - Parallel title 200 1ƀ‡aMeteorology‡dArchives for meteorology, geophysics, and bioclimatology	
250 - Edition Statement Indicators First - Undefined Second - Undefined Subfields ‡a - Edition statement Example 250 ƀƀ‡a16th ed.	205 - Edition Statement Indicators First - Undefined Second - Undefined Subfields ‡a Example 205 ƀƀ‡a16th ed.	
260 - Publication, Distribution, etc. Indicators First - Undefined Second - Undefined Subfields ‡a - Place of publication ‡b - Name of publisher ‡c - Date of publication Example 260 ƀƀ‡aCambridge [Cambridgeshire] :‡bUniversity of Cambridge Press, ‡c1980.	210 - Publication, Distribution, etc Indicators First - Undefined Second - Undefined Subfields ‡a ‡c ‡d Example 210 ƀƀ‡aCambridge [Cambridgeshire] : ‡cUniversity of Cambridge Press, ‡d1980.	
300 - Physical Description Indicators	215 - Physical Description Indicators	

First - Undefined Second - Undefined Subfields ‡a - Extent of item ‡e - Accompanying material Example 300 ƀƀ‡a274 p.:‡eteacher's manual	First - Undefined Second - Undefined Subfields ‡a ‡e Example 215 ƀƀ‡a274 p.:‡eteacher's manual	
500 - General Note Indicators First - Undefined Second - Undefined Subfields ‡a - General note Example 500 ƀƀ‡aThree-dimensional film: Natural vision. 500 ƀƀ‡aSlides in pocket. 500 ƀƀ‡aIncludes index.	300 - Notes Indicators First - Undefined Second - Undefined Subfields ‡a Examples 300 ƀƀ‡aThree-dimensional film: Natural vision. 300 ƀƀ‡aSlides in pocket. 300 ƀƀ‡aIncludes index.	
780 - Preceding Entry Indicators First 0 - Display note 1 - Do not display note Second 0 - Continues 1 - Continues in part Subfields (*See notes*) ‡a - Main entry heading ‡b - Edition ‡d - Place, publisher, and date of publication ‡t - Title	430 - Continues Indicators Second 1 0 First - Undefined Subfields ‡a ‡e ‡c ‡t ‡x	Subfields: *Other subfield values are also defined for field 780 in MARC 21.*

‡x - ISSN (*See notes*) Example 780 00‡aAmerican Hospital Association.‡tBulletin of the American Hospital Association	Example 430 ƀ1‡aAmerican Hospital Association.‡tBulletin of the American Hospital Association	
650 - Topical Name Used as Subject Indicators (*See notes*) First 0 - No level specified 1 - Primary 2 - Secondary Second 0 - Library of Congress Subject Headings 4 - Source not specified Subfields (*See notes*) ‡a - Main subject ‡x - Subject subdivision ‡y - Chronological subdivision ‡z - Geographic subdivision ‡v - Form subdivision Example 650 07‡aEducational buildings ‡zWashington (D.C.)‡y1890-1910.	606 - Topical Name Used as Subject Indicators First 0 1 2 Second ƀ - Undefined Subfields ‡a ‡x ‡z ‡y ‡j Example 606 0ƀ‡aEducational buildings ‡yWashington (D.C.)‡z1890-1910.	***Other indicator and subfield values are also defined for field 650 in MARC 21.***
653 - Uncontrolled subject Terms Indicators First 0 - No level specified 1 - Primary 2 - Secondary	610 - Uncontrolled subject Terms Indicators First 0 1 2	

Second - Undefined Subfield ‡a - Subject term Example 653 0b ‡aMan‡aEyes ‡aDiseases	Second Undefined Subfield ‡a Example 610 0b‡aMan‡aEyes ‡aDiseases	
084 - Other Class Number Indicators First - Undefined Second - Undefined Subfields ‡a - Class number ‡b - Item number ‡2 - Source of number Example 084 bb‡aW1‡bRE359‡2usnlm	686 - Other Class Number Indicators First - Undefined Second - Undefined Subfields ‡a ‡b ‡d Example 686 bb‡aW1‡bRE359‡dusnlm	
100 - Personal Name Primary Indicators First 0 - Forename 1 - Surname Second - Undefined Subfields ‡a - Personal name *(See notes)* Example 100 1b‡aLawrence, David Herbert	700 - Personal Name Primary Indicators Second 0 - Name entered under forename or direct order 1 First - Undefined Subfields ‡a ‡b - Part of name other than entry element Example 700 b1‡aLawrence‡bDavid	Subfield: *Subfield ‡a in MARC 21 includes both the entry element and part of name other than the entry element.*

	Herbert	
700 - Personal Name Alternative Indicators First 0 - Forename 1 - Surname Second ƀ - No information provided Subfields ‡a - Personal name (*See notes*) Example 700 1ƀ‡aParker, R.S.	701 - Personal Name Alternative Indicators Second 0 - Name entered under forename or direct order 1 First - Undefined Subfields ‡a ‡b - Part of name other than entry element Example 701 ƀ1‡aParker,‡bR.S.	Subfield: *Subfield ‡a in MARC 21 includes both the entry element and part of name other than the entry element.*
110 - Corporate Body Name - Primary Indicators First 0 - Inverted name 1 - Jurisdiction name 2 - Direct order Second - Undefined Subfields ‡a - Name of the main body ‡b - Subdivision of main body Example 110 1ƀ‡aUnited States.‡bCourt	710 - Corporate Body Name - Primary Indicators First 0 - Corporate name *(See notes)* Second 0 1 2 Subfields ‡a ‡b Example 710 01‡aUnited States. ‡bCourt of Appeals (2nd Circuit)	*Meeting names are entered in MARC 21 field 111 (Meeting name). See below for mapping.*

of Appeals (2nd Circuit)		
111 - Meeting name Primary Indicators First 0 - Inverted name 1 - Jurisdiction name 2 - Direct order Second - Undefined Subfields ‡a - Meeting name ‡e - Subdivision of meeting Example 111 2ƀ‡aWhite House Conference on Library and Information Services ‡eOhio Conference Delegation.	710 - Corporate Body Name - Primary Indicators First 1 - Meeting *(See notes)* Second 0 1 2 Subfields ‡a ‡b Example 710 12‡aWhite House Conference on Library and Information Services‡bOhio Conference Delegation.	*Corporate names are entered in MARC 21 field 110 (Main entry corporate name). See above for mapping.*
710 - Corporate Name Alternate Indicators First 0 - Inverted name 1 - Jurisdiction name 2 - Direct order Second ƀ - No information provided	711 - Corporate Body Name - Alternate Indicators First 0 - Corporate name *(See notes)* Second 0 1 2	*Meeting added entry names are entered in MARC 21 field 711 (Added Entry Meeting name). See below for mapping.*

<table>
<tr><td>Subfields

‡a - Name of the main body
‡b - Subdivision of main body

Example

710 2b‡aCatholic Church. ‡bPope (1958-1963 : John XXIII).</td><td>Subfields

‡a
‡b

Example

711 02‡aCatholic Church. ‡bPope (1958-1963 : John XXIII).</td><td></td></tr>
<tr><td>711 -Meeting name Alternate

Indicators

First
0 - Inverted name
1 - Jurisdiction name

2 - Direct order

Second
b - No information provided

Subfields

‡a - Meeting name
‡e - Subdivision meeting name

Example

711 2b‡aMostly Mozart Festival. ‡eOrchestra.</td><td>711 - Corporate Body Name - Alternate

Indicators

First
1 - Meeting name
(See notes)

Second
0
1

2

Subfields

‡a
‡b

Example

711 12‡aMostly Mozart Festival. ‡bOrchestra.</td><td>Corporate added entry names are entered in MARC 21 field 710 (Added Entry Corporate name). See above for mapping.</td></tr>
<tr><td>710 - Corporate Name Secondary

Indicators</td><td>712 - Corporate Body Name - Secondary

Indicators

First
0 - Corporate name
(See notes)</td><td>Meeting added entry names are entered in MARC 21 field 711 (Added Entry Meeting name). See below for mapping.</td></tr>
</table>

First 0 - Inverted name 1 - Jurisdiction name 2 - Direct order Second ɓ - No information provided Subfields ‡a - Name of the main body ‡b - Subdivision of main body Example 710 1ɓ‡aMinnesota. ‡bConstitutional Convention	Second 0 1 2 Subfields ‡a ‡b Example 712 01‡aMinnesota. ‡bConstitutional Convention	
711 -Meeting Name Secondary Indicators First 0 - Inverted name 1 - Jurisdiction name 2 - Name in direct order Second ɓ - No information provided Subfields ‡a - Meeting name ‡e - Subdivision meeting name Example 711 2ɓ‡aOlympic Games ‡eOrganizing Committee.‡eArts	712 - Corporate Body Name - Secondary Indicators First 1 - Meeting name *(See notes)* Second 0 1 2 Subfields ‡a ‡b Example 712 12‡aOlympic Games ‡bOrganizing Committee. ‡bArts	*Corporate added entry names are entered in MARC 21 field 710 (Added Entry Corporate name). See above for mapping*

and Culture Program.‡eVisual Arts Section.	and Culture Program.‡bVisual Arts Section.	

LOCAL FIELDS

Indian UniMARC	MARC 21	Notes
903 - Location	850 - Holdings Institution *(See notes)* Indicators First - Undefined Second - Undefined Subfields ‡a - Holding institution	*For more detailed holdings information, use field 852 (Location) below.*
852 - Location Indicators First - Shelving Scheme Second - Shelving order Subfields *(See note)* ‡a - Location ‡b - Sublocation or collection ‡c - Shelving location	903 - Location	*Other indicator and subfield values are also defined for field 852.*

6

MARC 21 FORMAT FOR AUTHORITY DATA

1. GENERAL INFORMATION:

This document lists all valid and obsolete data elements that may appear in MARC 21 authority records. It is intended to meet the need for a simple data element list to support MARC system development and online validation of MARC data elements. This listing does not include any descriptions or examples of MARC data elements. Descriptions and examples can be found in the MARC 21 Concise Authority Format.

2. LEADER AND DIRECTORY

Leader

A fixed field that comprises the first 24 character positions (00-23) of each record and provides information for the processing of the record.

Character Positions

00-04 - Record length

05 - Record status

A one-character code that indicates the relation of the record to a file.

a - Increase in encoding level

c - Corrected or revised

d - Deleted

n - New

o - Obsolete

s - Deleted: heading split into two or more headings

x - Deleted; heading replaced by another heading

06 - Type of record

A one-character code that indicates the characteristics of and defines the components of the record.

z - Authority data

07-08 - Undefined character positions

09 - Character coding scheme

- MARC-8

a - UCS/Unicode

10 - Indicator count

11 - Sub field code length

12-16 - Base address of data

17 - Encoding level

n - Complete authority record

o - Incomplete authority record

18-19 - Undefined character positions

20-23 - Entry map

20 - Length of the length-of-field portion

21 - Length of the starting-character-position portion

22 - Length of the implementation-defined portion

23 - Undefined

Directory

A computer-generated index to the location of the variable control and data fields within a record. The Directory immediately follows the Leader at character position 24 and consists of a series of fixed length (12 character positions) entries that give the tag, length, and starting character position of each variable field

Character Positions

00-02 - Tag

03-06 - Field length

07-11 - Starting character position

3. CONTROL FIELDS (00X)

Fields 001-008 contain the record control number and other control and coded information that are used in processing MARC authority records. Each control field is identified by a field tag in the Directory and contains either a single data element or a series of fixed-length data elements identified by relative character position. Variable control fields contain neither indicator positions nor subfield codes.

001 - CONTROL NUMBER (NR)

The control number assigned by the organization creating, using, or distributing the record.

Example:

001	n##86742756#
001	0010C0086##

003 - CONTROL NUMBER IDENTIFIER (NR)

The MARC code for the organization whose control number is contained in field 001 (Control Number). The source of the code is the MARC Code List for Organizations that is maintained by the Library of Congress (http://www.loc.gov/marc/organizations). For Canadian organizations, the source of the code is Symbols and Interlibrary Loan Policies in Canada that is maintained by the National Library of Canada (http://www.nlc-bnc.ca/6/16/s16-202-e.html).

Example:

003	DLC
003	CaOONL

005 - DATE AND TIME OF LATEST TRANSACTION (NR)

Sixteen characters that indicate the date and time of the latest record transaction and serve as a version identifier for the record. The data and time are recorded according to Representation of Dates and Times (ISO 8601) in the pattern yyyymmdd.

Example:

005 19940223151047.0

008 - FIXED-LENGTH DATA ELEMENTS (NR)

Forty character positions (00-39) that contain positionally-defined data elements that provide coded information about the record as a whole or about special aspects of the 1XX heading or 4XX/5XX tracing fields. Undefined character positions contain either a blank (#) or a fill character (|). Each defined character position must contain either a defined code or a fill character. The fill character may be used (in certain character positions) when a cataloging organization makes no attempt to code the character position. Field 008 is not repeatable.

Character positions

00-05 Date entered on file

The computer-generated, six-character numeric string that indicates the date the MARC record was created. The date is recorded in the pattern yymmdd.

008/06 - Direct or Indirect Geographic Subdivision

A one-character code that indicates whether the 1XX heading may be subdivided geographically when used as a subject heading and, if so, the method of subdivision used.

Not subdivided geographically

The heading may not be subdivided geographically.

d Subdivided geographically — direct

The heading may be followed immediately by the name of the specific place to which it is limited without the interposition of a subdivision for the larger geographic entity.

i Subdivided geographically — indirect

The name of the larger geographic entity is interposed between the heading and the subdivision for the specific place to which the heading is limited.

008/07 - Romanization Scheme

A one-character code that indicates whether the 1XX field contains the romanized form of the heading and, if so, identifies the romanization scheme used.

a International standard

b National standard

c National library association standard

d National library or bibliographic agency standard

e Local standard

08 Language of Catalog

A one-character alphabetic code that indicates whether the heading in the 1XX field and its associated reference structure are valid according to the rules used in establishing headings for English-language catalogs, French-language catalogs, or both

No information provided

b English and French

e English only

f French only

09 - Kind of record

a - Established heading

b - Untraced reference

c - Traced reference

d – Subdivision

e - Node label

f - Established heading and subdivision

g - Reference and subdivision

10 - Descriptive cataloging rules

A one-character code that identifies the descriptive cataloging rules used to formulate the 1XX name, name/title, or uniform title heading in established heading or reference records.

a - Earlier rules

b - AACR 1

c - AACR 2

d - AACR 2 compatible heading

n - Not applicable

z - Other

| - No attempt to code

11. Subject heading system/thesaurus

A one-character code that identifies the subject heading system/ thesaurus building conventions used to formulate the 1XX heading in established heading, reference, subdivision, or node label records.

a - Library of Congress Subject Headings

b - LC subject headings for children's literature

c - Medical Subject Headings

d - National Agricultural Library subject authority file

k - Canadian Subject Headings

n - Not applicable

r - Art and Architecture Thesaurus

s - Sears List of Subject Headings

v - Répertoire de vedettes-matière

z - Other

| - No attempt to code

12 - Type of series

A one-character code that indicates the type of series heading contained in the 1XX field in an established heading record.

a - Monographic series

b - Multipart item

c - Series-like phrase

n - Not applicable

z - Other

| - No attempt to code

13 - Numbered or unnumbered series

A one-character code that indicates the numbering characteristics of the series (or series-like phrase) represented by the 1XX heading.

a - Numbered

b - Unnumbered

c - Numbering varies

n - Not applicable

| - No attempt to code

14 - Heading use—main or added entry

A one-character code that indicates whether the 1XX heading is appropriate for use as a main or added entry in bibliographic records.

- Undetermined [OBSOLETE]

a - Appropriate

b - Not appropriate

c - Heading is appropriate for use as a main or added entry [OBSOLETE]

u - Unknown [OBSOLETE]

| - No attempt to code

15 - Heading use—subject added entry

A one-character code that indicates whether the 1XX heading is appropriate for use as a subject added entry in bibliographic records.

- Undetermined [OBSOLETE]

a - Appropriate

b - Not appropriate

c - Heading is appropriate for use as a subject [OBSOLETE]

u - Unknown [OBSOLETE]

| - No attempt to code

16 - Heading use—series added entry

A one-character code that indicates whether the 1XX heading is appropriate for use as a series added entry in bibliographic records.

- Undetermined [OBSOLETE]

a - Appropriate

b - Not appropriate

c - Heading is appropriate for use as a series [OBSOLETE]

u - Unknown [OBSOLETE]

| - No attempt to code

17 - Type of subject subdivision

A one-character code that indicates the type of subject subdivision heading contained in the 1XX field of a subdivision record, an established heading and subdivision record, or a reference and subdivision record.

- Value used in records before definition of this character position [OBSOLETE]

a - Topical

b - Form

c - Chronological

d - Geographic

e - Language

n - Not applicable

| - No attempt to code

18-27 - Undefined character positions

28 - Type of government agency

A one-character code that indicates whether the 1XX heading represents a government agency and, if so, the jurisdictional level of the agency.

- Not a government agency

a - Autonomous or semi-autonomous component

c - Multilocal

f - Federal/national

i - International intergovernmental

l - Local

m - Multistate

o - Government agency—type undetermined

s - State, provincial, territorial, dependent, etc.

u - Unknown if heading is government agency

z - Other

| - No attempt to code

29 - Reference evaluation

A one-character code that indicates whether the 4XX/5XX tracing fields in a record have been evaluated for consistency with the rules used to formulate the 1XX heading in the record.

- Value used in records before definition of this character position [OBSOLETE]

a - Tracings are consistent with the heading

b - Tracings are not necessarily consistent with the heading

n - Not applicable

| - No attempt to code

30 - Undefined character position

31 - Record update in process

A one-character code that indicates whether a change in any field in a record is being considered.

a - Record can be used

b - Record is being updated

| - No attempt to code

32 - Undifferentiated personal name

A one-character code that indicates whether a personal name heading contained in field 100 in an established heading record or a reference record is used by one person or by two or more persons.

a - Differentiated personal name

b - Undifferentiated personal name

n - Not applicable

| - No attempt to code

33 - Level of establishment

A one-character code that indicates the extent to which the formulation of the 1XX heading conforms to the descriptive cataloging rules coded in 008/10 and/or the subject heading system/ thesaurus conventions coded in 008/11.

a - Fully established

b - Memorandum

c - Provisional

d - Preliminary

n - Not applicable

| - No attempt to code

34-37 - Undefined character positions

35-37 - Language of heading code [OBSOLETE]

38 - Modified record

A one-character code indicates whether the record is modified from its intended content.

- Not modified

s - Shortened

x - Missing characters

| - No attempt to code

39 - Cataloging source

A one-character code that indicates the creator of the original authority record. The NUC symbol for or the name of the organization may be contained in subfield $a of field 040 (Cataloging Source)

- National bibliographic agency

a - National Agricultural Library [OBSOLETE]

b - National Library of Medicine [OBSOLETE]

c - Cooperative cataloging program

d - Other

u - Unknown

| - No attempt to code

4. VARIABLE FIELDS

(i) Number and Code Fields (01X-09X)

Fields 010-09X contain control numbers, linking standard numbers, classification and call numbers, codes, and other data elements relating to the authority record.

010 - LIBRARY OF CONGRESS CONTROL NUMBER (NR)

A unique number assigned to a record by LC or a Linked Systems Project partner contributing authority records to the National Coordinated Cataloging Operations database. (010 is an agency-assigned field.)

Indicators

First - Undefined

- Undefined

Second - Undefined

- Undefined

Sub field Codes

$a - LC control number (NR)

$z - Canceled/invalid LC control number (R)

$8 - Field link and sequence number (R)

014 - LINK TO BIBLIOGRAPHIC RECORD FOR SERIAL OR MULTIPART ITEM (R)

The control number copied from field 001 of a MARC 21 bibliographic record for a serial or a multipart item that is cataloged as a set.

Indicators

First - Undefined

- Undefined

Second - Undefined

-Undefined

Sub field Codes

$a - Control number of related bibliographic record (NR)

$6 - Linkage (NR)

$8 - Field link and sequence number (R)

016 - NATIONAL BIBLIOGRAPHIC AGENCY CONTROL NUMBER (R)

Unique numbers that have been assigned to a record by a national bibliographic agency other than the Library of Congress.

Indicators

First - National bibliographic agency

- National Library of Canada

7 - Agency identified in subfield $2

Second - Undefined

- Undefined

Subfield Codes

$a - Record control number (NR)

$z - Canceled/invalid record control number (R)

$2 - Source (NR)

$8 - Field link and sequence number (R)

020 - INTERNATIONAL STANDARD BOOK NUMBER (R)

The ISBN, terms of availability, and any cancelled/invalid ISBN copied from field 020 of a MARC 21 bibliographic record for a multipart item that is cataloged as a set (The ISBN is an agency-assigned data element.)

Indicators

First - Undefined

- Undefined

Second - Undefined

- Undefined

Subfield Codes

$a - International Standard Book Number (NR)

$c - Terms of availability (NR)

$z - Canceled/invalid ISBN (R)

$6 - Linkage (NR)

$8 - Field link and sequence number (R)

022 - INTERNATIONAL STANDARD SERIAL NUMBER (R)

The ISSN and/or any incorrect and cancelled ISSNs copied from field 022 of a MARC 21 bibliographic record for a serial. (The ISSN is an agency-assigned data element.)

Indicators

First - Undefined

- Undefined

Second - Undefined

- Undefined

Subfield Codes

$a - International Standard Serial Number (NR)

$y - Incorrect ISSN (R)

$z - Canceled ISSN (R)

$6 - Linkage (NR)

$8 - Field link and sequence number (R)

035 - SYSTEM CONTROL NUMBER (R)

A control number of a system other than the one whose control number is contained in field 001 or 010 of the authority record.

Indicators

First - Undefined

- Undefined

Second - Undefined

- Undefined

Subfield Codes

$a - System control number (NR)

$z - Canceled/invalid system control number (R)

$6 - Linkage (NR)

$8 - Field link and sequence number (R)

040 - CATALOGING SOURCE (NR)

The MARC code or the name of the organization(s) that created the original authority record, assigned MARC content designation and transcribed the record into machine-readable form, or modified an existing MARC record. These data and the code in 008/39 (Cataloging source) specify the parties responsible for the authority record.

For U.S. organizations and countries other than Canada, the source of the code is the MARC Code List for Organizations (http://www.loc.gov/marc/organizations/). For Canadian organizations, the source of the code is Symbols and Interlibrary Loan Policies in Canada that is maintained by the National Library of Canada (http://www.nlc-bnc.ca/6/16/s16-202-e.html).

One or more codes that indicate an authentication center has reviewed a national database record. The codes are associated with specifically designated authentication agencies.

Indicators

First - Undefined

- Undefined

Second - Undefined

- Undefined

Subfield Codes

$a - Original cataloging agency (NR)

$b - Language of cataloging (NR)

$c - Transcribing agency (NR)

$d - Modifying agency (R)

$e - Description conventions (NR)

$f - Subject heading or thesaurus conventions (NR)

$6 - Linkage (NR)

$8 - Field link and sequence number (R)

042 - AUTHENTICATION CODE (NR)

One or more codes that indicate an authentication center has reviewed a national database record. The codes are associated with specifically designated authentication agencies.

Indicators

First - Undefined

- Undefined

Second - Undefined

- Undefined

Subfield Code

$a - Authentication code (R)

sanb - South African National Bibliography Project

043 - GEOGRAPHIC AREA CODE (NR)

Up to three MARC codes for geographic areas associated with the 1XX heading in an established heading record or a subdivision record. The code is seven characters in length. The code is taken from the MARC Code List for Geographic Areas (http://www.loc.gov/marc/geoareas/) and is an authoritative-agency data element.

Indicators

First - Undefined

- Undefined

Second - Undefined

- Undefined

Subfield Codes

$a - Geographic area code (R)

$b - Local GAC code (R)

$c - ISO code (R)

$2 - Source of local code (R)

$6 - Linkage (NR)

$8 - Field link and sequence number (R)

045 - TIME PERIOD OF HEADING (NR)

A time period code (subfield $a) and/or a formatted time period (subfield $b or $c) associated with the 1XX heading in an established heading record or a subdivision record.

Indicators

First - Type of time period in subfield $b or $c

- Subfield $b or $c not present

0 - Single date/time

1 - Multiple single dates/times

2 - Range of dates/times

Second - Undefined

- Undefined

Subfield Codes

$a - Time period code (R)

$b - Formatted 9999 B.C. through C.E. time period (R)

$c - Formatted pre-9999 B.C. time period (R)

$6 - Linkage (NR)

$8 - Field link and sequence number (R)

050 - LIBRARY OF CONGRESS CALL NUMBER (R)

A call/and or class number for a series when all or part of the series is classified as a collected set or with the main series. The classification number is taken from the Library of Congress Classification and/or the LC Classification Additions and Changes.

Indicators

First - Undefined

- Undefined

Second - Source of call number

0 - Assigned by LC

4 - Assigned by agency other than LC

Subfield Codes

$a - Classification number (NR)

$b - Item number (NR)

$d - Volumes/dates to which call number applies (NR)

$5 - Institution to which field applies (R)

$6 - Linkage (NR)

$8 - Field link and sequence number (R)

052 - GEOGRAPHIC CLASSIFICATION (R)

A code for a geographic area associated with the 151 field in an established heading record or a subdivision record for a geographic name. The geographic classification code is derived from the Library of Congress Classification Class G and expanded Cutter number lists for place names. (The geographic classification area code and the subarea code are authoritative-agency data elements.)

Indicators

First - Code source

- Library of Congress Classification

0 - U.S. Dept. of Defense Classification [OBSOLETE]

1 - U.S. Dept. of Defense Classification

7 - Source specified in subfield $2

Second - Undefined

- Undefined

Subfield Codes

$a - Geographic classification area code (NR)

$b - Geographic classification subarea code (R)

$d - Populated place name (R)

$2 - Code source (NR)

$6 - Linkage (NR)

$8 - Field link and sequence number (R)

053 - LC CLASSIFICATION NUMBER (R)

A single LC classification number or a range of numbers associated with a 1XX heading in an established heading record or a subdivision record. The classification number is taken from the Library of Congress Classification and/or the LC Classification Additions and Changes. The hyphen (-) between the two class numbers in a range of numbers may be generated based on the presence of both subfields $a and $b. (053 is an authoritative-agency data element.)

Indicators

First - Undefined

- Undefined

Second - Source of classification number

0 - Assigned by LC

4 - Assigned by agency other than LC

Subfield Codes

$a - Classification number element—single number or beginning number of span (NR)

$b - Classification number element—ending number of span (NR)

$c - Explanatory term (NR)

$5 - Institution to which field applies (R)

$6 - Linkage (NR)

$8 - Field link and sequence number (R)

055 - NATIONAL LIBRARY OF CANADA CALL NUMBER (R)

The call number for a series assigned in Canada if the institution has classified all of part of the series as a collected set. The second indicator values distinguish between content actually assigned by the National Library of Canada and that assigned by an organization other than NLC.

Indicators

First - Undefined

- Undefined

Second - Source of call number

0 - Assigned by NLC

4 - Assigned by agency other than NLC

Subfield Codes

$a - Classification number (NR)

$b - Item number (NR)

$d - Volumes/dates to which call number applies (NR)

$5 - Institution to which field applies (R)

$6 - Linkage (NR)

$8 - Field link and sequence number (R)

060 - NATIONAL LIBRARY OF MEDICINE CALL NUMBER (R)

A call number for a series when all or part of the series is classified as a collected set or with the main series. The classification number is taken from the National Library of Medicine Classification schedules QS-QZ and W or from the Library of Congress Classification schedules as used by NLM for peripheral and related topics.

Indicators

First - Undefined

- Undefined

Second - Source of call number

0 - Assigned by NLM

4 - Assigned by agency other than NLM

Subfield Codes

$a - Classification number (NR)

$b - Item number (NR)

$d - Volumes/dates to which call number applies (NR)

$5 - Institution to which field applies (R)

$6 - Linkage (NR)

$8 - Field link and sequence number (R)

065 - OTHER CLASSIFICATION NUMBER (R)

Indicators

First - Undefined

- Undefined

Second - Undefined

- Undefined

Subfield Codes

$a - Classification number element-single number or beginning of span (NR)

$b - Classification number element-ending number of span (NR)

$c - Explanatory term (NR)

$2 - Number source (NR)

$5 - Institution to which field applies (R)

$6 - Linkage (NR)

$8 - Field link and sequence number (R)

066 - CHARACTER SETS PRESENT (NR)

Information that indicates that the character set present in a record is other than the default MARC Latin sets (ANSEL and ASCII). A detailed description of the standard escape sequences used in MARC records is provided in MARC 21 Specifications for Record Structure, Character Sets and Exchange Media.

Indicators

First - Undefined

- Undefined

Second - Undefined

- Undefined

Subfield Codes

$a - Primary G0 character set (NR)

$b - Primary G1 character set (NR)

$c - Alternate G0 or G1 character set (R)

070 - NATIONAL AGRICULTURAL LIBRARY CALL NUMBER (R)

A call number assigned by the National Agricultural Library to a series when all or part of the series is classified as a collected set or with the main series. (070 is an agency-assigned field.)

Indicators

First - Undefined

- Undefined

Second - Undefined

- Undefined

Subfield Codes

$a - Classification number (NR)

$b - Item number (NR)

$d - Volume/dates to which call number applies (NR)

$6 - Linkage (NR)

$8 - Field link and sequence number (R)

072 - SUBJECT CATEGORY CODE (R)

A code for the subject category that is associated with the 1XX field in an established heading record or a node label record.

Indicators

First - Undefined

- Undefined

Second - Code source

- No information provided

0 - NAL subject category code list

7 - Source specified in subfield $2

Subfield Codes

$a - Subject category code (NR)

$x - Subject category code subdivision (R)

$2 - Code source (NR)

$6 - Linkage (NR)

$8 - Field link and sequence number (R)

073 - SUBDIVISION USAGE (NR)

A code specifying the topical or geographic subject terms with which the 1XX heading in a subdivision record may be used in a particular thesaurus.

Indicators

First - Undefined

- Undefined

Second - Undefined

- Undefined

Subfield Codes

$a - Subdivision usage (R)

$z - Code source (NR)

$6 - Linkage (NR)

$8 - Field link and sequence number (R)

082 - DEWEY DECIMAL CALL NUMBER (R)

A call number for a series when all or part of the series is classified as a collected set or with the main series. The classification number is taken from the Dewey Decimal Classification; the Abridged Dewey Decimal Classification; and/or the DC&: Dewey Decimal Classification Additions, Notes and Decisions.

Indicators

First - Type of edition

0 - Full

1 - Abridged

Second - Source of call number

- No information provided

0 - Assigned by LC

4 - Assigned by agency other than LC

Subfield Codes

$a - Classification number (NR)

$b - Item number (NR)

$d - Volumes/dates to which call number applies (NR)

$2 - Edition number (NR)

$5 - Institution to which field applies (R)

$6 - Linkage (NR)

$8 - Field link and sequence number (R)

083 - DEWEY DECIMAL CLASSIFICATION NUMBER (R)

A single Dewey classification number or a range of numbers associated with a 1XX heading in an established heading record or a subdivision record. The classification number is taken from the Dewey Decimal Classification and Relative Index; the Abridged Dewey Decimal Classification and Relative Index; and/or the DC&: Dewey Decimal Classification Additions, Notes and Decisions.

The hyphen (-) between the two class numbers in a range of numbers may be generated based on the presence of both subfields $a and $b; the parentheses that may enclose an explanatory term in subfield $c in an established heading record; the abbreviation T before the table in subfield $z; the dash (-) between the table number and the class number in subfields $z and $a; and the abbreviation dc before the edition number in subfield $2 may be system generated

Indicators

First - Type of edition

0 - Full

1 - Abridged

Second - Source of classification number

0 - Assigned by LC

4 - Assigned by agency other than LC

Subfield Codes

$a - Classification number element—single number or beginning number of span (NR)

$b - Classification number element—ending number of span (NR)

$c - Explanatory term (NR)

$z - Table identification—table number (NR)

$2 - Edition number (NR)

$5 - Institution to which field applies (R)

$6 - Linkage (NR)

$8 - Field link and sequence number (R)

086 - GOVERNMENT DOCUMENT CALL NUMBER (R)

A government document call number for a series when all or part of the series is classified as a collected set or with a main series (646, Series Classification Practice, subfield $a, code c or m). The organization assigning the number may be identified in subfield $5.

Field 086 may also contain the volumes/dates to which the number applies. Varying call numbers for different ranges of volumes/dates within a series or different copies or sets are contained in separate occurrences of field 086.

Indicators

First - Number source

- Source specified in subfield $2

0 - Superintendent of Documents Classification System

1 - Government of Canada Publications: Outline of

Classification

Second - Undefined

- Undefined

Subfield Codes

$a - Call number (NR)

$d - Volumes/dates to which call number applies (NR)

$z - Canceled/invalid call number (NR)

$2 - Number source (NR)

$5 - Institution to which field applies (R)

$6 - Linkage (NR)

$8 - Field link and sequence number (R)

087 - GOVERNMENT DOCUMENT CLASSIFICATION NUMBER (R)

A government document call number for a series when all or part of the series is classified as a collected set or with a main series (646, Series Classification Practice, subfield $a, code c or m). The organization assigning the number may be identified in subfield $5.

Field 086 may also contain the volumes/dates to which the number applies. Varying call numbers for different ranges of volumes/ dates within a series or different copies or sets are contained in separate occurrences of field 086.

Indicators

First - Number source

- Source specified in subfield $2

0 - Superintendent of Documents Classification System

1 - Government of Canada Publications: Outline of Classification

Second - Undefined

- Undefined

Subfield Codes

$a - Classification number element—Single number or

beginning number of span (NR)

$b - Classification number element—Ending number of span (NR)

$c - Explanatory information (NR)

$2 - Number source (NR)

$6 - Linkage (NR)

$8 - Field link and sequence number (R)

09X - LOCAL CALL NUMBERS

The 090-099 fields are reserved for a locally-assigned call number for a series when all or part of the series is classified as a collected set or with the main series.

090 - LOCAL CALL NUMBER (SERIES)[OBSOLETE]

Indicators

First - Undefined

- Undefined

Second - Undefined

- Undefined

Subfield Codes

$a - Classification number (NR)

$b - Item number (NR)

$d - Volume/dates to which call number applies (NR)

(ii) Heading Fields (1XX)

Fields 100-185 contain names, uniform titles, and terms used in headings or subdivisions to headings. They are usually constructed according to generally accepted cataloging and thesaurus-building rules. In a MARC authority record, a heading is the content of a 1XX, 4XX, or 5XX field that documents the form of name, title, or term used for indexing and retrieval or organizational purposes in a file. The content designation of the subelements of each type of heading is consistent across the 1XX heading and 4XX/5XX tracing fields.

* **GENERAL INFORMATION**

Two types of headings are defined in the authorities format:

* **Established heading** - The authoritative form of a heading that is used as a main entry (1XX), added entry (700-730), or series added entry (440 or 800-830), or as the lead element in a subject access (600-651, 654-657) field in bibliographic records. In authority records, established headings are used in fields 100-155 (headings) and fields 500-555 (tracings) for established heading (008/09, Kind of record, code a or f) and subdivision (008/09, Kind of record, code d) records.

Unestablished heading - A heading used within an authority file to organize or to refer. The unestablished heading may be a variant to the established form, a heading used only for authority file organizational purposes, or an incomplete piece of an established heading. This heading is not used in bibliographic records. In established heading records an unestablished heading may be used in a 4XX (tracing) field. In reference, subdivision, reference and subdivision, and node label records, the 1XX (heading) field contains an unestablished heading.

Both established and unestablished headings may be names, name/title combinations, uniform titles, topical terms, genre/form terms, subdivisions, extended subject headings or node labels.

* **Name Heading** - A heading that is a personal, corporate, meeting, or jurisdiction (including geographic) name.
* **Name/Title Heading** - A heading consisting of both a name and a title portion. The name portion may be a personal, corporate, meeting, or jurisdiction name. The title portion may be a uniform or conventional title, a title page title of a work, or a series title.
* **Uniform Title Heading** - A heading consisting of a uniform or conventional title, a title page title, or a series title that is not entered under a personal, corporate, meeting, or jurisdiction name in a name/title heading construction.
* **Topical Term Heading** - A heading consisting of a topical subject term.

* **Genre/Form Term Heading** - A heading consisting of a genre/form subject term.
* **Subdivision Heading** - A heading consisting of a general (topical or language), form, geographic, or chronological subject subdivision term. An extended subdivision heading contains more than one subject subdivision term (subfields $v, $x, $y, and $z).
* **Extended Subject Heading** - A name, name/title, uniform title, topical term or genre/form term heading that includes one or more general, form, geographic, or chronological subject subdivision terms (subfield $v, $x, $y, or $z).
* **Node label heading** - A heading consisting of a term used in the systematic section of a thesaurus to indicate the logical basis on which a category is divided. The dash (—) that precedes a subject subdivision is not carried in the MARC record; it may be generated based on the presence of subfields $v, $x, $y, or $z.

Heading Usage in Bibliographic Records

Only the 1XX field in established heading records may be used as access points in bibliographic records. Name, name/title, and uniform title headings may be used as main or added entries (008/14, code a); name, name/title, uniform title, topical term, genre/form, and extended subject headings may be used as subject added entries (008/15, code a), and name/title and uniform title headings may be used as series added entries (008/16, code a). Subdivision headings may be used only in extended subject heading added entries.

Heading Usage in Authority Structures

A heading may be categorized as being suitable for either a name or a subject authority structure. Headings that are formulated using descriptive cataloging conventions (008/10) are suitable for a name authority structure. These headings encompass name, name/title, and uniform title headings in established heading and established heading and subdivision records and unestablished forms of these types of headings in reference records. Certain note and tracing and reference fields are used only in records for headings suitable for name authority structures.

Headings that are formulated using subject heading system /thesaurus building conventions (008/11) are suitable for a subject authority structure. These headings encompass names, name/title combinations, uniform titles, topical terms, and genre/form headings (and extended subject headings using these types of headings) in established heading and established heading and subdivision records. Unestablished forms of these types of headings are used in reference and, reference and subdivision records. Unestablished headings are also used in subdivision and node label records Certain note and tracing and reference fields in the format are used only in records for headings suitable for subject authority structures

100 - HEADING—PERSONAL NAME(NR)

An established personal name used in name, name/title, or extended subject heading established heading records or an unestablished personal name used in these types of headings in reference records.

Indicators

First - Type of personal name entry element

0 - Forename

1 - Surname

1 - Single surname [OBSOLETE]

2 - Multiple surname [OBSOLETE]

3 - Family name

Second - Undefined

- Undefined

Second - Nonfiling characters [OBSOLETE]

0-9 - Number of nonfiling characters present [OBSOLETE]

Subfield Codes

$a - Personal name (NR)

$b - Numeration (NR)

$c - Titles and other words associated with a name (R)

$d - Dates associated with a name (NR)

$e - Relator term (R)

$f - Date of a work (NR)

$g - Miscellaneous information (NR)

$h - Medium (NR)

$j - Attribution qualifier (R)

$k - Form subheading (R)

$l - Language of a work (NR)

$m - Medium of performance for music (R)

$n - Number of part/section of a work (R)

$o - Arranged statement for music (NR)

$p - Name of part/section of a work (R)

$q - Fuller form of name (NR)

$r - Key for music (NR)

$s - Version (NR)

$t - Title of a work (NR)

$v - Form subdivision (R)

$x - General subdivision (R)

$y - Chronological subdivision (R)

$z - Geographic subdivision (R)

$6 - Linkage (NR)

$8 - Field link and sequence number (R)

Examples :

100	1	#$aOlema, Adam, $d1603-1671
100	1	#$aDe Anala, Anna
100	1	1#$aMcGraw, Hal
100	1	#$aO'Brib, Gerard
100	1	#$aAleixandre Ferrandis, N.

110 - HEADING—CORPORATE NAME (NR)

An established corporate name used in a name, name/title, or extended subject heading in established heading records or an unestablished corporate name used in these types of headings in reference records.

Indicators

First - Type of corporate name entry element

0 - Inverted name

1 - Jurisdiction name

2 - Name in direct order

Second - Undefined

- Undefined

Second - Nonfiling characters [OBSOLETE]

0-9 - Number of nonfiling characters present [OBSOLETE]

Subfield Codes

$a - Corporate name or jurisdiction name as entry element (NR)

$b - Subordinate unit (R)

$c - Location of meeting (NR)

$d - Date of meeting or treaty signing (R)

$e - Relator term (R)

$f - Date of a work (NR)

$g - Miscellaneous information (NR)

$h - Medium (NR)

$k - Form subheading (R)

$l - Language of a work (NR)

$m - Medium of performance for music (R)

$n - Number of part/section/meeting (R)

$o - Arranged statement for music (NR)

$p - Name of part/section of a work (R)

$r - Key for music (NR)

$s - Version (NR)

$t - Title of a work (NR)

$v - Form subdivision (R)

$x - General subdivision (R)

$y - Chronological subdivision (R)

$z - Geographic subdivision (R)

$6 - Linkage (NR)

$8 - Field link and sequence number (R)

Examples :

110 2#$aNizarian Brooks Chorale

110 2#$aField & Young (Jersey City, N.J.)

110 1#$aPennsylvania. $bState Board of Examiners of Nursing Home Administrators

110 2#$aUniversity of Hyderabad $bExperimental Music Studios

110 2#$aIndian Family Planning Council

110 2#$aPRONAPADE (Firm)

110 1#$aNotre-Dame de Laeken (Belgium : Parish)

111 - HEADING—MEETING NAME(NR)

An established meeting name used in a name, name/title, or extended subject heading in established heading records or an unestablished meeting name used in these types of headings in reference records.

Indicators

First - Type of meeting name entry element

0 - Inverted name

1 - Jurisdiction name

2 - Name in direct order

Second - Undefined

- Undefined

Second - Nonfiling characters [OBSOLETE]

0-9 - Number of nonfiling characters present [OBSOLETE]

Subfield Codes

$a - Meeting name or jurisdiction name as entry element (NR)

$b - Number (NR) [OBSOLETE]

$c - Location of meeting (NR)

$d - Date of meeting (NR)

$e - Subordinate unit (R)

$f - Date of a work (NR)

$g - Miscellaneous information (NR)

$h - Medium (NR)

$k - Form subheading (R)

$l - Language of a work (NR)

$n - Number of part/section/meeting (R)

$p - Name of part/section of a work (R)

$q - Name of meeting following jurisdiction name entry element (NR)

$s - Version (NR)

$t - Title of a work (NR)

$v - Form subdivision (R)

$x - General subdivision (R)

$y - Chronological subdivision (R)

$z - Geographic subdivision (R)

$6 - Linkage (NR)

$8 - Field link and sequence number (R)

Examples :

111 2#$aSymposium Internacional In Memoriam $d(1970 : $cGuanajuato, Mexico)

111 2#$Indian University Symposium $d(1983)

111 2#$aInternational Congress Philology $n(17th : $d1993 : $cAix-en-Provence, France). $tActes du XVIIeme Congres international

111 2#$aInternational Symposium on Quality Control (1974-)

111 2#$aIllinois White House Conference on Children

$d(1980 : $cSpringfield, Ill.). $eChicago Regional Committee

130 - HEADING—UNIFORM TITLE (NR)

An established uniform title used in a title or extended subject heading in established heading records or an unestablished uniform title used in these types of headings in reference records.

Indicators

First - Undefined

- Undefined

Nonfiling characters

0-9 - Number of nonfiling characters

Subfield Codes

$a - Uniform title (NR)

$d - Date of treaty signing (R)

$f - Date of a work (NR)

$g - Miscellaneous information (NR)

$h - Medium (NR)

$k - Form subheading (R)

$l - Language of a work (NR)

$m - Medium of performance for music (R)

$n - Number of part/section of a work (R)

$o - Arranged statement for music (NR)

$p - Name of part/section of a work (R)

$r - Key for music (NR)

$s - Version (NR)

$t - Title of a work (NR)

$v - Form subdivision (R)

$x - General subdivision (R)

$y - Chronological subdivision (R)

$z - Geographic subdivision (R)

$6 - Linkage (NR)

$8 - Field link and sequence number (R)

Examples :

130 #0$a"Hsuan lai hsi kan" hsi lieh

130 #0$aElektroshlakovyi pereplav

130 #0$aHabakkuk commentary

130 #0$aResources information se

148 - HEADING—CHRONOLOGICAL TERM (NR)

Indicators

First - Undefined

- Undefined

Second - Undefined

- Undefined

Subfield Codes

$a - Chronological term (NR)

$v - Form subdivision (R)

$x - General subdivision (R)

$y - Chronological subdivision (R)

$z - Geographic subdivision (R)

$6 - Linkage (NR)

$8 - Field link and sequence number (R)

150 - HEADING—TOPICAL TERM (NR)

An established topical term used in main or extended subject headings in established heading records or an unestablished topical term used in these types of headings in subdivision, reference, or node label records.

Indicators

First - Undefined

- Undefined

Second - Undefined

- Undefined

Second - Nonfiling characters [OBSOLETE]

0-9 - Number of nonfiling characters present [OBSOLETE]

Subfield Codes

$a - Topical term or geographic name entry element (NR)

$b - Topical term following geographic name entry element (NR)

$v - Form subdivision (R)

$x - General subdivision (R)

$y - Chronological subdivision (R)

$z - Geographic subdivision (R)

$6 - Linkage (NR)

$8 - Field link and sequence number (R)

Examples :

150 ##$aBlood

150 ##$acatalogs by source

150 ##$aCharacters and characteristics in literature

150 ##$aBull Run, 2nd Battle, 1862

150 ##$aScuba diving $vPeriodicals

150 ##$aConflict of laws $xSupport (Domestic relations)

151 - HEADING—GEOGRAPHIC NAME (NR)

An established geographic name used in main or extended subject headings in established heading records or an unestablished geographic name used in these types of headings in subdivision or reference records.

Indicators

First - Undefined

- Undefined

Second - Undefined

- Undefined

Second - Nonfiling characters [OBSOLETE]

0-9 - Number of nonfiling characters present [OBSOLETE]

Subfield Codes

$a - Geographic name (NR)

$b - Name following place as entry element (NR) [OBSOLETE]

$v - Form subdivision (R)

$x - General subdivision (R)

$y - Chronological subdivision (R)

$z - Geographic subdivision (R)

$6 - Linkage (NR)

$8 - Field link and sequence number (R)

Examples :

151 ##$aAmazon River

151 ##$aCommunist countries

151 ##$aHalley's comet

151 ##$aInterstate 70

151 ##$aMason and Dixon's Line

151 ##$aHimalaya Mountains

155 - HEADING—GENRE/FORM TERM (NR)

A genre or form term used as a heading in an established heading record, an established heading and reference record, a traced or an untraced reference record, or a reference and subdivision record. The term may consist of more than one word.

Indicators

First - Undefined

- Undefined

Second - Undefined

- Undefined

Subfield Codes

$a - Genre/form term (NR)

$v - Form subdivision (R)

$x - General subdivision (R)

$y - Chronological subdivision (R)

$z - Geographic subdivision (R)

$6 - Linkage (NR)

$8 - Field link and sequence number (R)

Examples :

155 ##$aBird's-eye views $y1874

155 ##$aCartoons $vPeriodicals

155 ##$aDictionaries $xFrench $y18th century

155 ##$aHymnals $zMassachusetts $y18th century

155 ##$aPhotographs $vPeriodicals

180 - HEADING—GENERAL SUBDIVISION (NR)

A topical, form, or language term used as a heading in a subdivision record.

Indicators

First - Undefined

- Undefined

Second - Undefined

- Undefined

Subfield Codes

$v - Form subdivision (R)

$x - General subdivision (R)

$y - Chronological subdivision (R)

$z - Geographic subdivision (R)

$6 - Linkage (NR)

$8 - Field link and sequence number (R)

Examples :

180 ##$xRussian $vDictionaries

180 ##$xPolitical aspects

180 ##$xRhetoric $xAbility testing

180 ##$xArabic [or, Italian, etc.]

180 ##$xCivilization $y16th century

180 ##$xHistory $y18th century $xExhibition

181 - HEADING—GEOGRAPHIC SUBDIVISION (NR)

A geographic name or term used as a heading in a subdivision record.

Indicators

First - Undefined

- Undefined

Second - Undefined

- Undefined

Subfield Codes

$v - Form subdivision (R)

$x - General subdivision (R)

$y - Chronological subdivision (R)

$z - Geographic subdivision (R)

$6 - Linkage (NR)

$8 - Field link and sequence number (R)

Examples :

181 ##$zParis (France) $vPhotographs

181 ##$zMississippi $zTippah County $xHistory

181 ##$zWashington (D.C.) $y1890-1910

181 ##$zHudson River Valley (N.Y. and N.J.)

181 ##$zNew York (State) $zBuffalo

181 ##$zFrance $zLoire River Valley

182 - HEADING—CHRONOLOGICAL SUBDIVISION (NR)

A chronological term used as a heading in a subdivision record.

Indicators

First - Undefined

- Undefined

Second - Undefined

- Undefined

Subfield Codes

$v - Form subdivision (R)

$x - General subdivision (R)

$y - Chronological subdivision (R)

$z - Geographic subdivision (R)

$6 - Linkage (NR)

$8 - Field link and sequence number (R)

Examples :

182 ##$y1981- $vPeriodicals

182 ##$y1981- $xFrench

182 ##$yTo 1500

182 ##$y18th century

182 ##$yEarly church, ca. 30-600

185 - HEADING—FORM SUBDIVISION (NR)

A form or genre term used as a heading in a subdivision record.

Indicators

First - Undefined

- Undefined

Second - Undefined

- Undefined

Subfield Codes

$v - Form subdivision (R)

$x - General subdivision (R)

$y - Chronological subdivision (R)

$z - Geographic subdivision (R)

$6 - Linkage (NR)

$8 - Field link and sequence number (R)

Examples :

185 ##$vFiction

185 ##$vAbbreviations

185 ##$vIndexes $vPeriodicals

185 ##$vcase studies $vsoftware

185 ##$vDictionaries $xSpanish

(iii) Complex Subject References (2XX-3XX)

Introduction

A cross reference leads from an unauthorized heading to an authorized heading (see reference) or from one authorized heading to another (see also reference). Actual cross references are generally not carried explicitly in authority records. Instead, variant form and related headings are carried in authority records in either tracing or reference note fields. Cross reference displays may be generated by combining the contents of a tracing or a reference note field and the 1XX heading field of a record.

In the MARC 21 Authority format, a variety of tracing and reference fields are defined to allow the generation of simple and complex references. These data elements are divided into the following groups where descriptions of specific fields can be found:

Complex Subject Reference Fields (2XX-3XX)

See From Tracing Fields (4XX)

See Also From Tracing Fields (5XX)

Complex Name Reference Fields (663-666)

260 - COMPLEX SEE REFERENCE—SUBJECT (R)

Indicators

First - Undefined

- Undefined

Second - Undefined

- Undefined

Subfield Codes

$a - Heading referred to (R)

$i - Explanatory text (R)

$6 - Linkage (NR)

$8 - Field link and sequence number (R)

360 - COMPLEX SEE ALSO REFERENCE—SUBJECT (R)

Indicators

First - Undefined

- Undefined

Second - Undefined

- Undefined

Subfield Codes

$a - Heading referred to (R)

$i - Explanatory text (R)

$6 - Linkage (NR)

$8 - Field link and sequence number (R)

(iv) See From Tracing Fields (4XX)

400 - SEE FROM TRACING—PERSONAL NAME (R)

Indicators

First - Type of personal name entry element

0 - Forename

1 - Surname

1 - Single surname [OBSOLETE]

2 - Multiple surname [OBSOLETE]

3 - Family name

Second - Undefined

- Undefined

Second - Nonfiling characters [OBSOLETE]

0-9 - Number of nonfiling characters present [OBSOLETE]

Subfield Codes

$a - Personal name (NR)

$b - Numeration (NR)

$c - Titles and other words associated with a name (R)

$d - Dates associated with a name (NR)

$e - Relator term (R)

$f - Date of a work (NR)

$g - Miscellaneous information (NR)

$h - Medium (NR)

$i - Reference instruction phrase (NR)

$j - Attribution qualifier (R)

$k - Form subheading (R)

$l - Language of a work (NR)

$m - Medium of performance for music (R)

$n - Number of part/section of a work (R)

$o - Arranged statement for music (NR)

$p - Name of part/section of a work (R)

$q - Fuller form of name (NR)

$r - Key for music (NR)

$s - Version (NR)

$t - Title of a work (NR)

$v - Form subdivision (R)

$w - Control subfield (NR)

0 - Special relationship

1 - Tracing use restriction

2 - Earlier form of heading

3 - Reference display

$x - General subdivision (R)

$y - Chronological subdivision (R)

$z - Geographic subdivision (R)

$5 - Institution to which field applies (R)

$6 - Linkage (NR)

$8 - Field link and sequence number (R)

410 - SEE FROM TRACING—CORPORATE NAME (R)

Indicators

First - Type of corporate name entry element

0 - Inverted name

1 - Jurisdiction name

2 - Name in direct order

Second - Undefined

- Undefined

Second - Nonfiling characters [OBSOLETE]

0-9 - Number of nonfiling characters present [OBSOLETE]

Subfield Codes

$a - Corporate name or jurisdiction name as entry element (NR)

$b - Subordinate unit (R)

$c - Location of meeting (NR)

$d - Date of meeting or treaty signing (R)

$e - Relator term (R)

$f - Date of a work (NR)

$g - Miscellaneous information (NR)

$h - Medium (NR)

$i - Reference instruction phrase (NR)

$k - Form subheading (R)

$l - Language of a work (NR)

$m - Medium of performance for music (R)

$n - Number of part/section/meeting (R)

$o - Arranged statement for music (NR)

$p - Name of part/section of a work (R)

$r - Key for music (NR)

$s - Version (NR)

$t - Title of a work (NR)

$v - Form subdivision (R)

$w - Control subfield (NR)

0 - Special relationship

1 - Tracing use restriction

2 - Earlier form of heading

3 - Reference display

$x - General subdivision (R)

$y - Chronological subdivision (R)

$z - Geographic subdivision (R)

$5 - Institution to which field applies (R)

$6 - Linkage (NR)

$8 - Field link and sequence number (R)

411 - SEE FROM TRACING—MEETING NAME (R)

Indicators

First - Type of meeting name entry element

0 - Inverted name

1 - Jurisdiction name

2 - Name in direct order

Second - Undefined

- Undefined

Second - Nonfiling characters [OBSOLETE]

0-9 - Number of nonfiling characters present [OBSOLETE]

Subfield Codes

$a - Meeting name or jurisdiction name as entry element (NR)

$b - Number (NR) [OBSOLETE]

$c - Location of meeting (NR)

$d - Date of meeting (NR)

$e - Subordinate unit (R)

$f - Date of a work (NR)

$g - Miscellaneous information (NR)

$h - Medium (NR)

$i - Reference instruction phrase (NR)

$k - Form subheading (R)

$l - Language of a work (NR)

$n - Number of part/section/meeting (R)

$p - Name of part/section of a work (R)

$q - Name of meeting following jurisdiction name entry element (NR)

$s - Version (NR)

$t - Title of a work (NR)

$v - Form subdivision (R)

$w - Control subfield (NR)

0 - Special relationship

1 - Tracing use restriction

2 - Earlier form of heading

3 - Reference display

$x - General subdivision (R)

$y - Chronological subdivision (R)

$z - Geographic subdivision (R)

$5 - Institution to which field applies (R)

$6 - Linkage (NR)

$8 - Field link and sequence number (R)

430 - SEE FROM TRACING—UNIFORM TITLE (R)

Indicators

First - Undefined

- Undefined

Second - Nonfiling characters

0-9 Number of nonfiling characters

Subfield Codes

$a - Uniform title (NR)

$d - Date of treaty signing (R)

$f - Date of a work (NR)

$g - Miscellaneous information (NR)

$h - Medium (NR)

$i - Reference instruction phrase (NR)

$k - Form subheading (R)

$l - Language of a work (NR)

$m - Medium of performance for music (R)

$n - Number of part/section of a work (R)

$o - Arranged statement for music (NR)

$p - Name of part/section of a work (R)

$r - Key for music (NR)

$s - Version (NR)

$t - Title of a work (NR)

$v - Form subdivision (R)

$w - Control subfield (NR)

0 - Special relationship

1 - Tracing use restriction

2 - Earlier form of heading

3 - Reference display

$x - General subdivision (R)

$y - Chronological subdivision (R)

$z - Geographic subdivision (R)

$5 - Institution to which field applies (R)

$6 - Linkage (NR)

$8 - Field link and sequence number (R)

448 - SEE FROM TRACING—CHRONOLOGICAL TERM (R)

Indicators

First - Undefined

- Undefined

Second - Undefined

- Undefined

Subfield Codes

$a - Chronological term (NR)

$i - Reference instruction phrase (NR)

$v - Form subdivision (R)

$w - Control subfield (NR)

0 - Special relationship

1 - Tracing use restriction

2 - Earlier form of heading

3 - Reference display

$x - General subdivision (R)

$y - Chronological subdivision (R)

$z - Geographic subdivision (R)

$5 - Institution to which field applies (R)

$6 - Linkage (NR)

$8 - Field link and sequence number (R)

450 - SEE FROM TRACING—TOPICAL TERM (R)

Indicators

First - Undefined

- Undefined

Second - Undefined

- Undefined

Second - Nonfiling characters [OBSOLETE]

0-9 - Number of nonfiling characters present [OBSOLETE]

Subfield Codes

$a - Topical term or geographic name entry element (NR)

$b - Topical term following geographic name entry element (NR)

$i - Reference instruction phrase (NR)

$v - Form subdivision (R)

$w - Control subfield (NR)

0 - Special relationship

1 - Tracing use restriction

2 - Earlier form of heading

3 - Reference display

$x - General subdivision (R)

$y - Chronological subdivision (R)

$z - Geographic subdivision (R)

$5 - Institution to which field applies (R)

$6 - Linkage (NR)

$8 - Field link and sequence number (R)

451 - SEE FROM TRACING—GEOGRAPHIC NAME (R)

Indicators

First - Undefined

- Undefined

Second - Undefined

- Undefined

Second - Nonfiling characters [OBSOLETE]

0-9 - Number of nonfiling characters present [OBSOLETE]

Subfield Codes

$a - Geographic name (NR)

$b - Name following place as entry element (NR) [OBSOLETE]

$i - Reference instruction phrase (NR)

$v - Form subdivision (R)

$w - Control subfield (NR)

0 - Special relationship

1 - Tracing use restriction

2 - Earlier form of heading

3 - Reference display

$x - General subdivision (R)

$y - Chronological subdivision (R)

$z - Geographic subdivision (R)

$5 - Institution to which field applies (R)

$6 - Linkage (NR)

$8 - Field link and sequence number (R)

455 - SEE FROM TRACING—GENRE/FORM TERM (R)

Indicators

First - Undefined

- Undefined

Second - Undefined

- Undefined

Subfield Codes

$a - Genre/form term (NR)

$i - Reference instruction phrase (NR)

$v - Form subdivision (R)

$w - Control subfield (NR)

0 - Special relationship

1 - Tracing use restriction

2 - Earlier form of heading

3 - Reference display

$x - General subdivision (R)

$y - Chronological subdivision (R)

$z - Geographic subdivision (R)

$5 - Institution to which field applies (R)

$6 - Linkage (NR)

$8 - Field link and sequence number (R)

480 - SEE FROM TRACING—GENERAL SUBDIVISION (R)

Indicators

First - Undefined

- Undefined

Second - Undefined

- Undefined

Subfield Codes

$i - Reference instruction phrase (NR)

$v - Form subdivision (R)

$w - Control subfield (NR)

0 - Special relationship

1 - Tracing use restriction

2 - Earlier form of heading

3 - Reference display

$x - General subdivision (R)

$y - Chronological subdivision (R)

$z - Geographic subdivision (R)

$5 - Institution to which field applies (R)

$6 - Linkage (NR)

$8 - Field link and sequence number (R)

481 - SEE FROM TRACING—GEOGRAPHIC SUBDIVISION (R)

Indicators

First - Undefined

- Undefined

Second - Undefined

- Undefined

Subfield Codes

$i - Reference instruction phrase (NR)

$v - Form subdivision (R)

$w - Control subfield (NR)

0 - Special relationship

1 - Tracing use restriction

2 - Earlier form of heading

3 - Reference display

$x - General subdivision (R)

$y - Chronological subdivision (R)

$z - Geographic subdivision (R)

$5 - Institution to which field applies (R)

$6 - Linkage (NR)

$8 - Field link and sequence number (R)

482 - SEE FROM TRACING—CHRONOLOGICAL SUBDIVISION (R)

Indicators

First - Undefined

- Undefined

Second - Undefined

- Undefined

Subfield Codes

$i - Reference instruction phrase (NR)

$v - Form subdivision (R)

$w - Control subfield (NR)

0 - Special relationship

1 - Tracing use restriction

2 - Earlier form of heading

3 - Reference display

$x - General subdivision (R)

$y - Chronological subdivision (R)

$z - Geographic subdivision (R)

$5 - Institution to which field applies (R)

$6 - Linkage (NR)

$8 - Field link and sequence number (R)

485 - SEE FROM TRACING—FORM SUBDIVISION (R)

Indicators

First - Undefined

- Undefined

Second - Undefined

- Undefined

Subfield Codes

$i - Reference instruction phrase (NR)

$v - Form subdivision (R)

$w - Control subfield (NR)

0 - Special relationship

1 - Tracing use restriction

2 - Earlier form of heading

3 - Reference display

$x - General subdivision (R)

$y - Chronological subdivision (R)

$z - Geographic subdivision (R)

$5 - Institution to which field applies (R)

$6 - Linkage (NR)

$8 - Field link and sequence number (R)

(v) See Also From Tracing Fields (5XX)

500 - SEE ALSO FROM TRACING—PERSONAL NAME (R)

Indicators

First - Type of personal name entry element

0 - Forename

1 - Surname

1 - Single surname [OBSOLETE]

2 - Multiple surname [OBSOLETE]

3 - Family name

Second - Undefined

\# - Undefined

Second - Nonfiling characters [OBSOLETE]

0-9 - Number of nonfiling characters present [OBSOLETE]

Subfield Codes

$a - Personal name (NR)

$b - Numeration (NR)

$c - Titles and other words associated with a name (R)

$d - Dates associated with a name (NR)

$e - Relator term (R)

$f - Date of a work (NR)

$g - Miscellaneous information (NR)

$h - Medium (NR)

$i - Reference instruction phrase (NR)

$j - Attribution qualifier(R)

$k - Form subheading (R)

$l - Language of a work (NR)

$m - Medium of performance for music (R)

$n - Number of part/section of a work (R)

$o - Arranged statement for music (NR)

$p - Name of part/section of a work (R)

$q - Fuller form of name (NR)

$r - Key for music (NR)

$s - Version (NR)

$t - Title of a work (NR)

$v - Form subdivision (R)

$w - Control subfield (NR)

0 - Special relationship

1 - Tracing use restriction

2 - Earlier form of heading

3 - Reference display

$x - General subdivision (R)

$y - Chronological subdivision (R)

$z - Geographic subdivision (R)

$0 - Record control number (R)

$5 - Institution to which field applies (R)

$6 - Linkage (NR)

$8 - Field link and sequence number (R)

510 - SEE ALSO FROM TRACING—CORPORATE NAME (R)

Indicators

First - Type of corporate name entry element

0 - Inverted name

1 - Jurisdiction name

2 - Name in direct order

Second - Undefined

- Undefined

Second - Nonfiling characters [OBSOLETE]

0-9 - Number of nonfiling characters present [OBSOLETE]

Subfield Codes

$a - Corporate name or jurisdiction name as entry element (NR)

$b - Subordinate unit (R)

$c - Location of meeting (NR)

$d - Date of meeting or treaty signing (R)

$e - Relator term (R)

$f - Date of a work (NR)

$g - Miscellaneous information (NR)

$h - Medium (NR)

$i - Reference instruction phrase (NR)

$k - Form subheading (R)

$l - Language of a work (NR)

$m - Medium of performance for music (R)

$n - Number of part/section/meeting (R)

$o - Arranged statement for music (NR)

$p - Name of part/section of a work (R)

$r - Key for music (NR)

$s - Version (NR)

$t - Title of a work (NR)

$v - Form subdivision (R)

$w - Control subfield (NR)

0 - Special relationship

1 - Tracing use restriction

2 - Earlier form of heading

3 - Reference display

$x - General subdivision (R)

$y - Chronological subdivision (R)

$z - Geographic subdivision (R)

$0 - Record control number (R)

$5 - Institution to which field applies (R)

$6 - Linkage (NR)

$8 - Field link and sequence number (R)

511 - SEE ALSO FROM TRACING—MEETING NAME (R)

Indicators

First - Type of meeting name entry element

0 - Inverted name

1 - Jurisdiction name

2 - Name in direct order

Second - Undefined

- Undefined

Second - Nonfiling characters [OBSOLETE]

0-9 - Number of nonfiling characters present [OBSOLETE]

Subfield Codes

$a - Meeting name or jurisdiction name as entry element (NR)

$b - Number (NR) [OBSOLETE]

$c - Location of meeting (NR)

$d - Date of meeting (NR)

$e - Subordinate unit (R)

$f - Date of a work (NR)

$g - Miscellaneous information (NR)

$h - Medium (NR)

$i - Reference instruction phrase (NR)

$k - Form subheading (R)

$l - Language of a work (NR)

$n - Number of part/section/meeting (R)

$p - Name of part/section of a work (R)

$q - Name of meeting following jurisdiction name entry element (NR)

$s - Version (NR)

$t - Title of a work (NR)

$v - Form subdivision (R)

$w - Control subfield (NR)

0 - Special relationship

1 - Tracing use restriction

2 - Earlier form of heading

3 - Reference display

$x - General subdivision (R)

$y - Chronological subdivision (R)

$z - Geographic subdivision (R)

$0 - Record control number (R)

$5 - Institution to which field applies (R)

$6 - Linkage (NR)

$8 - Field link and sequence number (R)

530 - SEE ALSO FROM TRACING—UNIFORM TITLE

Indicators

First - Undefined

- Undefined

Second - Nonfiling characters

0-9 Number of nonfiling characters

Subfield Codes

$a - Uniform title (NR)

$d - Date of treaty signing (R)

$f - Date of a work (NR)

$g - Miscellaneous information (NR)

$h - Medium (NR)

$i - Reference instruction phrase (NR)

$k - Form subheading (R)

$l - Language of a work (NR)

$m - Medium of performance for music (R)

$n - Number of part/section of a work (R)

$o - Arranged statement for music (NR)

$p - Name of part/section of a work (R)

$r - Key for music (NR)

$s - Version (NR)

$t - Title of a work (NR)

$v - Form subdivision (R)

$w - Control subfield (NR)

0 - Special relationship

1 - Tracing use restriction

2 - Earlier form of heading

3 - Reference display

$x - General subdivision (R)

$y - Chronological subdivision (R)

$z - Geographic subdivision (R)

$0 - Record control number (R)

$5 - Institution to which field applies (R)

$6 - Linkage (NR)

$8 - Field link and sequence number (R)

548 - SEE ALSO FROM TRACING—CHRONOLOGICAL TERM (R)

Indicators

First - Undefined

- Undefined

Second - Undefined

- Undefined

Subfield Codes

$a - Chronological term (NR)

$i - Reference instruction phrase (NR)

$v - Form subdivision (R)

$w - Control subfield (NR)

0 - Special relationship

1 - Tracing use restriction

2 - Earlier form of heading

3 - Reference display

$x - General subdivision (R)

$y - Chronological subdivision (R)

$z - Geographic subdivision (R)

$0 - Record control number (R)

$5 - Institution to which field applies (R)

$6 - Linkage (NR)

$8 - Field link and sequence number (R)

550 - SEE ALSO FROM TRACING—TOPICAL TERM (R)

Indicators

First - Undefined

- Undefined

Second - Undefined

- Undefined

Second - Nonfiling characters [OBSOLETE]

0-9 - Number of nonfiling characters present [OBSOLETE]

Subfield Codes

$a - Topical term or geographic name entry element (NR)

$b - Topical term following geographic name entry element (NR)

$i - Reference instruction phrase (NR)

$v - Form subdivision (R)

$w - Control subfield (NR)

0 - Special relationship

1 - Tracing use restriction

2 - Earlier form of heading

3 - Reference display

$x - General subdivision (R)

$y - Chronological subdivision (R)

$z - Geographic subdivision (R)

$0 - Record control number (R)

$5 - Institution to which field applies (R)

$6 - Linkage (NR)

$8 - Field link and sequence number (R)

551 - SEE ALSO FROM TRACING—GEOGRAPHIC NAME (R)

Indicators

First - Undefined

- Undefined

Second - Undefined

- Undefined

Second - Nonfiling characters [OBSOLETE]

0-9 - Number of nonfiling characters present [OBSOLETE]

Subfield Codes

$a - Geographic name (NR)

$b - Name following place as entry element (NR) [OBSOLETE]

$i - Reference instruction phrase (NR)

$v - Form subdivision (R)

$w - Control subfield (NR)

0 - Special relationship

1 - Tracing use restriction

2 - Earlier form of heading

3 - Reference display

$x - General subdivision (R)

$y - Chronological subdivision (R)

$z - Geographic subdivision (R)

$0 - Record control number (R)

$5 - Institution to which field applies (R)

$6 - Linkage (NR)

$8 - Field link and sequence number (R)

555 - SEE ALSO FROM TRACING—GENRE/FORM TERM (R)

Indicators

First - Undefined

- Undefined

Second - Undefined

- Undefined

Subfield Codes

$a - Genre/form term (NR)

$i - Reference instruction phrase (NR)

$v - Form subdivision (R)

$w - Control subfield (NR)

0 - Special relationship

1 - Tracing use restriction

2 - Earlier form of heading

3 - Reference display

$x - General subdivision (R)

$y - Chronological subdivision (R)

$z - Geographic subdivision (R)

$0 - Record control number (R)

$5 - Institution to which field applies (R)

$6 - Linkage (NR)

$8 - Field link and sequence number (R)

580 - SEE ALSO FROM TRACING—GENERAL SUBDIVISION (R)

Indicators

First - Undefined

- Undefined

Second - Undefined

- Undefined

Subfield Codes

$i - Reference instruction phrase (NR)

$v - Form subdivision (R)

$w - Control subfield (NR)

0 - Special relationship

1 - Tracing use restriction

2 - Earlier form of heading

3 - Reference display

$x - General subdivision (R)

$y - Chronological subdivision (R)

$z - Geographic subdivision (R)

$0 - Record control number (R)

$5 - Institution to which field applies (R)

$6 - Linkage (NR)

$8 - Field link and sequence number (R)

581 - SEE ALSO FROM TRACING—GEOGRAPHIC SUBDIVISION (R)

Indicators

First - Undefined

- Undefined

Second - Undefined

- Undefined

Subfield Codes

$i - Reference instruction phrase (NR)

$v - Form subdivision (R)

$w - Control subfield (NR)

0 - Special relationship

1 - Tracing use restriction

2 - Earlier form of heading

3 - Reference display

$x - General subdivision (R)

$y - Chronological subdivision (R)

$z - Geographic subdivision (R)

$0 - Record control number (R)

$5 - Institution to which field applies (R)

$6 - Linkage (NR)

$8 - Field link and sequence number (R)

582 - SEE ALSO FROM TRACING—CHRONOLOGICAL SUBDIVISION (R)

Indicators

First - Undefined

- Undefined

Second - Undefined

- Undefined

Subfield Codes

$i - Reference instruction phrase (NR)

$v - Form subdivision (R)

$w - Control subfield (NR)

0 - Special relationship

1 - Tracing use restriction

2 - Earlier form of heading

3 - Reference display

$x - General subdivision (R)

$y - Chronological subdivision (R)

$z - Geographic subdivision (R)

$0 - Record control number (R)

$5 - Institution to which field applies (R)

$6 - Linkage (NR)

$8 - Field link and sequence number (R)

585 - SEE ALSO FROM TRACING—FORM SUBDIVISION (R)

Indicators

First - Undefined

- Undefined

Second - Undefined

- Undefined

Subfield Codes

$i - Reference instruction phrase (NR)

$v - Form subdivision (R)

$w - Control subfield (NR)

0 - Special relationship

1 - Tracing use restriction

2 - Earlier form of heading

3 - Reference display

$x - General subdivision (R)

$y - Chronological subdivision (R)

$z - Geographic subdivision (R)

$0 - Record control number (R)

$5 - Institution to which field applies (R)

$6 - Linkage (NR)

$8 - Field link and sequence number (R)

(vii) Series Treatment Fields (64X)

640 - SERIES DATES OF PUBLICATION AND/OR SEQUENTIAL DESIGNATION (R)

Indicators

First - Note format style

0 - Formatted style

1 - Unformatted style

Second - Undefined

- Undefined

Subfield Codes

$a - Dates of publication and/or sequential designation (NR)

$z - Source of information (NR)

$6 - Linkage (NR)

$8 - Field link and sequence number (R)

641 - SERIES NUMBERING PECULIARITIES (R)

Indicators

First - Undefined

- Undefined

Second - Undefined

- Undefined

Subfield Codes

$a - Numbering peculiarities note (NR)

$z - Source of information (NR)

$6 - Linkage (NR)

$8 - Field link and sequence number (R)

642 - SERIES NUMBERING EXAMPLE (R)

Indicators

First - Undefined

- Undefined

Second - Undefined

- Undefined

Subfield Codes

$a - Series numbering example (NR)

$d - Volumes/dates to which series numbering example applies (NR)

$5 - Institution/copy to which field applies (R)

$6 - Linkage (NR)

$8 - Field link and sequence number (R)

643 - SERIES PLACE AND PUBLISHER/ISSUING BODY (R)

Indicators

First - Undefined

- Undefined

Second - Undefined

- Undefined

Subfield Codes

$a - Place (R)

$b - Publisher/issuing body (R)

$d - Volumes/dates to which place and publisher/issuing body apply (NR)

$6 - Linkage (NR)

$8 - Field link and sequence number (R)

644 - SERIES ANALYSIS PRACTICE (R)

Indicators

First - Undefined

- Undefined

Second - Undefined

- Undefined

Subfield Codes

$a - Series analysis practice (NR)

f - Analyzed in full

p - Analyzed in part

n - Not analyzed

$b - Exceptions to analysis practice (NR)

$d - Volumes/dates to which analysis practice applies (NR)

$5 - Institution/copy to which field applies (R)

$6 - Linkage (NR)

$8 - Field link and sequence number (R)

645 - SERIES TRACING PRACTICE (R)

Indicators

First - Undefined

- Undefined

Second - Undefined

- Undefined

Subfield Codes

$a - Series tracing practice (NR)

t - Traced as a series added entry

n - Not traced as a series added entry

$d - Volumes/dates to which tracing practice applies (NR)

$5 - Institution/copy to which field applies (R)

$6 - Linkage (NR)

$8 - Field link and sequence number (R)

646 - SERIES CLASSIFICATION PRACTICE (R)

Indicators

First - Undefined

- Undefined

Second - Undefined

- Undefined

Subfield Codes

$a - Series classification practice (NR)

c - Volumes are classified as a collection

m - Volumes are classified with main or other series

s - Volumes are classified separately

$d - Volumes/dates to which classification practice applies (NR)

$5 - Institution to which field applies (R)

$6 - Linkage (NR)

$8 - Field link and sequence number (R)

(vii) Complex Name References (663-666)

663 - COMPLEX SEE ALSO REFERENCE—NAME (NR)

Indicators

First - Undefined

- Undefined

Second - Undefined

- Undefined

Subfield Codes

$a - Explanatory text (R)

$b - Heading referred to (R)

$t - Title referred to (R)

$6 - Linkage (NR)

$8 - Field link and sequence number (R)

664 - COMPLEX SEE REFERENCE—NAME (NR)

Indicators

First - Undefined

- Undefined

Second - Undefined

- Undefined

Subfield Codes

$a - Explanatory text (R)

$b - Heading referred to (R)

$t - Title referred to (R)

$6 - Linkage (NR)

$8 - Field link and sequence number (R)

665 - HISTORY REFERENCE (NR)

Indicators

First - Undefined

- Undefined

Second - Undefined

- Undefined

Subfield Codes

$a - History reference (R)

$6 - Linkage (NR)

$8 - Field link and sequence number (R)

666 - GENERAL EXPLANATORY REFERENCE—NAME (NR)

Indicators

First - Undefined

- Undefined

Second - Undefined

- Undefined

Subfield Codes

$a - General explanatory reference (R)

$6 - Linkage (NR)

$8 - Field link and sequence number (R)

(viii) Note Fields (667-68X)

667 - NONPUBLIC GENERAL NOTE (R)

Indicators

First - Undefined

- Undefined

Second - Undefined

- Undefined

Subfield Codes

$a - Nonpublic general note (NR)

$5 - Institution to which field applies (R)

$6 - Linkage (NR)

$8 - Field link and sequence number (R)

668 - CHARACTERS IN NONROMAN ALPHABETS (R) [OBSOLETE]

Indicators

First - Undefined

- Undefined

Second - Undefined

- Undefined

Subfield Codes

$a - Characters in nonroman alphabet (NR)

670 - SOURCE DATA FOUND (R)

Indicators

First - Undefined

- Undefined

Second - Undefined

- Undefined

Subfield Codes

$a - Source citation (NR)

$b - Information found (NR)

$u - Uniform Resource Identifier (R)

$6 - Linkage (NR)

$8 - Field link and sequence number (R)

675 - SOURCE DATA NOT FOUND (NR)

Indicators

First - Undefined

- Undefined

Second - Undefined

- Undefined

Subfield Codes

$a - Source citation (R)

$6 - Linkage (NR)

$8 - Field link and sequence number (R)

678 - BIOGRAPHICAL OR HISTORICAL DATA (R)

Indicators

First - Type of data

- No information provided

0 - Biographical sketch

1 - Administrative history

Second - Undefined

- Undefined

Subfield Codes

$a - Biographical or historical data (R)

$b - Expansion (NR)

$u - Uniform Resource Identifier (R)

$6 - Linkage (NR)

$8 - Field link and sequence number (R)

680 - PUBLIC GENERAL NOTE (R)

Indicators

First - Undefined

- Undefined

Second - Undefined

- Undefined

Subfield Codes

$a - Heading or subdivision term (R)

$i - Explanatory text (R)

$5 - Institution to which field applies (R)

$6 - Linkage (NR)

$8 - Field link and sequence number (R)

681 - SUBJECT EXAMPLE TRACING NOTE (R)

Indicators

First - Undefined

- Undefined

Second - Undefined

- Undefined

Subfield Codes

$a - Subject heading or subdivision term (R)

$i - Explanatory text (R)

$6 - Linkage (NR)

$8 - Field link and sequence number (R)

682 - DELETED HEADING INFORMATION (NR)

Indicators

First - Undefined

- Undefined

Second - Undefined

- Undefined

Subfield Codes

$a - Replacement heading (R)

$i - Explanatory text (R)

$6 - Linkage (NR)

$8 - Field link and sequence number (R)

688 - APPLICATION HISTORY NOTE (R)

Indicators

First - Undefined

- Undefined

Second - Undefined

- Undefined

Subfield Codes

$a - Application history note (NR)

$5 - Institution to which field applies (R)

$6 - Linkage (NR)

$8 - Field link and sequence number (R)

(ix) Heading Linking Entry Fields (7XX)

HEADING LINKING ENTRIES—GENERAL INFORMATION

700 - ESTABLISHED HEADING LINKING ENTRY—PERSONAL NAME (R)

Indicators

First - Type of personal name entry element

0 - Forename

1 - Surname

1 - Single surname [OBSOLETE]

2 - Multiple surname [OBSOLETE]

3 - Family name

Second - Thesaurus

0 - Library of Congress Subject Headings/Name authority file

1 - LC subject headings for children's literature

2 - Medical Subject Headings/NLM name authority file

3 - National Agricultural Library subject authority file

4 - Source not specified

5 - Canadian Subject Headings/NLC name authority file

6 - Répertoire de vedettes-matière

7 - Source specified in subfield $2

Subfield Codes

$a - Personal name (NR)

$b - Numeration (NR)

$c - Titles and other words associated with a name (R)

$d - Dates associated with a name (NR)

$e - Relator term (R)

$f - Date of a work (NR)

$g - Miscellaneous information (NR)

$h - Medium (NR)

$j - Attribution qualifier (R)

$k - Form subheading (R)

$l - Language of a work (NR)

$m - Medium of performance for music (R)

$n - Number of part/section of a work (R)

$o - Arranged statement for music (NR)

$p - Name of part/section of a work (R)

$q - Fuller form of name (NR)

$r - Key for music (NR)

$s - Version (NR)

$t - Title of a work (NR)

$v - Form subdivision (R)

$w - Control subfield (NR)

/0 - Link display

/1 - Replacement complexity

$x - General subdivision (R)

$y - Chronological subdivision (R)

$z - Geographic subdivision (R)

$0 - Record control number (R)

$2 - Source of heading or term (NR)

$5 - Institution to which field applies (R)

$6 - Linkage (NR)

$8 - Field link and sequence number (R)

710 - ESTABLISHED HEADING LINKING ENTRY—CORPORATE NAME (R)

Indicators

First - Type of corporate name entry element

0 - Inverted name

1 - Jurisdiction name

2 - Name in direct order

Second - Thesaurus

0 - Library of Congress Subject Headings/Name authority file

1 - LC subject headings for children's literature

2 - Medical Subject Headings/NLM name authority file

3 - National Agricultural Library subject authority file

4 - Source not specified

5 - Canadian Subject Headings/NLC name authority file

6 - Répertoire de vedettes-matière

7 - Source specified in subfield $2

Subfield Codes

$a - Corporate name or jurisdiction name as entry element (NR)

$b - Subordinate unit (R)

$c - Location of meeting (NR)

$d - Date of meeting or treaty signing (R)

$e - Relator term (R)

$f - Date of a work (NR)

$g - Miscellaneous information (NR)

$h - Medium (NR)

$k - Form subheading (R)

$l - Language of a work (NR)

$m - Medium of performance for music (R)

$n - Number of part/section/meeting (R)

$o - Arranged statement for music (NR)

$p - Name of part/section of a work (R)

$r - Key for music (NR)

$s - Version (NR)

$t - Title of a work (NR)

$v - Form subdivision (R)

$w - Control subfield (NR)

/0 - Link display

/1 - Replacement complexity

$x - General subdivision (R)

$y - Chronological subdivision (R)

$z - Geographic subdivision (R)

$0 - Record control number (R)

$2 - Source of heading or term (NR)

$5 - Institution to which field applies (R)

$6 - Linkage (NR)

$8 - Field link and sequence number (R)

711 - ESTABLISHED HEADING LINKING ENTRY—MEETING NAME (R)

Indicators

First - Type of meeting name entry element

0 - Inverted name

1 - Jurisdiction name

2 - Name in direct order

Second - Thesaurus

0 - Library of Congress Subject Headings/Name authority file

1 - LC subject headings for children's literature

2 - Medical Subject Headings/NLM name authority file

3 - National Agricultural Library subject authority file

4 - Source not specified

5 - Canadian Subject Headings/NLC name authority file

6 - Répertoire de vedettes-matière

7 - Source specified in subfield $2

Subfield Codes

$a - Meeting name or jurisdiction name as entry element (NR)

$c - Location of meeting (NR)

$d - Date of meeting (NR)

$e - Subordinate unit (R)

$f - Date of a work (NR)

$g - Miscellaneous information (NR)

$h - Medium (NR)

$k - Form subheading (R)

$l - Language of a work (NR)

$n - Number of part/section/meeting (R)

$p - Name of part/section of a work (R)

$q - Name of meeting following jurisdiction name entry element (NR)

$s - Version (NR)

$t - Title of a work (NR)

$v - Form subdivision (R)

$w - Control subfield (NR)

/0 - Link display

/1 - Replacement complexity

$x - General subdivision (R)

$y - Chronological subdivision (R)

$z - Geographic subdivision (R)

$0 - Record control number (R)

$2 - Source of heading or term (NR)

$5 - Institution to which field applies (R)

$6 - Linkage (NR)

$8 - Field link and sequence number (R)

730 - ESTABLISHED HEADING LINKING ENTRY—UNIFORM TITLE (R)

Indicators

First - Undefined

- Undefined

Second - Thesaurus

0 - Library of Congress Subject Headings/Name authority file

1 - LC subject headings for children's literature

2 - Medical Subject Headings/NLM name authority file

3 - National Agricultural Library subject authority file

4 - Source not specified

5 - Canadian Subject Headings/NLC name authority file

6 - Répertoire de vedettes-matière

7 - Source specified in subfield $2

Subfield Codes

$a - Uniform title (NR)

$d - Date of treaty signing (R)

$f - Date of a work (NR)

$g - Miscellaneous information (NR)

$h - Medium (NR)

$k - Form subheading (R)

$l - Language of a work (NR)

$m - Medium of performance for music (R)

$n - Number of part/section of a work (R)

$o - Arranged statement for music (NR)

$p - Name of part/section of a work (R)

$r - Key for music (NR)

$s - Version (NR)

$t - Title of a work (NR)

$v - Form subdivision (R)

$w - Control subfield (NR)

/0 - Link display

/1 - Replacement complexity

$x - General subdivision (R)

$y - Chronological subdivision (R)

$z - Geographic subdivision (R)

$0 - Record control number (R)

$2 - Source of heading or term (NR)

$5 - Institution to which field applies (R)

$6 - Linkage (NR)

$8 - Field link and sequence number (R)

748 - ESTABLISHED HEADING LINKING ENTRY—CHRONOLOGICAL TERM (R)

Indicators

First - Undefined

- Undefined

Second - Thesaurus

0 - Library of Congress Subject Headings/Name authority file

1 - LC subject headings for children's literature

2 - Medical Subject Headings/NLM name authority file

3 - National Agricultural Library subject authority file

4 - Source not specified

5 - Canadian Subject Headings/NLC name authority file

6 - Répertoire de vedettes-matière

7 - Source specified in subfield $2

Subfield Codes

$a - Chronological term (NR)

$v - Form subdivision (R)

$w - Control subfield (NR)

/0 - Link display

/1 - Replacement complexity

$x - General subdivision (R)

$y - Chronological subdivision (R)

$z - Geographic subdivision (R)

$0 - Record control number (R)

$2 - Source of heading or term (NR)

$5 - Institution to which field applies (R)

$6 - Linkage (NR)

$8 - Field link and sequence number (R)

750 - ESTABLISHED HEADING LINKING ENTRY—TOPICAL TERM (R)

Indicators

First - Undefined

- Undefined

Second - Thesaurus

0 - Library of Congress Subject Headings/Name authority file

1 - LC subject headings for children's literature

2 - Medical Subject Headings/NLM name authority file

3 - National Agricultural Library subject authority file

4 - Source not specified

5 - Canadian Subject Headings/NLC name authority file

6 - Répertoire de vedettes-matière

7 - Source specified in subfield $2

Subfield Codes

$a - Topical term or geographic name entry element (NR)

$b - Topical term following geographic name as entry element (NR)

$v - Form subdivision (R)

$w - Control subfield (NR)

/0 - Link display

/1 - Replacement complexity

$x - General subdivision (R)

$y - Chronological subdivision (R)

$z - Geographic subdivision (R)

$0 - Record control number (R)

$2 - Source of heading or term (NR)

$5 - Institution to which field applies (R)

$6 - Linkage (NR)

$8 - Field link and sequence number (R)

751 - ESTABLISHED HEADING LINKING ENTRY—GEOGRAPHIC NAME (R)

Indicators

First - Undefined

- Undefined

Second - Thesaurus

0 - Library of Congress Subject Headings/Name authority file

1 - LC subject headings for children's literature

2 - Medical Subject Headings/NLM name authority file

3 - National Agricultural Library subject authority file

4 - Source not specified

5 - Canadian Subject Headings/NLC name authority file

6 - Répertoire de vedettes-matière

7 - Source specified in subfield $2

Subfield Codes

$a - Geographic name (NR)

$v - Form subdivision (R)

$w - Control subfield (NR)

/0 - Link display

/1 - Replacement complexity

$x - General subdivision (R)

$y - Chronological subdivision (R)

$z - Geographic subdivision (R)

$0 - Record control number (R)

$2 - Source of heading or term (NR)

$5 - Institution to which field applies (R)

$6 - Linkage (NR)

$8 - Field link and sequence number (R)

755 - ESTABLISHED HEADING LINKING ENTRY—GENRE/FORM TERM (R)

Indicators

First - Undefined

- Undefined

Second - Thesaurus

0 - Library of Congress Subject Headings/Name authority file

1 - LC subject headings for children's literature

2 - Medical Subject Headings/NLM name authority file

3 - National Agricultural Library subject authority file

4 - Source not specified

5 - Canadian Subject Headings/NLC name authority file

6 - Répertoire de vedettes-matière

7 - Source specified in subfield $2

Subfield Codes

$a - Genre/form term as entry element (NR)

$v - Form subdivision (R)

$w - Control subfield (NR)

/0 - Link display

/1 - Replacement complexity

$x - General subdivision (R)

$y - Chronological subdivision (R)

$z - Geographic subdivision (R)

$0 - Record control number (R)

$2 - Source of heading or term (NR)

$5 - Institution to which field applies (R)

$6 - Linkage (NR)

$8 - Field link and sequence number (R)

780 - SUBDIVISION LINKING ENTRY—GENERAL SUBDIVISION (R)

Indicators

First - Undefined

- Undefined

Second - Thesaurus

0 - Library of Congress Subject Headings/Name authority file

1 - LC subject headings for children's literature

2 - Medical Subject Headings/NLM name authority file

3 - National Agricultural Library subject authority file

4 - Source not specified

5 - Canadian Subject Headings/NLC name authority file

6 - Répertoire de vedettes-matière

7 - Source specified in subfield $2

Subfield Codes

$v - Form subdivision (R)

$w - Control subfield (NR)

/0 - Link display

/1 - Replacement complexity

$x - General subdivision (R)

$y - Chronological subdivision (R)

$z - Geographic subdivision (R)

$0 - Record control number (R)

$2 - Source of heading or term (NR)

$5 - Institution to which field applies (R)

$6 - Linkage (NR)

$8 - Field link and sequence number (R)

781 - SUBDIVISION LINKING ENTRY—GEOGRAPHIC SUBDIVISION (R)

Indicators

First - Undefined

- Undefined

Second - Thesaurus

0 - Library of Congress Subject Headings/Name authority file

1 - LC subject headings for children's literature

2 - Medical Subject Headings/NLM name authority file

3 - National Agricultural Library subject authority file

4 - Source not specified

5 - Canadian Subject Headings/NLC name authority file

6 - Répertoire de vedettes-matière

7 - Source specified in subfield $2

Subfield Codes

$v - Form subdivision (R)

$w - Control subfield (NR)

/0 - Link display

/1 - Replacement complexity

$x - General subdivision (R)

$y - Chronological subdivision (R)

$z - Geographic subdivision (R)

$0 - Record control number (R)

$2 - Source of heading or term (NR)

$5 - Institution to which field applies (R)

$6 - Linkage (NR)

$8 - Field link and sequence number (R)

782 - SUBDIVISION LINKING ENTRY—CHRONOLOGICAL SUBDIVISION (R)

Indicators

First - Undefined

- Undefined

Second - Thesaurus

0 - Library of Congress Subject Headings/Name authority file

1 - LC subject headings for children's literature

2 - Medical Subject Headings/NLM name authority file

3 - National Agricultural Library subject authority file

4 - Source not specified

5 - Canadian Subject Headings/NLC name authority file

6 - Répertoire de vedettes-matière

7 - Source specified in subfield $2

Subfield Codes

$v - Form subdivision (R)

$w - Control subfield (NR)

/0 - Link display

/1 - Replacement complexity

$x - General subdivision (R)

$y - Chronological subdivision (R)

$z - Geographic subdivision (R)

$0 - Record control number (R)

$2 - Source of heading or term (NR)

$5 - Institution to which field applies (R)

$6 - Linkage (NR)

$8 - Field link and sequence number (R)

785 - SUBDIVISION LINKING ENTRY—FORM SUBDIVISION (R)

Indicators

First - Undefined

- Undefined

Second - Thesaurus

0 - Library of Congress Subject Headings/Name authority file

1 - LC subject headings for children's literature

2 - Medical Subject Headings/NLM name authority file

3 - National Agricultural Library subject authority file

4 - Source not specified

5 - Canadian Subject Headings/NLC name authority file

6 - Répertoire de vedettes-matière

7 - Source specified in subfield $2

Subfield Codes

$v - Form subdivision (R)

$w - Control subfield (NR)

/0 - Link display

/1 - Replacement complexity

$x - General subdivision (R)

$y - Chronological subdivision (R)

$z - Geographic subdivision (R)

$0 - Record control number (R)

$2 - Source of heading or term (NR)

$5 - Institution to which field applies (R)

$6 - Linkage (NR)

$8 - Field link and sequence number (R)

788 - COMPLEX LINKING ENTRY DATA (NR)

Indicators

First - Undefined

- Undefined

Second - Thesaurus

0 - Library of Congress Subject Headings/Name authority file

1 - LC subject headings for children's literature

2 - Medical Subject Headings/NLM name authority file

3 - National Agricultural Library subject authority file

4 - Source not specified

5 - Canadian Subject Headings/NLC name authority file

6 - Répertoire de vedettes-matière

7 - Source specified in subfield $2

Subfield Codes

$a - Heading referred to (R)

$i - Explanatory text (R)

$2 - Source of heading or term (NR)

$5 - Institution to which field applies (R)

$6 - Linkage (NR)

$8 - Field link and sequence number (R)

(x) Location and Alternate Graphics (8XX)

856 - ELECTRONIC LOCATION AND ACCESS (R)

Indicators

First - Access method

- No information provided

0 - Email

1 - FTP

2 - Remote login (Telnet)

3 - Dial-up

4 - HTTP

7 - Method specified in subfield $2

Second - Relationship

- No information provided

0 - Resource

1 - Version of resource

2 - Related resource

8 - No display constant generated

Subfield Codes

$a - Host name (R)

$b - Access number (R)

$c - Compression information (R)

$d - Path (R)

$f - Electronic name (R)

$g - Uniform Resource Name [OBSOLETE](R)

$h - Processor of request (NR)

$i - Instruction (R)

$j - Bits per second (NR)

$k - Password (NR)

$l - Logon (NR)

$m - Contact for access assistance (R)

$n - Name of location of host (NR)

$o - Operating system (NR)

$p - Port (NR)

$q - Electronic format type (NR)

$r - Settings (NR)

$s - File size (R)

$t - Terminal emulation (R)

$u - Uniform Resource Identifier (R)

$v - Hours access method available (R)

$w - Record control number (R)

$x - Nonpublic note (R)

$y - Link text (R)

$z - Public note (R)

$2 - Access method (NR)

$3 - Materials specified (NR)

$6 - Linkage (NR)

$8 - Field link and sequence number (R)

880 - ALTERNATE GRAPHIC REPRESENTATION (R)

Indicators

First - Same as associated field

Second - Same as associated field

Subfield Codes

$6 - Linkage (NR)

$a-z - Same as associated field

$0-5 - Same as associated field

$7-9 - Same as associated field

7

MARC 21 FORMAT FOR BIBLIOGRAPHIC RECORD

1. Leader and Directory

LEADER

A fixed field that comprises the first 24 character positions (00-23) of each record and provides information for the processing of the record.

Character Positions

00-04 - Logical record length

The computer-generated, five-character numeric string that specifies the length of the entire record. The number is right justified and each unused position contains a zero.

05 - Record status

A one-character code that indicates the relation of the record to a file.

a - Increase in encoding level

c - Corrected or revised

d - Deleted

n - New

p - Increase in encoding level from prepublication

06 - Type of record

A one-character code that indicates the characteristics of and defines the components of the record.

a - Language material

c - Notated music

d - Manuscript notated music

e - Cartographic material

f - Manuscript cartographic material

g - Projected medium

i - Nonmusical sound recording

j - Musical sound recording

k - Two-dimensional nonprojectable graphic

m - Computer file

o - Kit

p - Mixed material

r - Three-dimensional artifact or naturally occurring object

t - Manuscript language material

07 - Bibliographic level

A one-character code that indicates the bibliographic level of the record.

a - Monographic component part

b - Serial component part

c - Collection

d - Subunit

i - Integrating resource

m - Monograph/item

s - Serial

08 - Type of control

- No specific type

a - Archival

09 - Character coding scheme

A one-character code that identifies the character-coding scheme used in the record.

- MARC-8

a - UCS/Unicode

10 - Indicator count

The computer-generated number 2 that indicates the number of character
positions used for indicators in a variable data field.

11 - Subfield code count

The computer-generated number 2 that indicates the number of character positions used for each subfield code in a variable data field.

12-16 - Base address of data

The computer-generated, five-character numeric string that indicates the first character position of the first variable control field in a record. The number is right justified and each unused position contains a zero.

17 - Encoding level

- Full level

1 - Full level, material not examined

2 - Less-than-full level, material not examined

3 - Abbreviated level

4 - Core level

5 - Partial (preliminary) level

7 - Minimal level

8 - Prepublication level

u - Unknown

z - Not applicable

18 - Descriptive cataloging form

A one character code that indicates the descriptive cataloging form reflected in the record. Subfield e (Description conventions) of field 040 (Cataloging Source) may contain additional information on the cataloging conventions used.

- Non-ISBD

a - AACR 2

i - ISBD

u - Unknown

19 - Linked record requirement

- Related record not required

r - Related record required

20-23 - Entry map

Four computer-generated, single-digit numeric characters that indicate the structure of each entry in the Directory.

20 - Length of the length-of-field portion

21 - Length of the starting-character-position portion

22 - Length of the implementation-defined portion

23 - Undefined Entry map character position

DIRECTORY

A computer-generated index to the location of the variable control and data fields within a record. The Directory immediately follows the Leader at character position 24 and consists of a series of fixed-length (12 character positions) entries that give the tag, length, and starting character position of each variable field

Character Positions

00-02 - Tag

Three numeric or alphabetic (uppercase or lowercase, but not both) characters that identify an associated field

03-06 - Field length

Four numeric characters that indicate the length of the field, including indicators, subfield codes, data, and the field terminator. The number is right justified and each unused position contains a zero.

07-11 - Starting character position

Five numeric characters that indicate the starting character position of the field relative to the Base address of data (Leader/12-16) of the record. The number is right justified and each unused position contains a zero.

2. Control Fields (001-006)

Fields 001-006 contain control numbers and other control and coded information that are used in processing MARC bibliographic records. Each control field is identified by a field tag in the Directory and contains either a single data element or a series of fixed-length data elements identified by relative character position. Variable control fields contain neither indicator positions nor subfield codes.

001 - CONTROL NUMBER (NR)

The control number assigned by the organization creating, using, or distributing the record. The MARC code for the organization is contained in field 003 (Control Number Identifier).

003 - CONTROL NUMBER IDENTIFIER (NR)

The MARC code for the organization whose control number is contained in field 001 (Control Number). The source of the code is the MARC Code List for Organizations that is maintained by the Library of Congress.

005 - DATE AND TIME OF LATEST TRANSACTION (NR)

Sixteen characters that indicate the date and time of the latest record transaction and serve as a version identifier for the record. They are recorded according to Representation of Dates and Times (ISO 8601). The date requires 8 numeric characters in the pattern yyyymmdd. The time requires 8 numeric characters in the in the pattern hhmmss.f, expressed in terms of the 24-hour (00-23) clock.

006 - FIXED-LENGTH DATA ELEMENTS—ADDITIONAL MATERIAL

GENERAL INFORMATION (R)

This field contains 18 character positions (00-17) that provide for coding information about special aspects of the item being cataloged that cannot be coded in field 008 (Fixed-Length Data Elements). It is used in cases when an item has multiple characteristics. It is also used to record the coded serial aspects of nontextual serials.

The field has a tree structure, whereby the code given in 006/00 (Form of material) determines the data elements defined for subsequent character positions. Except for code s (Serial), the codes in field 006/00 correspond to those in Leader/06 (Type of record). For each occurrence of field 006, the codes defined for character positions 01-17 will be the same as those defined in the corresponding field 008, character positions 18-34. Configurations of field 006 are given in the following order: books, computer file, map, music, serials, visual material, and mixed material.

006 - Books

006 - Computer Files

006 - Maps

006 - Mixed Materials

006 - Music

006 - Serials

006 - Visual Materials

006—BOOKS

Character Positions

00 - Form of material

a - Language material

t - Manuscript language material

01-04 - Illustrations

Up to four one-character codes (recorded in alphabetical order) that indicate the presence of types of illustrations in the item. If fewer than four codes are assigned, the codes are left justified and each unused position contains a blank (#).

No illustrations

a Illustrations

b Maps

c Portraits

d Charts

e Plans

f Plates
g Music
h Facsimiles
i Coats of arms
j Genealogical tables
k Forms
l Samples
m Phonodisc, phonowire, etc.
o Photographs
p Illuminations
| No attempt to code

05 - Target audience

Target Audience

A one-character code that indicates the audience for which the item is intended.

Unknown or not specified
a Preschool
b Primary
c Elementary and junior high
d Secondary (senior high)
e Adult
f Specialized
g General
j Juvenile
| No attempt to code

06 - Form of item

A two-character code that indicates the form of composition of printed or manuscript music or a musical sound recording. The codes are based on Library of Congress subject headings. If more than one code is appropriate, the code mu (Multiple forms) is used in 008/18-19 and all appropriate specific codes are given in field 047 (Form of Composition).

an	Anthems
bd	Ballads
bg	Bluegrass music
bl	Blues
bt	Ballets
ca	Chaconnes
cb	Chants, Other religions
cc	Chant, Christian
cg	Concerti grossi
ch	Chorales
cl	Chorale preludes
cn	Canons and rounds
co	Concertos
cp	Chansons, polyphonic
cr	Carols
cs	Chance Compositions
ct	Cantatas
cy	Country music
cz	Canzonas
df	Dance forms

Separate codes are defined for mazurkas, minuets, pavans, polonaises, and waltzes.

dv	Divertimentos, serenades, cassations, divertissements, notturni
fg	Fugues
fm	Folk music
ft	Fantasias
gm	Gospel music
hy	Hymns
jz	Jazz
mc	Musical revues and comedies

md	Madrigals
mi	Minuets
mo	Motets
mp	Motion picture music
mr	Marches
ms	Masses
mu	Multiple forms
mz	Mazurkas
nc	Nocturnes
nn	Not applicable
op	Operas
or	Oratorios
ov	Overtures
pg	Program music
pm	Passion music
po	Polonaises
pp	Popular music
pr	Preludes
ps	Passacaglias
pt	Part-songs
pv	Pavans
rc	Rock music
rd	Rondos
rg	Ragtime music
ri	Ricercars
rp	Rhapsodies
rq	Requiems
sg	Songs
sn	Sonatas
sp	Symphonic poems
sq	Square dance music

st Studies and exercises

su Suites

sy Symphonies

tc Toccatas

ts Trio-sonatas

uu Unknown

vr Variations

wz Waltzes

zz Other

|| No attempt to code

07-10 - Nature of contents

Up to four one-character codes (recorded in alphabetical order) that indicate whether a significant part of the item is or contains certain types of material. If fewer than four codes are assigned, the codes are left justified and each unused position contains a blank (#).

No specified nature of contents

a Abstracts/summaries

The item is or contains abstracts or summaries of other publications.

b Bibliographies

c Catalogs

d Dictionaries

This code is also used for a glossary or a gazetteer.

e Encyclopedias

f Handbooks

g Legal articles

i Indexes

The item is or contains an index to bibliographical material other than itself.

j Patent document

k Discographies

l Legislation

The item is or contains full or partial texts of enactments of legislative bodies or texts of rules and regulations issued by executive or administrative agencies.

m Theses

Indicates that the item is a thesis, dissertation, or work identified as having been created to satisfy the requirements for an academic certification or degree.

n Surveys of literature in a subject area

The item is or contains authored surveys that summarize what has been published about a subject.

o Reviews

The item is or contains critical reviews of published or performed works.

p Programmed texts

q Filmographies

r Directories

s Statistics

t Technical reports

v Legal cases and case notes

w Law reports and digests

z Treaties

Indicates that the item is a treaty or accord negotiated between two or more parties to settle a disagreement, establish a relationship, grant rights, etc.

| No attempt to code

11 - Government publication

A one-character code that indicates whether the item is published or produced by or for a government agency, and, if so, the jurisdictional level of the agency.

Not a government publication

a Autonomous or semi-autonomous component

c Multilocal

f Federal/national

i International intergovernmental

l Local

m Multistate

o Government publication¾level undetermined

s State, provincial, territorial, dependent, etc.

u Unknown if item is government publication

z Other

| No attempt to code

12 - Conference publication

A one-character code that indicates whether the item OR serial consists of the proceedings, reports, or summaries of a conference.

0 Not a conference publication

1 Conference publication

| No attempt to code

13 - Festschrift

A one-character code that indicates whether the item is a festschrift.

0 Not a festschrift

1 Festschrift

| No attempt to code

14 - Index

A one-character code that indicates whether the item (in the case of a Book) includes an index to its own contents, or whether accompanying material (in the case of a Map) includes a location index or gazetteer.

0 No index

1 Index present

| No attempt to code

15 - Undefined

16 - Literary form

Indicates the literary form of an item. Numeric codes 0 and 1 provide a generic identification of whether or not the item is a work of fiction. Alphabetic codes may be used to identify specific literary forms.

0 Not fiction (not further specified)

1 Fiction (not further specified)

c Comic strips

d Dramas

e Essays

f Novels

h Humor, satires, etc.

Indicates that the item is a humorous work, satire, or of a similar literary form.

i Letters

Indicates that the item is a single letter or collection of correspondence.

j Short stories

Indicates that the item is a short story or collection of short stories.

m Mixed forms

Indicates that the item represents a variety of literary forms (e.g., poetry and short stories).

p Poetry

s Speech

u Unknown

| No attempt to code

17 - Biography

A one-character code that indicates whether the item contains biographical material, and, if so, what the biographical characteristics are.

No biographical material

a Autobiography

b Individual biography

c Collective biography

d Contains biographical information

| No attempt to code

006—COMPUTER FILES/ELECTRONIC RESOURCES

Character Positions

00 - Form of material

m - Computer file/Electronic resource

01-04 - Undefined

05 - Target audience

A one-character code that indicates the audience for which the item is intended.

Unknown or not specified

a Preschool

b Primary

c Elementary and junior high

d Secondary (senior high)

e Adult

f Specialized

g General

j Juvenile

| No attempt to code

06-08 - Undefined

09 - Type of computer file

A one-character code that indicates the type of computer file described in the bibliographic record.

a Numeric data

b Computer nprogram

c Representational

Pictorial or graphic information that can be manipulated inconjunction with other types of files to produce graphic patterns that can be used to interpret and give meaning to the information.

d Document

e Bibliographic data

f Font

g Game

h Sound

i Interactive multimedia

j Online system or service

m Combination

u Unknown

z Other

| No attempt to code

10 - Undefined

11 - Government publication

A one-character code that indicates whether theitem is published or produced by or for a government agency, and, if so, the jurisdictional level of the agency.

Not a government publication

a Autonomous or semi-autonomous component

c Multilocal

f Federal/national

i International intergovernmental

l Local

m Multistate

o Government publication¾level undetermined

s State, provincial, territorial, dependent, etc.

u Unknown if item is government publication

z Other

| No attempt to code

12-17 - Undefined

006—MAPS

Character Positions

00 - Form of material

e - Cartographic material

f - Manuscript cartographic material

01-04 - Relief

Up to four one-character codes that indicate the relief type specified on the item. Codes are recorded in order of their importance to the described item. If fewer than four codes are assigned, the codes are left justified and each unused position contains a blank (#).

#	No relief shown
a	Contours
b	Shading
c	Gradient and bathymetric tints
d	Hachures
e	Bathymetry/soundings
f	Form lines
g	Spot heights
i	Pictorially
j	Land forms
k	Bathymetry/isolines
m	Rock drawings
z	Other relief type
|	No attempt to code

05-06 - Projection

A two-character code that indicates the projection used in producing the item.

##	Projection not specified
aa	Aitoff
ab	Gnomic

Lambert's azimuthal equal area
Orthographic
Azimuthal equidistant
Stereographic
General vertical near-sided
Modified sterographic for Alaska
Chamberlin trimetric
Polar sterographic
Azimuthal, specific type unknown
Azimuthal, other
Gall
Goode's homolographic
Lambert's cylindrical equal area
Mercator
Miller
Mollweide
Sinusoidal
Transverse Mercator
Gauss-Kruger
Equirectangular
Oblique Mercantor
Robinson
Space oblique Mercantor
Cylindrical, specific type unknown
Cylindrical, other
Alber's equal area
Bonne
Lambert's conformal conic
Equidistant conic
Polyconic

cu Conic, specific type unknown

cz Conic, other

da Armadillo

db Butterfly

dc Eckert

dd Goode's homolosine

de Miller's bipolar oblique conformal conic

df Van Der Grinten

dg Dimaxion

dh Cordiform

dl Lambert conformal

zz Other

| No attempt to code

07 - Undefined

08 - Type of cartographic material

A one-character code that indicates the type of nonbook cartographic item described in the bibliographic record.

a Single map

b Map series

A number of related but physically separate and bibliographically distinct cartographic units intended by the producer or issuing body to form a single group.

c Map serial

A cartographic publication issued in successive parts bearing numerical or chronological designations and intended to be continued indefinitely.

d Globe

e Atlas

f Separate map supplement to another work

g Map bound as part of another work

u Unknown

z Other

| No attempt to code

09-10 - Undefined

11 - Government publication

A one-character code that indicates whether the item is published or produced by or for a government agency, and, if so, the jurisdictional level of the agency.

Not a government publication

a Autonomous or semi-autonomous component

c Multilocal

f Federal/national

i International intergovernmental

l Local

m Multistate

o Government publication¾level undetermined

s State, provincial, territorial, dependent, etc.

u Unknown if item is government publication

z Other

| No attempt to code

12 - Form of item

A one-character code that indicates the form of material for the item.

None of the following

a Microfilm

b Microfiche

c Microopaque

d Large print

f Braille

r Regular print reproduction

Eye-readable print.

s Electronic

No attempt to code

13 - Undefined

14 - Index

A one-character code that indicates whether the item (in the case of a Book) includes an index to its own contents, or whether accompanying material (in the case of a Map) includes a location index or gazetteer.

0 No index

1 Index present

| No attempt to code

15 - Undefined

16-17 - Special format characteristics

Up to two one-character codes that indicate the special format characteristics of the map. Codes are recorded in order of their importance to the described item. If only one code is assigned, it is left justified and the unused position contains a blank (#).

No specified special format characteristics Manuscript

j Picture card, post card

k Calendar

l Puzzle

n Game

o Wall map

p Playing cards

q Large print

r Loose-leaf

z Other

| No attempt to code

006—MIXED MATERIALS

Character Positions

00 - Form of material

p - Mixed material

01-05 - Undefined

06 - Form of item

A one-character code that indicates the form of material for the item.

None of the following

a Microfilm

b Microfiche

c Microopaque

d Large print

f Braille

r Regular print reproduction

Eye-readable print.

s Electronic

No attempt to code

07-17 - Undefined

006—MUSIC

Character Positions

00 - Form of material

c - Notated music

d - Manuscript notated music

i - Nonmusical sound recording

j - Musical sound recording

01-02 - Form of composition

A two-character code that indicates the form of composition of printed or manuscript music or a musical sound recording. The codes are based on Library of Congress subject headings. If more than one code is appropriate, the code mu (Multiple forms) is used in 008/18-19 and all appropriate specific codes are given in field 047 (Form of Composition).

an Anthems
bd Ballads
bg Bluegrass music
bl Blues
bt Ballets
ca Chaconnes
cb Chants. Other religions
cc Chant. Christian
cg Concerti grossi
ch Chorales
cl Chorale preludes
cn Canons and rounds
co Concertos
cp Chansons, polyphonic
cr Carols
cs Chance Compositions
ct Cantatas
cy Country music
cz Canzonas
df Dance forms

Separate codes are defined for mazurkas, minuets, pavans, polonaises, and waltzes.

dv Divertimentos, serenades, cassations, divertissements, notturni
fg Fugues
fm Folk music
ft Fantasias
gm Gospel music
hy Hymns
jz Jazz
mc Musical revues and comedies

md	Madrigals
mi	Minuets
mo	Motets
mp	Motion picture music
mr	Marches
ms	Masses
mu	Multiple forms
mz	Mazurkas
nc	Nocturnes
nn	Not applicable
op	Operas
or	Oratorios
ov	Overtures
pg	Program music
pm	Passion music
po	Polonaises
pp	Popular music
pr	Preludes
ps	Passacaglias
pt	Part-songs
pv	Pavans
rc	Rock music
rd	Rondos
rg	Ragtime music
ri	Ricercars
rp	Rhapsodies
rq	Requiems
sg	Songs
sn	Sonatas
sp	Symphonic poems
sq	Square dance music

st Studies and exercises

su Suites

sy Symphonies

tc Toccatas

ts Trio-sonatas

uu Unknown

vr Variations

wz Waltzes

zz Other

|| No attempt to code

03 - Format of music

04 - Music parts

05 - Target audience

A one-character code that indicates the audience for which the item is intended.

\# Unknown or not specified

a Preschool

b Primary

c Elementary and junior high

d Secondary (senior high)

e Adult

f Specialized

g General

j Juvenile

| No attempt to code

06 - Form of item

A one-character code that indicates the form of material for the item.

\# None of the following

a Microfilm

b Microfiche

c Microopaque

d Large print

f Braille

r Regular print reproduction

Eye-readable print.

s Electronic

| No attempt to code

07-12 - Accompanying matter

Up to six one-character codes (recorded in alphabetical order) that indicate the contents of program notes and other accompanying material for the sound recording, manuscript music, or printed music. If fewer than six codes are assigned, the codes are left justified and each unused position contains a blank (#).

No accompanying matter

a Discography

b Bibliography

c Thematic index

d Libretto or text

e Biography of composer or author

f Biography of performer or history of ensemble

g Technical and/or historical information on instruments

h Technical information on music

i Historical information

k Ethnological information

r Instructional materials

s Music

z Other

| No attempt to code

13-14 - Literary text for sound recordings

Up to two one-character codes (recorded in the order of the following list) that indicate the type of literary text contained in the nonmusical sound recording. If only one code is assigned, it is left justified and the unused position contains a blank (#).

- # Item is a musical sound recording
- a Autobiography
- b Biography
- c Conference proceedings
- d Drama
- e Essays
- f Fiction
- g Reporting
- h History
- i Instruction
- j Language instruction
- k Comedy
- l Lectures, speeches
- m Memoirs
- n Not applicable
- o Folktales
- p Poetry
- r Rehearsals
- s Sounds
- t Interviews
- z Other
- | No attempt to code

15 - Undefined

16 - Transposition and arrangement

17 - Undefined

006—CONTINUING RESOURCES (serial)

Character Positions

00 - Form of material

s - Serial/Integrating resource

01 - Frequency

A one-character code that indicates the frequency of the serial; used in conjunction with 008/19 (Regularity).

#	No determinable frequency Frequency is intentionally irregular.
a	Annual
b	Bimonthly Includes 6, 7, or 8 numbers a year.
c	Semiweekly
d	Daily
e	Biweekly
f	Semiannual Includes 2 numbers a year.
g	Biennial
h	Triennial
i	Three times a week
j	Three times a month
m	Monthly Includes 9, 10, 11, or 12 numbers a year.
q	Quarterly Includes 4 numbers a year.
s	Semimonthly
t	Three times a year
u	Unknown
w	Weekly
z	Other
|	No attempt to code

02 - Regularity

03 - ISSN center

04 - Type of continuing resource

05 - Form of original item

06 - Form of item

07 - Nature of entire work

08-10 - Nature of contents

11 - Government publication

12 - Conference publication

13-15 - Undefined

16 - Original alphabet or script of title

17 - Entry convention

006—VISUAL MATERIALS

Character Positions

00 - Form of material

g - Projected medium

k - Two-dimensional nonprojectable graphic

o - Kit

r - Three-dimensional artifact or naturally occurring object

01-03 - Running time

04 - Undefined

05 - Target audience

06-10 - Undefined

11 - Government publication

12 - Form of item

13-15 - Undefined

16 - Type of visual material

17 - Technique

3. CONTROL FIELD 007

007 - PHYSICAL DESCRIPTION FIXED FIELD

GENERAL INFORMATION (R)

007—MAP

Character Positions

00 - Category of material

a - Map

01 - Specific material designation

d - Atlas

g - Diagram

j - Map

k - Profile

q - Model

r - Remote-sensing image

s - Section

u - Unspecified

y - View

z - Other

| - No attempt to code

02 - Undefined

03 - Color

a - One color

c - Multicolored

| - No attempt to code

04 - Physical medium

a - Paper

b - Wood

c - Stone

d - Metal

e - Synthetic

f - Skin

g - Textile

j - Glass

p - Plaster

q - Flexible base photographic, positive

r - Flexible base photographic, negative

s - Non-flexible base photographic, positive

t - Non-flexible base photographic, negative

u - Unknown

y - Other photographic medium

z - Other

| - No attempt to code

05 - Type of reproduction

f - Facsimile

n - Not applicable

u - Unknown

z - Other

| - No attempt to code

06 - Production/reproduction details

a - Photocopy, blueline print

b - Photocopy

c - Pre-production

d - Film

u - Unknown

z - Other

| - No attempt to code

07 - Positive/negative aspect

a - Positive

b - Negative

m - Mixed polarity

n - Not applicable

| - No attempt to code

007—ELECTRONIC RESOURCE

Character Positions

00 - Category of material

c - Computer file

01 - Specific material designation

a - Tape cartridge

b - Chip cartridge

c - Computer optical disc cartridge

f - Tape cassette

h - Tape reel

j - Magnetic disc

m - Magneto-optical disc

o - Optical disc

r - Remote

u - Unspecified

z - Other

| - No attempt to code

02 - Undefined

03 - Color

a - One color

b - Black-and-white

c - Multicolored

g - Gray scale

m - Mixed

n - Not applicable

u - Unknown

z - Other

| - No attempt to code

04 - Dimensions

a - 3 1/2 in.

e - 12 in.

g - 4 3/4 in. or 12 cm.

i - 1 1/8 x 2 3/8 in.

j - 3 7/8 x 2 1/2 in.

n - Not applicable

o - 5 1/4 in.

u - Unknown

v - 8 in.

z - Other

| - No attempt to code

05 - Sound

- No sound (silent)

a - Sound on medium

u - Unknown

| - No attempt to code

06-08 - Image bit depth

001-999 - Exact bit depth

mmm - Multiple

nnn - Not applicable

— - Unknown

||| - No attempt to code

09 - File formats

a - One

m - Multiple

u - Unknown

| - No attempt to code

10 - Quality assurance target(s)

a - Absent

n - Not applicable

p - Present

u - Unknown

| - No attempt to code

11 - Antecedent/source

a - File reproduced from original

b - File reproduced from microform

c - File reproduced from an electronic resource

d - File reproduced from an intermediate (not microform)

m - Mixed

n - Not applicable

u - Unknown

| - No attempt to code

12 - Level of compression

a - Uncompressed

b - Lossless

d - Lossy

m - Mixed

u - Unknown

| - No attempt to code

13 - Reformatting quality

a - Access

n - Not applicable

p - Preservation

r - Replacement

u - Unknown

| - No attempt to code

007—GLOBE

Character Positions

00 - Category of material

d - Globe

01 - Specific material designation

a - Celestial globe

b - Planetary or lunar globe

c - Terrestrial globe

e - Earth moon globe

u - Unspecified

z - Other

| - No attempt to code

02 - Undefined

03 - Color

a - One color

c - Multicolored

| - No attempt to code

04 - Physical medium

a - Paper

b - Wood

c - Stone

d - Metal

e - Synthetic

f - Skin

g - Textile

p - Plaster

u - Unknown

z - Other

| - No attempt to code

05 - Type of reproduction

f - Facsimile

n - Not applicable

u - Unknown

z - Other

| - No attempt to code

007—TACTILE MATERIAL

Character Positions

00 - Category of material

f - Tactile material

01 - Specific material designation

a - Moon

b - Braille

c - Combination

d - Tactile, with no writing system

u - Unspecified

z - Other

| - No attempt to code

02 - Undefined

03-04 - Class of braille writing

- No specified class of braille writing

a - Literary braille

b - Format code braille

c - Mathematics and scientific braille

d - Computer braille

e - Music braille

m - Multiple braille types

n - Not applicable

u - Unknown

z - Other

| - No attempt to code

05 - Level of contraction

a - Uncontracted

b - Contracted

m - Combination

n - Not applicable

u - Unknown

z - Other

| - No attempt to code

06-08 - Braille music format

- No specified braille music format

a - Bar over bar

b - Bar by bar

c - Line over line

d - Paragraph

e - Single line

f - Section by section

g - Line by line

h - Open score

i - Spanner short form scoring

j - Short form scoring

k - Outline

l - Vertical score

n - Not applicable

u - Unknown

| - No attempt to code

09 - Specific physical characteristics

a - Print/braille

b - Jumbo or enlarged braille

n - Not applicable

u - Unknown

z - Other

| - No attempt to code

007—PROJECTED GRAPHIC

Character Positions

00 - Category of material

g - Projected graphic

01 - Specific material designation

c - Filmstrip cartridge

d - Filmslip

f - Other filmstrip type

o - Filmstrip roll

s - Slide

t - Transparency

u - Unspecified

z - Other

| - No attempt to code

02 - Undefined

03 - Color

a - One color

b - Black-and-white

c - Multicolored

h - Hand colored

m - Mixed

n - Not applicable

u - Unknown

z - Other

| - No attempt to code

04 - Base of emulsion

d - Glass

e - Synthetic

j - Safety film

k - Film base, other than safety film

m - Mixed collection

o - Paper

u - Unknown

z - Other

| - No attempt to code

05 - Sound on medium or separate

- No sound (silent)

a - Sound on medium

b - Sound separate from medium

u - Unknown

| - No attempt to code

06 - Medium for sound

- No sound (silent)

a - Optical sound track on motion picture film

b - Magnetic sound track on motion picture film

c - Magnetic audio tape in cartridge

d - Sound disc

e - Magnetic audio tape on reel

f - Magnetic audio tape in cassette

g - Optical and magnetic sound track on motion picture film

h - Videotape

i - Videodisc

u - Unknown

z - Other

| - No attempt to code

07 - Dimensions

a - Standard 8 mm.

b - Super 8 mm./single 8 mm.

c - 9.5 mm.

d - 16 mm.

e - 28 mm.

f - 35 mm.

g - 70 mm.

j - 2x2 in. or 5x5 cm.

k - 2 1/4 x 2 1/4 in. or 6x6 cm.

s - 4x5 in. or 10x13 cm.

t - 5x7 in. or 13x18 cm.

u - Unknown

v - 8x10 in. or 21x26 cm.

w - 9x9 in. or 23x23 cm.

x - 10x10 in. or 26x26 cm.

y - 7x7 in. or 18x18 cm.

z - Other

| - No attempt to code

08 - Secondary support material

- No secondary support

c - Cardboard

d - Glass

e - Synthetic

h - Metal

j - Metal and glass

k - Synthetic and glass

m - Mixed collection

u - Unknown

z - Other

| - No attempt to code

007—MICROFORM

Character Positions

00 - Category of material

h - Microform

01 - Specific material designation

a - Aperture card

b - Microfilm cartridge

c - Microfilm cassette

d - Microfilm reel

e - Microfiche

f - Microfiche cassette

g - Microopaque

u - Unspecified

z - Other

| - No attempt to code

02 - Undefined

03 - Positive/negative aspect

a - Positive

b - Negative

m - Mixed polarity

u - Unknown

| - No attempt to code

04 - Dimensions

a - 8 mm.

d - 16 mm.

f - 35 mm.

g - 70 mm.

h - 105 mm.

l - 3x5 in. or 8x13 cm.

m - 4x6 in. or 11x15 cm.

o - 6x9 in. or 16x23 cm.

p - 3 1/4 x 7 3/8 in. or 9x19 cm.

u - Unknown

z - Other

| - No attempt to code

05 - Reduction ratio range

a - Low reduction

b - Normal reduction

c - High reduction

d - Very high reduction

e - Ultra high reduction

u - Unknown

v - Reduction rate varies

| - No attempt to code

06-08 - Reduction ratio

09 - Color

b - Black-and-white (or monochrome)

c - Multicolored

m - Mixed

u - Unknown

z - Other

| - No attempt to code

10 - Emulsion on film

a - Silver halide

b - Diazo

c - Vesicular

m - Mixed emulsion

n - Not applicable

u - Unknown

z - Other

| - No attempt to code

11 - Generation

a - First generation (master)

b - Printing master

c - Service copy

m - Mixed generation

u - Unknown

| - No attempt to code

12 - Base of film

a - Safety base, undetermined

c - Safety base, acetate undetermined

d - Safety base, diacetate

p - Safety base, polyester

r - Safety base, mixed

t - Safety base, triacetate

i - Nitrate base

m - Mixed base (nitrate and safety)

n - Not applicable

u - Unknown

z - Other

| - No attempt to code

007—NONPROJECTED GRAPHIC

Character Positions

00 - Category of material

k - Nonprojected graphic

01 - Specific material designation

c - Collage

d - Drawing

e - Painting

f - Photomechanical print

g - Photonegative

h - Photoprint

i - Picture

j - Print

l - Technical drawing

n - Chart

o - Flash card

u - Unspecified

z - Other

| - No attempt to code

02 - Undefined

03 - Color

a - One color

b - Black-and-white

c - Multicolored

h - Hand colored

m - Mixed

u - Unknown

z - Other

| - No attempt to code

04 - Primary support material

a - Canvas

b - Bristol board

c - Cardboard/illustration board

d - Glass

e - Synthetic

f - Skin

g - Textile

h - Metal

m - Mixed collection

o - Paper

p - Plaster

q - Hardboard

r - Porcelain

s - Stone

t - Wood

u - Unknown

z - Other

| - No attempt to code

05 - Secondary support material

- No secondary support

a - Canvas

b - Bristol board

c - Cardboard/illustration board

d - Glass

e - Synthetic

f - Skin

g - Textile
h - Metal
m - Mixed collection
o - Paper
p - Plaster
q - Hardboard
r - Porcelain
s - Stone
t - Wood
u - Unknown
z - Other
| - No attempt to code

007—MOTION PICTURE

Character Positions

00 - Category of material
m - Motion picture
01 - Specific material designation
c - Film cartridge
f - Film cassette
r - Film reel
u - Unspecified
z - Other
| - No attempt to code
02 - Undefined
03 - Color
b - Black-and-white
c - Multicolored
h - Hand colored
m - Mixed
n - Not applicable

u - Unknown

z - Other

| - No attempt to code

04 - Motion picture presentation format

a - Standard sound aperture (reduced frame)

b - Nonanamorphic (wide-screen)

c - 3D

d - Anamorphic (wide-screen)

e - Other wide-screen format

f - Standard silent aperture (full frame)

u - Unknown

z - Other

| - No attempt to code

05 - Sound on medium or separate

- No sound (silent)

a - Sound on medium

b - Sound separate from medium

u - Unknown

| - No attempt to code

06 - Medium for sound

- No sound (silent)

a - Optical sound track on motion picture film

b - Magnetic sound track on motion picture film

c - Magnetic audio tape in cartridge

d - Sound disc

e - Magnetic audio tape on reel

f - Magnetic audio tape in cassette

g - Optical and magnetic sound track on motion picture film

h - Videotape

i - Videodisc

u - Unknown

z - Other

| - No attempt to code

07 - Dimensions

a - Standard 8 mm.

b - Super 8 mm./single 8 mm.

c - 9.5 mm.

d - 16 mm.

e - 28 mm.

f - 35 mm.

g - 70 mm.

u - Unknown

z - Other

| - No attempt to code

08 - Configuration of playback channels

k - Mixed

m - Monaural

n - Not applicable

q - Quadraphonic, multichannel, or surround

s - Stereophonic

u - Unknown

z - Other

| - No attempt to code

09 - Production elements

a - Workprint

b - Trims

c - Outtakes

d - Rushes

e - Mixing tracks

f - Title bands/intertitle rolls

g - Production rolls

n - Not applicable

z - Other

| - No attempt to code

10 - Positive/negative aspect

a - Positive

b - Negative

n - Not applicable

u - Unknown

z - Other

| - No attempt to code

11 - Generation

d - Duplicate

e - Master

o - Original

r - Reference print/viewing copy

u - Unknown

z - Other

| - No attempt to code

12 - Base of film

a - Safety base, undetermined

c - Safety base, acetate undetermined

d - Safety base, diacetate

p - Safety base, polyester

r - Safety base, mixed

t - Safety base, triacetate

i - Nitrate base

m - Mixed base (nitrate and safety)

n - Not applicable

u - Unknown

z - Other

| - No attempt to code

13 - Refined categories of color

a - 3 layer color
b - 2 color, single strip
c - Undetermined 2 color
d - Undetermined 3 color
e - 3 strip color
f - 2 strip color
g - Red strip
h - Blue or green strip
i - Cyan strip
j - Magenta strip
k - Yellow strip
l - S E N 2
m - S E N 3
n - Not applicable
p - Sepia tone
q - Other tone
r - Tint
s - Tinted and toned
t - Stencil color
u - Unknown
v - Hand colored
z - Other
| - No attempt to code
14 - Kind of color stock or print
a - Imbibition dye transfer prints
b - Three layer stock
c - Three layer stock, low fade
d - Duplitized stock
n - Not applicable
u - Unknown
z - Other

| - No attempt to code

15 - Deterioration stage

a - None apparent

b - Nitrate: suspicious odor

c - Nitrate: pungent odor

d - Nitrate: brownish, discoloration, fading, dusty

e - Nitrate: sticky

f - Nitrate: frothy, bubbles, blisters

g - Nitrate: congealed

h - Nitrate: powder

k - Non-nitrate: detectable deterioration (diacetate odor)

l - Non-nitrate: advanced deterioration

m - Non-nitrate: disaster

| - No attempt to code

16 - Completeness

c - Complete

i - Incomplete

n - Not applicable

u - Unknown

| - No attempt to code

17-22 - Film inspection date

007—KIT

Character Positions

00 - Category of material

o - Kit

01 - Specific material designation

u - Unspecified

| - No attempt to code

007—NOTATED MUSIC

Character Positions

00 - Category of material

q - Notated music

01 - Specific material designation

u - Unspecified

| - No attempt to code

007—REMOTE-SENSING IMAGE

Character Positions

00 - Category of material

r - Remote-sensing image

01 - Specific material designation

u - Unspecified

| - No attempt to code

02 - Undefined

03 - Altitude of sensor

a - Surface

b - Airborne

c - Spaceborne

n - Not applicable

u - Unknown

z - Other

| - No attempt to code

04 - Attitude of sensor

a - Low oblique

b - High oblique

c - Vertical

n - Not applicable

u - Unknown

| - No attempt to code

05 - Cloud cover

0 - 0-9%

1 - 10-19%

2 - 20-29%

3 - 30-39%

4 - 40-49%

5 - 50-59%

6 - 60-69%

7 - 70-79%

8 - 80-89%

9 - 90-100%

n - Not applicable

u - Unknown

| - No attempt to code

06 - Platform construction type

a - Balloon

b - Aircraft—low altitude

c - Aircraft—medium altitude

d - Aircraft—high altitude

e - Manned spacecraft

f - Unmanned spacecraft

g - Land-based remote-sensing device

h - Water surface-based remote-sensing device

i - Submersible remote-sensing device

n - Not applicable

u - Unknown

z - Other

| - No attempt to code

07 - Platform use category

a - Meteorological

b - Surface observing
c - Space observing
m - Mixed uses
n - Not applicable
u - Unknown
z - Other
| - No attempt to code
08 - Sensor type
a - Active
b - Passive
u - Unknown
z - Other
| - No attempt to code
09-10 - Data type
aa - Visible light
da - Near infrared
db - Middle infrared
dc - Far infrared
dd - Thermal infrared
de - Shortwave infrared (SWIR)
df - Reflective infrared
dv - Combinations
dz - Other infrared data
ga - Sidelooking airborne radar (SLAR)
gb - Synthetic aperture radar (SAR)-Single frequency
gc - SAR-multi-frequency (multichannel)
gd - SAR-like polarization
ge - SAR-cross polarization
gf - Infometric SAR
gg - polarmetric SAR
gu - Passive microwave mapping

gz - Other microwave data

ja - Far ultraviolet

jb - Middle ultraviolet

jc - Near ultraviolet

jv - Ultraviolet combinations

jz - Other ultraviolet data

ma - Multi-spectral, multidata

mb - Multi-temporal

mm - Combination of various data types

nn - Not applicable

pa - Sonar—water depth

pb - Sonar—bottom topography images, sidescan

pc - Sonar—bottom topography, near surface

pd - Sonar—bottom topography, near bottom

pe - Seismic surveys

pz - Other acoustical data

ra - Gravity anomalies (general)

rb - Free-air

rc - Bouger

rd - Isostatic

sa - Magnetic field

ta - radiometric surveys

uu - Unknown

zz - Other

|| - No attempt to code

007—SOUND RECORDING

Character Positions

00 - Category of material

s - Sound recording

01 - Specific material designation

d - Sound disc

e - Cylinder

g - Sound cartridge

i - Sound-track film

q - Roll

s - Sound cassette

t - Sound-tape reel

u - Unspecified

w - Wire recording

z - Other

| - No attempt to code

02 - Undefined

03 - Speed

a - 16 rpm

b - 33 1/3 rpm

c - 45 rpm

d - 78 rpm

e - 8 rpm

f - 1.4 m. per sec.

h - 120 rpm

i - 160 rpm

k - 15/16 ips

l - 1 7/8 ips

m - 3 3/4 ips

o - 7 1/2 ips

p - 15 ips

r - 30 ips

u - Unknown

z - Other

| - No attempt to code

04 - Configuration of playback channels

m - Monaural

q - Quadraphonic

s - Stereophonic

u - Unknown

z - Other

| - No attempt to code

05 - Groove width/groove pitch

m - Microgroove/fine

n - Not applicable

s - Coarse/standard

u - Unknown

z - Other

| - No attempt to code

06 - Dimensions

a - 3 in.

b - 5 in.

c - 7 in.

d - 10 in.

e - 12 in.

f - 16 in.

g - 4 3/4 in. or 12 cm.

j - 3 7/8 x 2 1/2 in.

o - 5 1/4 x 3 7/8 in.

n - Not applicable

s - 2 3/4 x 4 in.

u - Unknown

z - Other

| - No attempt to code

07 - Tape width

l - 1/8 in.

m - 1/4 in.

n - Not applicable

o - 1/2 in.

p - 1 in.

u - Unknown

z - Other

| - No attempt to code

08 - Tape configuration

a - Full (1) track

b - Half (2) track

c - Quarter (4) track

d - Eight track

e - Twelve track

f - Sixteen track

n - Not applicable

u - Unknown

z - Other

| - No attempt to code

09 - Kind of disc, cylinder or tape

a - Master tape

b - Tape duplication master

d - Disc master (negative)

i - Instantaneous (recorded on the spot)

m - Mass produced

n - Not applicable

r - Mother (positive)

s - Stamper (negative)

t - Test pressing

u - Unknown

z - Other

| - No attempt to code

10 - Kind of material

a - Lacquer coating

b - Cellulose nitrate

c - Acetate tape with ferrous oxide

g - Glass with lacquer

i - Aluminum with lacquer

r - Paper with lacquer or ferrous oxide

l - Metal

m - Plastic with metal

n - Not applicable [OBSOLETE]

p - Plastic

s - Shellac

u - Unknown

w - Wax

z - Other

| - No attempt to code

11 - Kind of cutting

h - Hill-and-dale cutting

l - Lateral or combined cutting

n - Not applicable

u - Unknown

| - No attempt to code

12 - Special playback characteristics

a - NAB standard

b - CCIR standard

c - Dolby-B encoded

d - dbx encoded

e - Digital recording

f - Dolby-A encoded

g - Dolby-C encoded

h - CX encoded

n - Not applicable

u - Unknown

z - Other

| - No attempt to code

13 - Capture and storage technique

a - Acoustical capture, direct storage

b - Direct storage, not acoustical

d - Digital storage

e - Analog electrical storage

u - Unknown

z - Other

| - No attempt to code

007—TEXT

Character Positions

00 - Category of material

t - Text

01 - Specific material designation

a - Regular print

b - Large print

c - Braille

d - Text in looseleaf binder

u - Unspecified

z - Other

| - No attempt to code

007—VIDEORECORDING

Character Positions

00 - Category of material

v - Videorecording

01 - Specific material designation

c - Videocartridge

d - Videodisc

f - Videocassette

r - Videoreel

u - Unspecified

z - Other

| - No attempt to code

02 - Undefined

03 - Color

a - One color

b - Black-and-white

c - Multicolored

m - Mixed

n - Not applicable

u - Unknown

z - Other

| - No attempt to code

04 - Videorecording format

a - Beta (1/2 in., videocassette)

b - VHS (1/2 in., videocassette)

c - U-matic (3/4 in., videocassette)

d - EIAJ (1/2 in. reel)

e - Type C (1 in., reel)

f - Quadruplex (1 in. or 2 in., reel)

g - Laserdisc

h - CED (Capacitance Electronic Disc) videodisc

i - Betacam (1/2 in., videocassette)

j - Betacam SP (1/2 in., videocassette)

k - Super-VHS (1/2 in., videocassette)

m - M-II (1/2 in., videocassette)

o - D-2 (3/4 in., videocassette)

p - 8 mm.

q - Hi-8 mm.

u - Unknown

v - DVD

z - Other

| - No attempt to code

05 - Sound on medium or separate

- No sound (silent)

a - Sound on medium

b - Sound separate from medium

u - Unknown

| - No attempt to code

06 - Medium for sound

- No sound (silent)

a - Optical sound track on motion picture film

b - Magnetic sound track on motion picture film

c - Magnetic audio tape in cartridge

d - Sound disc

e - Magnetic audio tape on reel

f - Magnetic audio tape in cassette

g - Optical and magnetic sound track on motion picture film

h - Videotape

i - Videodisc

u - Unknown

z - Other

| - No attempt to code

07 - Dimensions

a - 8 mm.

m - 1/4 in.

o - 1/2 in.

p - 1 in.

q - 2 in.

r - 3/4 in.

u - Unknown

z - Other

| - No attempt to code

08 - Configuration of playback channels

k - Mixed

m - Monaural

n - Not applicable

q - Quadraphonic, multichannel, or surround

s - Stereophonic

u - Unknown

z - Other

| - No attempt to code

007—UNSPECIFIED

Character Positions

00 - Category of material

z - Unspecified

01 - Specific material designation

m - Multiple physical forms

u - Unspecified

z - Other

| - No attempt to code

5. CONTROL FIELD 008

This field contains 40 character positions (00-39) that provide coded information about the record as a whole and about special bibliographic aspects of the item being cataloged. These coded data elements are potentially useful for retrieval and data management purposes.

The data elements are positionally-defined. Character positions that are not defined contain a blank (#). All defined character positions must contain a defined code; for some field 008 positions, this may be the fill character (|). The fill character may be used (in certain character positions) when a cataloging organization makes no attempt to code the character position. The fill character is not allowed in field 008 positions 00-05 (Date entered on file). Its use is discouraged in positions 07-10 (Date 1), 15-17 (Place of publication, production, or execution), and the 008 position defined for Form of item (either position 23 or 29 depending upon the 008 configuration)

Character positions 00-17 and 35-39 are defined the same across all types of material, with special consideration for position 06. The definition of character positions 18-34 was done independently for each type of material, although certain date elements are defined the same in the specifications for more than one type of material. When similar data elements are defined for inclusion in field 008 for different types of material, they occupy the same field 008 character positions.

In the following documentation, character positions are described in the order of their listing at the beginning of this section. Field 008 positions 00-17 and 35-39 for all types of material are described first, followed by seven groups of sections for positions 18-34, each relating to one of the seven types of material described in the Introduction.

008 - FIXED-LE008 - All Materials

008 - Books

008 - Computer Files

008 - Maps

008 - Music

008 - Serials

008 - Visual Materials

008 - Mixed Materials NGTH DATA ELEMENTS—GENERAL INFORMATION (NR)

008—ALL MATERIALS

Character Positions

00-05 - Date entered on file

06 - Type of date/Publication status

b - No dates given; B.C. date involved

c - Continuing resource currently published

c - Actual date and copyright date [OBSOLETE]

d - Continuing resource ceased publication

d - Detailed date [OBSOLETE]

e - Detailed date

i - Inclusive dates of collection

k - Range of years of bulk of collection

m - Multiple dates

n - Dates unknown

p - Date of distribution/release/issue and production/recording session when different

q - Questionable date

r - Reprint/reissue date and original date

s - Single known date/probable date

t - Publication date and copyright date

u - Continuing resource status unknown

| - No attempt to code

07-10 - Date 1

1-9 - Date digit

- Date element is not applicable

u - Date element is totally or partially unknown

| - No attempt to code

11-14 - Date 2

1-9 - Date digit

- Date element is not applicable

u - Date element is totally or partially unknown

| - No attempt to code

15-17 - Place of publication, production, or execution

35-37 - Language

38 - Modified record

- Not modified

d - Dashed-on information omitted

o - Completely romanized/printed cards romanized

r - Completely romanized/printed cards in script

s - Shortened

x - Missing characters

| - No attempt to code

39 - Cataloging source

- National bibliographic agency

a - National Agricultural Library [OBSOLETE]

b - National Library of Medicine [OBSOLETE]

c - Cooperative cataloging program

d - Other

n - Report to [OBSOLETE]

u - Unknown

| - No attempt to code

008—BOOKS

Character Positions

18-21 - Illustrations

- No illustrations

a - Illustrations

b - Maps

c - Portraits

d - Charts

e - Plans

f - Plates

g - Music

h - Facsimiles

i - Coats of arms

j - Genealogical tables

k - Forms

l - Samples

m - Phonodisc, phonowire, etc.

o - Photographs

p - Illuminations

| - No attempt to code

22 - Target audience

- Unknown or not specified

a - Preschool

b - Primary

c - Pre-adolescent

d - Adolescent

e - Adult

f - Specialized

g - General

j - Juvenile

| - No attempt to code

23 - Form of item

- None of the following

a - Microfilm

b - Microfiche

c - Microopaque

d - Large print

f - Braille

g - Punched paper tape [OBSOLETE]

h - Magnetic tape [OBSOLETE]

i - Multimedia [OBSOLETE]

r - Regular print reproduction

s - Electronic

z - Other form of reproduction [OBSOLETE]

| - No attempt to code

24-27 - Nature of contents

- No specified nature of contents

a - Abstracts/summaries

b - Bibliographies

c - Catalogs

d - Dictionaries

e - Encyclopedias

f - Handbooks

g - Legal articles

h - Handbooks [OBSOLETE]

i - Indexes

j - Patent document

k - Discographies

l - Legislation

m - Theses

n - Surveys of literature in a subject area

o - Reviews

p - Programmed texts

q - Filmographies

r - Directories

s - Statistics

t - Technical reports

u - Standards/specifications

v - Legal cases and case notes

w - Law reports and digests

y - Yearbooks [OBSOLETE]

z - Treaties

| - No attempt to code

28 - Government publication

- Not a government publication

a - Autonomous or semi-autonomous component

c - Multilocal

f - Federal/national

i - International intergovernmental

l - Local

m - Multistate

n - Government publication—level undetermined [OBSOLETE]

o - Government publication—level undetermined

s - State, provincial, territorial, dependent, etc.

u - Unknown if item is government publication

z - Other

| - No attempt to code

29 - Conference publication

0 - Not a conference publication

1 - Conference publication

| - No attempt to code

30 - Festschrift

0 - Not a festschrift

1 - Festschrift

| - No attempt to code

31 - Index

0 - No index

1 - Index present

| - No attempt to code

32 - Undefined

32 - Main entry in body of entry [OBSOLETE]

0 - Main entry not in body of entry

1 - Main entry in body of entry

| - No attempt to code

33 - Literary form

0 - Not fiction (not further specified)

1 - Fiction (not further specified)

c - Comic strips

d - Dramas

e - Essays

f - Novels

h - Humor, satires, etc.

i - Letters

j - Short stories

m - Mixed forms

p - Poetry

s - Speeched

u - Unknown

| - No attempt to code

34 - Biography

- No biographical material

a - Autobiography

b - Individual biography

c - Collective biography

d - Contains biographical information

| - No attempt to code

008—COMPUTER FILES

Character Positions

18-21 - Undefined

18 - Frequency [OBSOLETE]

- No determinable frequency

a - Annual

b - Bimonthly

c - Semiweekly

d - Daily

e - Biweekly

f - Semiannual

g - Biennial

h - Triennial

i - Three times a week

j - Three times a month

m - Monthly

n - Not applicable

q - Quarterly

s - Semimonthly

t - Three times a year

u - Unknown

w - Weekly

z - Other frequencies

19 - Regularity [OBSOLETE]

- Not applicable

n - Normalized irregular

r - Regular

u - Unknown

x - Completely irregular

22 - Target audience

- Unknown or not specified

a - Preschool

b - Primary

c - Pre-adolescent

d - Adolescent

e - Adult

f - Specialized

g - General

j - Juvenile

| - No attempt to code

23-25 - Undefined

26 - Type of computer file

a - Numeric data

b - Computer program

c - Representational

d - Document

e - Bibliographic data

f - Font

g - Game

h - Sound

i - Interactive multimedia

j - Online system or service

m - Combination

u - Unknown

z - Other

| - No attempt to code

27 - Undefined

27 - Type of machine [OBSOLETE]

a - Computer readable

z - Other

28 - Government publication

- Not a government publication

a - Autonomous or semi-autonomous component

c - Multilocal

f - Federal/national

i - International intergovernmental

l - Local

m - Multistate

o - Government publication—level undetermined

s - State, provincial, territorial, dependent, etc.

u - Unknown if item is government publication

z - Other

| - No attempt to code

29-34 - Undefined

008—MAPS

Character Positions

18-21 - Relief

- No relief shown

a - Contours

b - Shading

c - Gradient and bathymetric tints

d - Hachures

e - Bathymetry/soundings

f - Form lines

g - Spot heights

h - Color [OBSOLETE]

i - Pictorially

j - Land forms

k - Bathymetry/isolines

m - Rock drawings

z - Other relief type

| - No attempt to code

22-23 - Projection

- Projection not specified

aa - Aitoff

ab - Gnomic.

ac - Lambert`s azimuthal equal area

ad - Orthographic

ae - Azimuthal equidistant

af - Stereographic

ag - General vertical near-sided

am - Modified stereographic for Alaska

an - Chamberlin trimetric

ap - Polar stereographic

au - Azimuthal, specific type unknown

az - Azimuthal, other

ba - Gall

bb - Goode's homolographic

bc - Lambert's cylindrical equal area

bd - Mercator

be - Miller

bf - Mollweide

bg - Sinusoidal

bh - Transverse Mercator

bi - Gauss-Kruger

bj - Equirectangular

bo - Oblique Mercator

br - Robinson

bs - Space oblique Mercator

bu - Cylindrical, specific type unknown

bz - Cylindrical, other

ca - Alber's equal area

cb - Bonne

cc - Lambert's conformal conic

ce - Equidistant conic

cp - Polyconic

cu - Conic, specific type unknown

cz - Conic, other

da - Armadillo

db - Butterfly

dc - Eckert

dd - Goode's homolosine

de - Miller's bipolar oblique conformal conic

df - Van Der Grinten

dg - Dimaxion

dh - Cordiform

dl - Lambert conformal

zz - Other

| - No attempt to code

24 - Undefined

24 - Prime meridian [OBSOLETE]

- Prime meridian not specified

e - Greenwich

f - Ferro

g - Paris

h - Other [OBSOLETE]

p - Philadelphia

w - Washington, D.C.

z - Other

25 - Type of cartographic material

a - Single map

b - Map series

c - Map serial

d - Globe

e - Atlas

f - Separate map supplement to another work

g - Map bound as part of another work

u - Unknown

z - Other

| - No attempt to code

26-27 - Undefined

26-27 - Publisher code [OBSOLETE]

28 - Government publication

- Not a government publication

a - Autonomous or semi-autonomous component

c - Multilocal

f - Federal/national

i - International intergovernmental

l - Local

m - Multistate

o - Government publication—level undetermined

s - State, provincial, territorial, dependent, etc.

u - Unknown if item is government publication

z - Other

| - No attempt to code

29 - Form of item

- None of the following

a - Microfilm

b - Microfiche

c - Microopaque

d - Large print

f - Braille

r - Regular print reproduction

s - Electronic

| - No attempt to code

30 - Undefined

- Index

- No index

1 - Index present

| - No attempt to code

32 - Undefined

32 - Citation indicator [OBSOLETE]

33-34 - Special format characteristics

- No specified special format characteristics

a - Photocopy, blue line print [OBSOLETE]

b - Photocopy [OBSOLETE]

c - Negative photocopy [OBSOLETE]

d - Film negative [OBSOLETE]

e - Manuscript

f - Facsimile [OBSOLETE]

g - Relief model [OBSOLETE]

h - Rare [OBSOLETE]

j - Picture card, post card

k - Calendar

l - Puzzle

m - Braille [OBSOLETE]

n - Game

o - Wall map

p - Playing cards

q - Large print [OBSOLETE]

r - Loose-leaf

z - Other

| - No attempt to code

008—MUSIC

Character Positions

18-19 - Form of composition

an - Anthems

bd - Ballads

bg - Bluegrass music

bl - Blues

bt - Ballets

ca - Chaconnes

cb - Chants, Other religions

cc - Chant, Christian

cg - Concerti grossi

ch - Chorales

cl - Chorale preludes

cn - Canons and rounds

co - Concertos

cp - Chansons, polyphonic

cr - Carols

cs - Chance compositions

ct - Cantatas

cy - Country music

cz - Canzonas

df - Dance forms

dv - Divertimentos, serenades, cassations, divertissements, notturni

fg - Fugues

fm - Folk music

ft - Fantasias

gm - Gospel music

hy - Hymns

jz - Jazz

mc - Musical revues and comedies

md - Madrigals

mi - Minuets

mo - Motets

mp - Motion picture music

mr - Marches

ms - Masses

mu - Multiple forms

mz - Mazurkas

nc - Nocturnes

nn - Not applicable

op - Operas

or - Oratorios

ov - Overtures

pg - Program music

pm - Passion music

po - Polonaises

pp - Popular music

pr - Preludes

ps - Passacaglias

pt - Part-songs

pv - Pavans

rc - Rock music

rd - Rondos

rg - Ragtime music

ri - Ricercars

rp - Rhapsodies

rq - Requiems

sd - Square dance music

sg - Songs

sn - Sonatas

sp - Symphonic poems

st - Studies and exercises

su - Suites

sy - Symphonies

tc - Toccatas

ts - Trio-sonatas

uu - Unknown

vr - Variations

wz - Waltzes

zz - Other

|| - No attempt to code

20 - Format of music

a - Full score

b - Full score. miniature or study size

c - Accompaniment reduced for keyboard

d - Voice score

e - Condensed score or piano-conductor score

g - Close score

m - Multiple score formats

n - Not applicable

u - Unknown

z - Other

| - No attempt to code

21 - Music parts

- No parts in hand or not specified

d - Instrumental and vocal parts

e - Instrumental parts

f - Vocal parts

n - Not applicable

u - Unknown

| - No attempt to code

1 - Existence of parts [OBSOLETE]

- No parts exist

a - Parts exist

n - Not applicable

u - Unknown

22 - Target audience

- Unknown or not specified

a - Preschool

b - Primary

c - Pre-adolescent

d - Adolescent

e - Adult

f - Specialized

g - General

j - Juvenile

| - No attempt to code

23 - Form of item

- None of the following

a - Microfilm

b - Microfiche

c - Microopaque

d - Large print

f - Braille

g - Punched paper tape [OBSOLETE]

h - Magnetic tape [OBSOLETE]

i - Multimedia [OBSOLETE]

r - Regular print reproduction

s - Electronic

x - Other form of reproduction [OBSOLETE]

z - Other form of reproduction [OBSOLETE]

| - No attempt to code

24-29 - Accompanying matter

- No accompanying matter

a - Discography

b - Bibliography

c - Thematic index

d - Libretto or text

e - Biography of composer or author

f - Biography of performer or history of ensemble

g - Technical and/or historical information on instruments

h - Technical information on music

i - Historical information

j - Historical information other than music [OBSOLETE]

k - Ethnological information

n - Not applicable [OBSOLETE]

r - Instructional materials

s - Music

z - Other

| - No attempt to code

30-31 - Literary text for sound recordings

- Item is a musical sound recording

a - Autobiography

b - Biography

c - Conference proceedings

d - Drama

e - Essays

f - Fiction

g - Reporting

h - History

i - Instruction

j - Language instruction

k - Comedy

l - Lectures, speeches

m - Memoirs

n - Not applicable

o - Folktales

p - Poetry

r - Rehearsals

s - Sounds

t - Interviews

z - Other

- No attempt to code

32 - Main entry in body of entry [OBSOLETE]

0 - Main entry not in body of entry

1 - Main entry in body of entry

- No attempt to code

32 - Undefined

33 - Transposition and arrangement

- Not arrangement or transposition or not specified

a - Transposition

b - Arrangement

c - Both transposed and arranged

n - Not applicable

u - Unknown

| - No attempt to code

34 - Undefined

008—CONTINUING RESOURCES

Character Positions

18 - Frequency

- No determinable frequency

a - Annual

b - Bimonthly

c - Semiweekly

d - Daily

e - Biweekly

f - Semiannual

g - Biennial

h - Triennial

i - Three times a week

j - Three times a month

k - Continuously updated

m - Monthly

q - Quarterly

s - Semimonthly

t - Three times a year

u - Unknown

w - Weekly

z - Other

| - No attempt to code

19 - Regularity

n - Normalized irregular

r - Regular

u - Unknown

x - Completely irregular

| - No attempt to code

20 - ISSN center

- No ISSN center code assigned

0 - International Center

1 - United States

2 - United Kingdom

3 - Australia [OBSOLETE]

4 - Canada

5 - Moscow Regional Centre [OBSOLETE]

6 - Federal Republic of Germany [OBSOLETE]

7 - France [OBSOLETE]

8 - Argentina [OBSOLETE]

9 - Japan [OBSOLETE]

u - Unknown [OBSOLETE]

z - Other

| - No attempt to code

21 - Type of continuing resource

- None of the following

d - Updating database

l - Updating loose-leaf

m - Monographic series

n - Newspaper

p - Periodical

w - Updating Web site

| - No attempt to code

22 - Form of original item

- None of the following

a - Microfilm

b - Microfiche

c - Microopaque

d - Large print

e - Newspaper format

f - Braille

g - Punched paper tape [OBSOLETE]

h - Magnetic tape [OBSOLETE]

i - Multimedia [OBSOLETE]

s - Electronic

x - Other physical medium [OBSOLETE]

z - Other physical medium [OBSOLETE]

| - No attempt to code

23 - Form of item

- None of the following

a - Microfilm

b - Microfiche

c - Microopaque

d - Large print

f - Braille

g - Punched paper tape [OBSOLETE]

h - Magnetic tape [OBSOLETE]

i - Multimedia [OBSOLETE]

r - Regular print reproduction

s - Electronic

z - Other form of reproduction [OBSOLETE]

| - No attempt to code

24 - Nature of entire work

- No specified nature of entire work

a - Abstracts/summaries

b - Bibliographies

c - Catalogs

d - Dictionaries

e - Encyclopedias

f - Handbooks

g - Legal articles

h - Biography

i - Indexes

k - Discographies

l - Legislation

m - Theses

n - Surveys of literature in a subject area

n - Legal cases and case notes [OBSOLETE]

o - Reviews

p - Programmed texts

q - Filmographies

r - Directories

s - Statistics

t - Technical reports

u - Standards/specifications

v - Legal cases and case notes

w - Law reports and digests

y - Yearbooks [OBSOLETE]

z - Treaties

| - No attempt to code

25-27 - Nature of contents

- No specified nature of contents

a - Abstracts/summaries

b - Bibliographies

c - Catalogs

d - Dictionaries

e - Encyclopedias

f - Handbooks

g - Legal articles

h - Biography

i - Indexes

k - Discographies

l - Legislation

m - Theses

n - Surveys of literature in a subject area

n - Legal cases and case notes [OBSOLETE]

o - Reviews

p - Programmed texts

q - Filmographies

r - Directories

s - Statistics

t - Technical reports

u - Standards/specifications

v - Legal cases and case notes

w - Law reports and digests

y - Yearbooks [OBSOLETE]

z - Treaties

| - No attempt to code

28 - Government publication

- Not a government publication

a - Autonomous or semi-autonomous component

c - Multilocal

f - Federal/national

i - International intergovernmental

l - Local

m - Multistate

n - Government publication—level undetermined [OBSOLETE]

o - Government publication—level undetermined

s - State, provincial, territorial, dependent,etc.

u - Unknown if item is government publication

z - Other

| - No attempt to code

29 - Conference publication

0 - Not a conference publication

1 - Conference publication

| - No attempt to code

30-32 - Undefined

30 - Title page availability [OBSOLETE]

- No separate title page issued

a - In last issue of volume, loose

b - In last issue of volume, attached

c - In first issue of next volume, loose

d - In first issue of next volume, attached

e - Published separately, free upon request

f - Published separately, free, automatically sent

g - Published separately, purchase, request

u - Unknown

z - Other title page availability

| - No attempt to code

31 - Index availability [OBSOLETE]

- No index published

a - Each issue contains index to its own contents (no volume index), loose

b - In last issue of volume, loose, separately paged

c - In last issue of volume, loose, unpaged

d - In last issue of volume, attached

e - In first issue of next volume, loose, separately paged

f - In first issue of next volume, loose, unpaged

g - In first issue of next volume, attached

h - Published separately, free, automatically sent

i - Published separately, free, upon request

j - Published separately, bound from publisher, free, automatically sent

k - Published separately, bound from publisher, free, upon request l - Received separately, bound from publisher

m - Supplement or subseries, indexed in parent journal index

u - Unknown

z - Other index availability

| - No attempt to code

32 - Cumulative index availability [OBSOLETE]

0 - No cumulative index available

1 - Cumulative index available

u - Unknown

| - No attempt to code

33 - Original alphabet or script of title

- No alphabet or script given/no key title

a - Basic roman

b - Extended roman

c - Cyrillic

d - Japanese

e - Chinese

f - Arabic

g - Greek

h - Hebrew

i - Thai

j - Devanagari

k - Korean

l - Tamil

u - Unknown

z - Other

| - No attempt to code

34 - Entry convention

0 - Successive entry

1 - Latest entry

2 - Integrating entry

| - No attempt to code

008—VISUAL MATERIALS

Character Positions

18-20 - Running time for motion pictures and videorecordings

000 - Running time exceeds three characters

001-999 - Running time

Running time unknown

nnn - Not applicable

- No attempt to code

21 - Undefined

21 - In LC collection [OBSOLETE

- Not in LC

a - In LC, print note

b - In LC, do not print note

u - Unknown

22 - Target audience

- Unknown or not specified

a - Preschool

b - Primary

c - Pre-adolescent

d - Adolescent

e - Adult

f - Specialized

g - General

j - Juvenile

| - No attempt to code

23-27 - Undefined

23-27 - Accompanying matter [OBSOLETE]

- No accompanying matter

0 - No [OBSOLETE]

1 - Yes [OBSOLETE]

l - Stills

m - Script material

o - Posters

p - Pressbooks

q - Lobby cards

r - Instructional materials

s - Music

z - Other

| - No attempt to code

28 - Government publication

- Not a government publication

a - Autonomous or semi-autonomous component

c - Multilocal

f - Federal/national

i - International intergovernmental

l - Local

m - Multistate

n - Government publication—level undetermined [OBSOLETE]

o - Government publication—level undetermined

s - State, provincial, territorial, dependent, etc.

u - Unknown if item is government publication

z - Other

| - No attempt to code

29 - Form of item

- None of the following

a - Microfilm

b - Microfiche

c - Microopaque

d - Large print

f - Braille

r - Regular print reproduction

s - Electronic

| - No attempt to code

30-32 - Undefined

32 - Main entry in body of entry [OBSOLETE]

0 - Main entry not in body of entry

1 - Main entry in body of entry

| - No attempt to code

33 - Type of visual material

a - Art original

b - Kit

c - Art reproduction

d - Diorama

e - Electronic videorecording [OBSOLETE]

f - Filmstrip

g - Game

i - Picture

k - Graphic

l - Technical drawing

m - Motion picture

n - Chart

o - Flash card

p - Microscope slide

q - Model

r - Realia

s - Slide

t - Transparency

v - Videorecording

w - Toy

z - Other

| - No attempt to code

34 - Technique

- Not applicable [OBSOLETE]

a - Animation

c - Animation and live action

l - Live action

n - Not applicable

u - Unknown

z - Other technique

| - No attempt to code

008—MIXED MATERIALS

Character Positions

18-22 - Undefined

23 - Form of item

- None of the following

a - Microfilm

b - Microfiche

c - Microopaque

d - Large print

f - Braille

g - Punched paper tape [OBSOLETE]

h - Magnetic tape [OBSOLETE]

i - Multimedia [OBSOLETE]

j - Handwritten transcript [OBSOLETE]

p - Photocopy [OBSOLETE]

r - Regular print reproduction

s - Electronic

t - Typewritten transcript [OBSOLETE]

z - Other form of reproduction [OBSOLETE]

| - No attempt to code

24-34 - Undefined

30 - Case file indicator [OBSOLETE]

- No case file exists

c - Case file exists

32 - Processing status code [OBSOLETE]

a - Collection not in library

b - Completely processed

c - Processed but with unprocessed additions

d - Requires processing

e - Totally unprocessed

f - Under total cloture

u - Unknown

33 - Collection status code [OBSOLETE]

a - Discrete grouping of material

b - Accession

c - Active solicitation

d - Solicitation unsuccessful

e - Information file only

u - Unknown

34 - Level of collection control code [OBSOLETE]

a - Control on collection level

b - Control by series

c - Control by container

d - Control by folder

e - Control by item

u - Unknown

009 - PHYSICAL DESCRIPTION FIXED-FIELD FOR ARCHIVAL COLLECTION (VM) - [OBSOLETE]

Character Positions

00 - Genealogical stage

01 - Technical stage

02 - Color stage

03 - Film emulsion

04 - Film base

05 - Negative or positive sound

06 - Additional types of color

07 - Longitudinal shrinkage

08 - Perforation shrinkage

09 - Film deterioration

10 - Completeness

11-14 - Film inspection date

Variable Fields:

Number and Code Fields (01X-04X)

010 - LIBRARY OF CONGRESS CONTROL NUMBER (NR)

A unique number assigned to a MARC record by the Library of Congress. Valid MARC prefixes for LC control are published in MARC 21 Format for Bibliographic Data.

Indicators

First - Undefined # - Undefined

Second - Undefined # - Undefined

Subfield Codes

$a - LC control number (NR)

$b - NUCMC control number (R)

$z - Canceled/invalid LC control number (R)

$8 - Field link and sequence number (R)

Examples:

010 ##$a###68004897#

010 ##$a###79139101#/AC/MN

010 ##$a###73002284#//r752

010 ##$anuc76039265#

011 - LINKING LIBRARY OF CONGRESS CONTROL NUMBER (NR) [OBSOLETE]

Indicators

First – Undefined

- Undefined

Second - Undefined

- Undefined

Subfield Codes

$a - LINKING LC control number (R)

013 - PATENT CONTROL INFORMATION (R)

Contains information used to control patent documents. In

addition to information about patents. this field may contain information relating to inventors' certificates, utility certificates, utility models. patents or certificates of addition. inventors' certificates of addition. utility certificates of addition, and published applications for any of these.

Indicators

First - Undefined

- Undefined

Second - Undefined

- Undefined

Subfield Codes

$a - Number (NR)

$b - Country (NR)

$c - Type of number (NR)

$d - Date (R)

$e - Status (R)

$f - Party to document (R)

$6 - Linkage (NR)

$8 - Field link and sequence number (R)

015 - NATIONAL BIBLIOGRAPHY NUMBER (R)

The bibliography entry number for cataloging information that is derived from a national bibliography.

Indicators

First - Undefined

- Undefined

Second - Undefined

- Undefined

Subfield Codes

$a - National bibliography number (R)

$2 - Source (NR)

$6 - Linkage (NR)

$8 - Field link and sequence number (R)

Examples:

015 ##$aF84-3117

015 ##$aB67-20987 $aB67-20988 (pbk)

015 ##$aGFR67-A14-54 $aAu67- 6

015 ##$aF67-835 (v. 1) $aF67-9455 (v. 2)

016 - NATIONAL BIBLIOGRAPHIC AGENCY CONTROL NUMBER (R)

Unique numbers that have been assigned to a record by a national bibliographic agency other than the Library of Congress. The control number may also appear in field 001 (Control Number) in records distributed by the same national agency. This number is a record control number used in a national bibliographic agency system, rather than a number used for an entry in a national bibliographic, field 015 (National Bibliography Number).

Indicators

First - National bibliographic agency

- National Library of Canada

7 - Agency identified in subfield $2

Second - Undefined

- Undefined

Subfield Codes

$a - Record control number (NR)

$z - Canceled or invalid record control number (R)

$2 - Source (NR)

$8 - Field link and sequence number (R)

Examples:

016 ##$a#730032015 rev

016 ##$a#84074272XE#

016 7#$a94.763966.7 $2GyFmDB

016 7#$aPTBN000004618 $2PoLiBN

016 ##$a890000298##rev $z89000298##

16 7#$ab9117951 $zE000214460 $2Uk

17

017 - COPYRIGHT OR LEGAL DEPOSIT NUMBER (R)

The copyright registration or legal deposit number for an item that was acquired by copyright or legal deposit.

Indicators

First - Undefined

- Undefined

Second - Undefined

- Undefined

Subfield Code

$a - Copyright registration number (R)

$b - Assigning agency (NR)

$2 - Source (NR)

$6 - Linkage (NR)

$8 - Field link and sequence number (R)

Examples:

017 ##$aEU781596 $bU.S. Copyright Office

017 ##$aPA52-758 (English subtitled version) $aPA52-759 (English language dubbed version) $bU.S. Copyright Office

017 ##$aDL1377-1984 $bBibliotheque nationale de France

18 ##$aVA26037 $aVA26038 $aVA26039 $aVA26040 $aVA26041 $aVA26042 $aVA26043 $bU.S. Copyright Office

018 - COPYRIGHT ARTICLE-FEE CODE (NR)

Indicators

First - Undefined

- Undefined

Second - Undefined

- Undefined

Subfield Code

$a - Copyright article-fee code (NR)

$6 - Linkage (NR)

$8 - Field link and sequence number (R)

020 - INTERNATIONAL STANDARD BOOK NUMBER (R)

The ISBN assigned to a monographic publication by designated agencies in each country participating in the program The field may include terms of availability and cancelled or invalid ISBNs. The initialism ISBN, the phrase ISBN (invalid), and the hyphens embedded in the number are not carried in the MARC record. (The ISBN is an agency-assigned data element.)

Indicators

First - Undefined

- Undefined

Second - Undefined

- Undefined

Subfield Codes

$a - International Standard Book Number (NR)

$c - Terms of availability (NR)

$z - Canceled/invalid ISBN (R)

$6 - Linkage (NR)

$8 - Field link and sequence number (R)

Examples:

020 ##$a0491001304

020 ##$a0914378260 (pbk. : v. 1) c5.00

020 ##$a0394502884 (Random House) : c12 50

020 ##$a0877790019 (black leather) $z0877780116 c14.00

020 ##$a0456789012 (reel l)

020 ##c8.95

020 ##$cRs15.76 ($5.60 U.S.)

020 ##$cRental material

020 ##$cFor sale ($200.00 for 3/4 in.: $150.00 for 1/2 in.)

19 ##c3.60 (pbk.)

20

022 - INTERNATIONAL STANDARD SERIAL NUMBER (R)

The ISSN assigned to a serial publication by a national center under the auspices of the International Serials Data System (ISDS). The initialism ISSN and the phrases ISSN (incorrect) and ISSN (cancelled) are not carried in the MARC record. (The ISSN is an agency-assigned data element.)

Indicators

First - Level of international interest

- No level specified

0 - Serial of international interest

1 - Serial not of international interest

Second - Undefined

- Undefined

Subfield Codes

$a - International Standard Serial Number (NR)

$y - Incorrect ISSN (R)

$z - Canceled ISSN (R)

$6 - Linkage (NR)

$8 - Field link and sequence number (R)

Examples:

022 ##$a0376-4583

022 0#$a0046-225X $y0046- 2254

022 0#$a0145-0808 $z0361- 7106

21 0#$z0027-3473

024 - OTHER STANDARD IDENTIFIER (R)

A standard number or code published on an item which cannot

be accommodated in another field (e.g., field 020 (International Standard Book Number), 022 (International Standard Serial Number), 027 (Standard Technical Report Number)). The type of standard number or code is identified in the first indicator position or in subfield $2 (Source of number or code).

Indicators

First - Type of standard number or code

0 - International Standard Recording Code (ISRC)

1 - Universal Product Code (UPC)

2 - International Standard Music Number (ISMN)

3 - International Article Number (EAN)

4 - Serial Item and Contribution Identifier (SICI)

7 - Source specified in subfield $2

8 - Unspecified type of standard number or code

Second - Difference indicator

- No information provided

0 - No difference

1 - Difference

Subfield Codes

$a - Standard number or code (NR)

$c - Terms of availability (NR)

$d - Additional codes following the standard number or code (NR)

$z - Canceled/invalid standard number or code (R)

$2 - Source of number or code (NR)

$6 - Linkage (NR)

$8 - Field link and sequence number (R)

Examples:

024 0#$aFRZ039101231

024 10$a070993005955 $d35740

024 2#$aM571100511

024 30$a9780449906200 $d51000

24 41$a87562324754198634O134QTP1

025 - OVERSEAS ACQUISITION NUMBER (R)

Indicators

First - Undefined

- Undefined

Second - Undefined

- Undefined

Subfield Code

$a - Overseas acquisition number (R)

$8 - Field link and sequence number (R)

026 - FINGERPRINT IDENTIFIER (R)

Indicators

First - Undefined

- Undefined

Second - Undefined

- Undefined

Subfield Codes

$a - First and second groups of characters (R)

$b - Third and fourth groups of characters (R)

$c - Date (NR)

$d - Number of volume or part (R)

$e - Unparsed fingerprint (NR)

$2 - Source (NR)

$5 - Institution to which field applies (R)

$6 - Linkage (NR) $8 - Field link and sequence number (R)

027 - STANDARD TECHNICAL REPORT NUMBER (R)

Indicators

First - Undefined

- Undefined

Second - Undefined

- Undefined

Subfield Codes

$a - Standard technical report number (NR)

$z - Canceled/invalid number (R)

$6 - Linkage (NR)

$8 - Field link and sequence number (R)

028 - PUBLISHER NUMBER (R)

Indicators

First - Type of publisher number

0 - Issue number

1 - Matrix number

2 - Plate number

3 - Other music number

4 - Videorecording number

5 - Other publisher number

Second - Note/added entry controller

0 - No note, no added entry

1 - Note, added entry

2 - Note, no added entry

3 - No note, added entry

Subfield Codes

$a - Publisher number (NR)

$b - Source (NR)

$6 - Linkage (NR)

$8 - Field link and sequence number (R)

030 - CODEN DESIGNATION (R)

Indicators

First - Undefined

- Undefined

Second - Undefined

- Undefined

Subfield Codes

$a - CODEN (NR)

$z - Canceled/invalid CODEN (R)

$6 - Linkage (NR)

$8 - Field link and sequence number (R)

032 - POSTAL REGISTRATION NUMBER (R)

Indicators

First - Undefined

- Undefined

Second - Undefined

- Undefined

Subfield Codes

$a - Postal registration number (NR)

$b - Source (agency assigning number) (NR)

$6 - Linkage (NR)

$8 - Field link and sequence number (R)

033 - DATE/TIME AND PLACE OF AN EVENT (R)

Indicators

First - Type of date in subfield $a

- No date information

0 - Single date

1 - Multiple single dates

2 - Range of dates

Second - Type of event

- No information provided

0 - Capture

1 - Broadcast

2 - Finding

Subfield Codes

$a - Formatted date/time (R)

$b - Geographic classification area code (R)

$c - Geographic classification subarea code (R)

$3 - Materials specified (NR)

$6 - Linkage (NR)

$8 - Field link and sequence number (R)

034 - CODED CARTOGRAPHIC MATHEMATICAL DATA (R)

Indicators

First - Type of scale

0 - Scale indeterminable/No scale recorded

1 - Single scale

3 - Range of scales

Second - Type of ring

- Not applicable

0 - Outer ring

1 - Exclusion ring

Subfield Codes

$a - Category of scale (NR)

a - Linear scale

b - Angular scale

z - Other type of scale

$b - Constant ratio linear horizontal scale (R)

$c - Constant ratio linear vertical scale (R)

$d - Coordinates—westernmost longitude (NR)

$e - Coordinates—easternmost longitude (NR)

$f - Coordinates—northernmost latitude (NR)

$g - Coordinates—southernmost latitude (NR)

$h - Angular scale (R)

$j - Declination—northern limit (NR)

$k - Declination—southern limit (NR)

$m - Right ascension—eastern limit (NR)

$n - Right ascension—western limit (NR)

$p - Equinox (NR)

$s - G-ring latitude (R)

$t - G-ring longitude (R)

$6 - Linkage (NR)

$8 - Field link and sequence number (R)

035 - SYSTEM CONTROL NUMBER (R)

Indicators

First - Undefined

- Undefined

Second - Undefined

- Undefined

Subfield Codes

$a - System control number (NR)

$z - Canceled/invalid control number (R)

$6 - Linkage (NR)

$8 - Field link and sequence number (R)

036 - ORIGINAL STUDY NUMBER FOR COMPUTER DATA FILES (NR)

Indicators

First - Undefined

- Undefined

Second - Undefined

- Undefined

Subfield Codes

$a - Original study number (NR)

$b - Source (agency assigning number) (NR)

$6 - Linkage (NR)

$8 - Field link and sequence number (R)

037 - SOURCE OF ACQUISITION (R)

Indicators

First - Undefined

- Undefined

Second - Undefined

- Undefined

Subfield Codes

$a - Stock number (NR)

$b - Source of stock number/acquisition (NR)

$c - Terms of availability (R)

$f - Form of issue (R)

$g - Additional format characteristics (R)

$n - Note (R)

$6 - Linkage (NR)

$8 - Field link and sequence number (R)

038 - RECORD CONTENT LICENSOR (NR)

Indicators

First - Undefined

- Undefined

Second - Undefined

- Undefined

Subfield Codes

$a - Record content licensor (NR)

$6 - Linkage (NR)

$8 - Field link and sequence number (R)

040 - CATALOGING SOURCE (NR)

Indicators

First - Undefined

- Undefined

Second - Undefined

- Undefined

Subfield Codes

$a - Original cataloging agency (NR)

$b - Language of cataloging (NR)

$c - Transcribing agency (NR)

$d - Modifying agency (R)

$e - Description conventions (NR)

$6 - Linkage (NR)

$8 - Field link and sequence number (R)

041 - LANGUAGE CODE (R)

Indicators

First - Translation indication

0 - Item not a translation/does not include a translation

1 - Item is or includes a translation

Second - Source of code

- MARC language code

7 - Source specified in subfield $2

Subfield Codes

$a - Language code of text/sound track or separate title (R)

$b - Language code of summary or abstract/overprinted title or subtitle (R)

$d - Language code of sung or spoken text (R)

$e - Language code of librettos (R)

$f - Language code of table of contents (R)

$g - Language code of accompanying material other than librettos (R)

$h - Language code of original and/or intermediate translations of text (R)

$2 - Source of code (NR)

$6 - Linkage (NR)

$8 - Field link and sequence number (R)

042 - AUTHENTICATION CODE (NR)

Indicators

First - Undefined

- Undefined

Second - Undefined

- Undefined

Subfield Code

$a - Authentication code (R)

dc - Dublin Core

dhca - Dance Heritage Coalition Access Project

gamma - Georgia Archives & Manuscripts Automated Access Project

gils - Government Information Location Service

isds/c - ISSN Canada

lc - Library of Congress

lcac - LC Annotated Children's Cataloging Program

lccopycat - LC copy cataloging

lccopycat-nm - LC copy cataloging-Near Match

lcd - CONSER full authority application

lcderive - LC derived cataloging

lchlas - Handbook of Latin American Studies

lcllh - LC Law Library Hispanic

lcnccp - LC National Coordinated Cataloging Program

lcnitrate - LC nitrate film

lcnuc - National Union Catalog

lcode - LC overseas data entry

msc - CONSER minimal authority application

nlc - National Library of Canada

nlmcopyc - National Library of Medicine copy cataloging

nsdp - National Serial Data Program

ntccf - LC National Translations Center citation file

pcc - Program for Cooperative Cataloging

premarc - LC PreMARC Retrospective Conversion Project

sanb - South African National Bibliography Project

xisds/c - ISSN Canada does not consider item a serial

xlc - LC does not consider item a serial

xnlc - NLC does not consider item a serial

xnsdp - NSDP does not consider item a serial

043 - GEOGRAPHIC AREA CODE (NR)

Indicators

First - Undefined

- Undefined

Second - Undefined

- Undefined

Subfield Code

$a - Geographic area code (R)

$b - Local GAC code (R)

$c - ISO code (R)

$2 - Source of local code (R)

$6 - Linkage (NR)

$8 - Field link and sequence number (R)

044 - COUNTRY OF PUBLISHING/PRODUCING ENTITY CODE (NR)

Indicators

First - Undefined

- Undefined

Second - Undefined

- Undefined

Subfield Code

$a - Country of publishing/producing entity code (R)

$b - Local subentity code (R)

$c - ISO code (R)

$2 - Source of local subentity code (R)

$6 - Linkage (NR)

$8 - Field link and sequence number (R)

045 - TIME PERIOD OF CONTENT (NR)

Indicators

First - Type of time period in subfield $b or $c

- Subfield $b or $c not present

0 - Single date/time

1 - Multiple single dates/times

2 - Range of dates/times

Second - Undefined

- Undefined

Subfield Codes

$a - Time period code (R)

$b - Formatted 9999 B.C. through C.E. time period (R)

$c - Formatted pre-9999 B.C. time period (R)

$6 - Linkage (NR)

$8 - Field link and sequence number (R)

046 - SPECIAL CODED DATES (R)

Indicators

First - Undefined

- Undefined

Second - Undefined

- Undefined

Subfield Codes

$a - Type of date code (NR)

i - Inclusive dates of collection

k - Bulk of collection

m - Multiple dates

n - Unknown dates

p - Distribution/release/issue and production/recording session dates

q - Questionable date

r - Reissue and originaldates

s - Single known/probable date

t - Publication date and copyright dates

x - Incorrect dates

$b - Date 1 (B.C. date) (NR)

$c - Date 1 (C.E. date) (NR)

$d - Date 2 (B.C. date) (NR)

$e - Date 2 (C.E. date) (NR)

$j - Date resource modified (NR)

$k - Beginning or single date created (NR)

$l - Ending date created (NR)

$m - Beginning of date valid (NR)

$n - End of date valid (NR)

$2 - Source of date (NR)

$6 - Linkage (NR)

$8 - Field link and sequence number (R)

047 - FORM OF MUSICAL COMPOSITION CODE (NR)

Indicators

First - Undefined

- Undefined

Second - Undefined

- Undefined

Subfield Codes

$a - Form of musical composition code (R)

$8 - Field link and sequence number (R)

048 - NUMBER OF MUSICAL INSTRUMENTS OR VOICES CODE (R)

Indicators

First - Undefined

- Undefined

Second - Undefined

- Undefined

Subfield Codes

$a - Performer or ensemble (R)

$b - Soloist (R)

$8 - Field link and sequence number(R)

Instrument or Voices Codes

ba - Brass - Horn

bb - Brass—Trumpet

bc - Brass—Cornet

bd - Brass—Trombone

be - Brass—Tuba

bf - Brass—Baritone

bn - Brass—Unspecified

bu - Brass—Unknown

by - Brass—Ethnic

bz - Brass—Other

ca - Choruses—Mixed

cb - Choruses—Women's

cc - Choruses—Men's

cd - Choruses—Children's

cn - Choruses—Unspecified

cu - Choruses—Unknown

cy - Choruses—Ethnic

ea - Electronic—Synthesizer

eb - Electronic—Tape

ec - Electronic—Computer

ed - Electronic—Ondes Martinot

en - Electronic—Unspecified

eu - Electronic—Unknown

ez - Electronic—Other

ka - Keyboard—Piano

kb - Keyboard—Organ

kc - Keyboard—Harpsichord

kd - Keyboard—Clavichord

ke - Keyboard—Continuo

kf - Keyboard—Celeste

kn - Keyboard—Unspecified

ku - Keyboard—Unknown

ky - Keyboard—Ethnic

kz - Keyboard—Other

oa - Larger ensemble—Full orchestra

ob - Larger ensemble—Chamber orch.

oc - Larger ensemble—String orchestra

od - Larger ensemble—Band

oe - Larger ensemble—Dance orchestra

of - Larger ensemble—Brass band

on - Larger ensemble—Unspecified

ou - Larger ensemble—Unknown

oy - Larger ensemble—Ethnic

oz - Larger ensemble—Other

pa - Percussion—Timpani

pb - Percussion—Xylophone

pc - Percussion—Marimba

pd - Percussion—Drum
pn - Percussion—Unspecified
pu - Percussion—Unknown
py - Percussion—Ethnic
pz - Percussion—Other
sa - Strings, bowed—Violin
sb - Strings, bowed—Viola
sc - Strings, bowed—Violoncello
sd - Strings, bowed—Double bass
se - Strings, bowed—Viol
sf - Strings, bowed—Viola d'amore
sg - Strings, bowed—Viola da gamba
sn - Strings, bowed—Unspecified
su - Strings, bowed—Unknown
sy - Strings, bowed—Ethnic
sz - Strings, bowed—Other
ta - Strings, plucked—Harp
tb - Strings, plucked—Guitar
tc - Strings, plucked—Lute
td - Strings, plucked—Mandolin
tn - Strings, plucked—Unspecified
tu - Strings, plucked—Unknown
ty - Strings, plucked—Ethnic
tz - Strings, plucked—Other
va - Voices—Soprano
vb - Voices—Mezzo Soprano
vc - Voices—Alto
vd - Voices—Tenor
ve - Voices—Baritone
vf - Voices—Bass
vg - Voices—Counter tenor

vh - Voices—High voice

vi - Voices—Medium voice

vj - Voices—Low voice

vn - Voices—Unspecified

vu - Voices—Unknown

vy - Voices—Ethnic

wa - Woodwinds—Flute

wb - Woodwinds—Oboe

wc - Woodwinds—Clarinet

wd - Woodwinds—Bassoon

we - Woodwinds—Piccolo

wf - Woodwinds—English horn

wg - Woodwinds—Bass clarinet

wh - Woodwinds—Recorder

wi - Woodwinds—Saxophone

wn - Woodwinds—Unspecified

wu - Woodwinds—Unknown

wy - Woodwinds—Ethnic

wz - Woodwinds—Other

zn - Unspecified instruments

zu - Unknown

—Classification and Call Number Fields (05X-08X)—

Fields 050-088 fields contain classification and call numbers related to the item described in the bibliographic record. Identification of the character sets used in encoding the bibliographic data is also provided for by a field in this group.

050 - LIBRARY OF CONGRESS CALL NUMBER (R)

A classification or call number that is taken from Library of Congress Classification or LC Classification Additions and Changes The brackets that customarily surround alternate class/call numbers are not carried in the MARC record: they may be generated based on the presence of repeated $a subfields.

Indicators

First - Existence in LC collection

- No information provided

0 - Item is in LC

1 - Item is not in LC

Second - Source of call number

- No information provided [OBSOLETE]

0 - Assigned by LC

4 - Assigned by agency other than LC

Second - Series call number (SE) [OBSOLETE]

0 - No series involved

1 - Main series

2 - Subseries

3 - Sub-subseries

Subfield Codes

$a - Classification number (R)

$b - Item number (NR)

$d - Supplementary class number (MU) [OBSOLETE]

$3 - Materials specified (NR)

$6 - Linkage (NR)

$8 - Field lin

Examples:

050 4aNB933.F44 $bT6

050 10$aBJ1533.C4 $bL49

050 00$aJK609 $b.M2

050 00$aZ7164.N3 $bL34 no. 9 $aZ7165.R42 $aHC517.R42k and sequence number (R)

051 - LIBRARY OF CONGRESS COPY, ISSUE, OFFPRINT STATEMENT (R)

Indicators

First - Undefined

- Undefined

Second - Undefined

- Undefined

Second - Series call number (SE) [OBSOLETE]

0 - No series involved

1 - Main series

2 - Subseries

3 - Sub-subseries

Subfield Codes

$a - Classification number (NR)

$b - Item number (NR)

$c - Copy information (NR)

$8 - Field link and sequence number (R)

052 - GEOGRAPHIC CLASSIFICATION (R)

Indicators

First - Code source

- Library of Congress Classification

0 - U.S. Dept. of Defense Classification [OBSOLETE]

1 - U.S. Dept. of Defense Classification

7 - Source specified in subfield $2

Second - Undefined

- Undefined

Subfield Codes

$a - Geographic classification area code (NR)

$b - Geographic classification subarea code (R)

$c - Subject (MP) [OBSOLETE]

$d - Populated place name (R)

$2 - Code source (NR)

$6 - Linkage (NR)

$8 - Field link and sequence number (R)

055 - CLASSIFICATION NUMBERS ASSIGNED IN CANADA (R)

Indicators

First - Existence in NLC collection

- Information not provided

0 - Work held by NLC

1 - Work not held by NLC

Second - Type, completeness, source of class/call number

0 - LC-based call number assigned by NLC

1 - Complete LC class number assigned by NLC

2 - Incomplete LC class number assigned by NLC

3 - LC-based call number assigned by the contributing library

4 - Complete LC class number assigned by the contributing library

5 - Incomplete LC class number assigned by the contributing library

6 - Other call number assigned by NLC

7 - Other class number assigned by NLC

8 - Other call number assigned by the contributing library

9 - Other class number assigned by the contributing library

Subfield Codes

$a - Classification number (NR)

$b - Item number (NR)

$2 - Source of call/class number (NR)

$8 - Field link and sequence number (R)

060 - NATIONAL LIBRARY OF MEDICINE CALL NUMBER (R)

Indicators

First - Existence in NLM collection

- No information provided

0 - Item is in NLM

1 - Item is not in NLM

Second - Source of call number

- No information provided [OBSOLETE]

0 - Assigned by NLM

4 - Assigned by agency other than NLM

Second - Series call number (SE) [OBSOLETE]

0 - No series involved

1 - Main series

2 - Subseries

3 - Sub-subseries

Subfield Codes

$a - Classification number (R)

$b - Item number (NR)

$8 - Field link and sequence number (R)

061 - NATIONAL LIBRARY OF MEDICINE COPY STATEMENT (R)

Indicators

First - Undefined

- Undefined

Second - Undefined

- Undefined

Second - Series call number (SE) [OBSOLETE]

0 - No series involved

1 - Main series

2 - Subseries

3 - Sub-subseries

Subfield Codes

$a - Classification number (R)

$b - Item number (NR)

$c - Copy information (NR)

$8 - Field link and sequence number (R)

066 - CHARACTER SETS PRESENT (NR)

Indicators

First - Undefined

- Undefined

Second - Undefined

- Undefined

Subfield Codes

$a - Primary G0 character set (NR)

$b - Primary G1 character set (NR)

$c - Alternate G0 or G1 character set (R)

070 - NATIONAL AGRICULTURAL LIBRARY CALL NUMBER (R)

Indicators

First - Existence in NAL collection

0 - Item is in NAL

1 - Item is not in NAL

Second - Undefined

- Undefined

Second - Series call number (SE) [OBSOLETE]

0 - No series involved

1 - Main series

2 - Subseries

3 - Sub-subseries

Subfield Codes

$a - Classification number (R)

$b - Item number (NR)

$8 - Field link and sequence number (R)

071 - NATIONAL AGRICULTURAL LIBRARY COPY STATEMENT (R)

Indicators

First - Undefined

- Undefined

Second - Undefined

- Undefined

Second - Series call number (SE) [OBSOLETE]

0 - No series involved

1 - Main series

2 - Subseries

3 - Sub-subseries

Subfield Codes

$a - Classification number (R)

$b - Item number (NR)

$c - Copy information (NR)

$8 - Field link and sequence number (R)

072 - SUBJECT CATEGORY CODE (R)

Indicators

First - Undefined

- Undefined

Second - Code source

0 - NAL subject category code list

7 - Code source specified in subfield $2

Subfield Codes

$a - Subject category code (NR)

$x - Subject category code subdivision (R)

$2 - Code source (NR)

$6 - Linkage (NR)

$8 - Field link and sequence number (R)

074 - GPO ITEM NUMBER (R)

Indicators

First - Undefined

- Undefined

Second - Undefined

- Undefined

Subfield Codes

$a - GPO item number (NR)

$z - Canceled/invalid GPO item number (R)

$8 - Field link and sequence number (R)

080 - UNIVERSAL DECIMAL CLASSIFICATION NUMBER (R)

Indicators

First - Undefined

- Undefined

Second - Undefined

- Undefined

Subfield Code

$a - Universal Decimal Classification number (NR)

$b - Item number (NR)

$x - Common auxiliary subdivision (R)

$2 - Edition identifier (NR)

$6 - Linkage (NR)

$8 - Field link and sequence number (R)

082 - DEWEY DECIMAL CLASSIFICATION NUMBER (R)

The classification number is taken from Dewey Decimal Classification, Abridged Dewey Decimal Classification, and/or DC&: Dewey Decimal Classification Additions, Notes and Decisions, all of which are maintained by the Library of Congress. The brackets enclosing a DDC number that appear on printed products are not carried in the MARC record. They may be generated based on the field tag.

Indicators

First - Type of edition

- No edition information recorded (BK CF MU VM SE) [OBSOLETE]

0 - Full edition

1 - Abridged edition

2 - Abridged NST version (BK MU VM SE) [OBSOLETE]

Second - Source of classification number

- No information provided

0 - Assigned by LC

4 - Assigned by agency other than LC

Subfield Codes

$a - Classification number (R)

$b - Item number (NR)

$b - DDC number—abridged NST version (SE) [OBSOLETE]

$2 - Edition number (NR)

$6 - Linkage (NR)

$8 - Field link and sequence number (R)

084 - OTHER CLASSIFICATION NUMBER (R)

Indicators

First - Undefined

- Undefined

Second - Undefined

- Undefined

Subfield Codes

$a - Classification number (R)

$b - Item number (NR)

$2 - Source of number (NR)

$6 - Linkage (NR)

$8 - Field link and sequence number (R)

086 - GOVERNMENT DOCUMENT CLASSIFICATION NUMBER (R)

Indicators

First - Number source

- Source specified in subfield $2

- Undefined (BK MP MU VM SE) [OBSOLETE]

0 - Superintendent of Documents Classification System

1 - Government of Canada Publications: Outline of Classification

First - Government jurisdiction (BK MP MU VM SE) [OBSOLETE]

Second - Undefined

- Undefined

Subfield Codes

$a - Classification number (NR)

$z - Canceled/invalid classification number (R)

$2 - Number source (NR)

$6 - Linkage (NR)

$8 - Field link and sequence number (R)

088 - REPORT NUMBER (R)

Indicators

First - Undefined

- Undefined

Second - Undefined

- Undefined

Subfield Codes

$a - Report number (NR)

$z - Canceled/invalid report number (R)

$6 - Linkage (NR)

$8 - Field link and sequence number (R)

090 - LOCAL CALL NUMBER (BK AM CF MP MU VM SE) [OBSOLETE]

Indicators

First - Undefined

- Undefined

Second - Undefined

- Undefined

Subfield Codes

$a - Local class number (NR)

$b - Local Cutter number (NR)

090 - SHELF LOCATION (AM)[OBSOLETE]

Indicators

First - Undefined

- Undefined

Second - Undefined

- Undefined

Subfield Code

$a - Shelf location (NR)

091 - MICROFILM SHELF LOCATION (AM) [OBSOLETE]

Indicators

First - Undefined

- Undefined

Second - Undefined

- Undefined

Subfield Code

$a - Microfilm shelf location (NR)

—Main Entry Fields (1XX)—

Fields 100-130 contain a name or a uniform title heading used as a main entry in bibliographic records. Except for the definitions of indicator positions and subfield codes that are field specific, the content designation for each type of name and for uniform titles is consistent for Main Entry (100-130), Series Statement (400-440), Subject Access (600-630), Added Entry (700-730), and Series Added Entry (800-830) fields.

100 - Main Entry—Personal Name (NR)

110 - Main Entry—Corporate Name (NR)

111 - Main Entry—Meeting Name (NR)

130 - Main Entry—Uniform Title (NR)

100 - MAIN ENTRY—PERSONAL NAME (NR)

Indicators

First - Type of personal name entry element

0 - Forename

1 - Surname

2 - Multiple surname [OBSOLETE]

3 - Family name

Second - Undefined

- Undefined

Second - Main entry/subject relationship (BK MU SE) [OBSOLETE]

Subfield Codes

$a - Personal name (NR)

$b - Numeration (NR)

$c - Titles and other words associated with a name (R)

$d - Dates associated with a name (NR)

$e - Relator term (R)

$f - Date of a work (NR)

$g - Miscellaneous information (NR)

$j - Attribution qualifier (R)

$k - Form subheading (R)

$l - Language of a work (NR)

$n - Number of part/section of a work (R)

$p - Name of part/section of a work (R)

$q - Fuller form of name (NR)

$t - Title of a work (NR)

$u - Affiliation (NR)

$4 - Relator code (R)

$6 - Linkage (NR)

$8 - Field link and sequence number (R)

Examples:

100 0#$aAbraham, $cSaint.

100 0#$a110908.

100 0#$aDr. Z.

100 0#$aAuthor of The diary of a physician, $d1807-1877.

100 0#$aClaude, $cd'Abbeville, pere, $dd. 1632.

100 0#$aHoward.

100 1#$aWilliam, David.

100 1#$aChiang, Kai-shek, $d1887-1975.

100 1#$aWatson, $cRev.

100 1#$aQ., Mike.

100 1#$aBlackbeard, Author of, $d1777-1852.

100 1#$aLe Conte, John Eatton. $d1784-1860

100 1#$aEl-Abiad, Ahmed H., $d1926-

100 0#$aJohn Paul $bII. $cPope. $d1920-

100 1#$aWilliam$cDr

100 1#$aChurchill. Winston. $cSir. $d1874- 1965

100 1#$aWard, Humphrey, $cMrs., $d1851- 1920.

100 1#$aWalle-Lissnijder, $cvan de.

100 0#$aThomas, $cAquinas, Saint, $d1225?-1274.

100 0#$aBlack Foot, $cChief, $dd. 1877 $c(Spirit)

100 1#$aLevi, James, $dfl. 1706-1739.

100 1#$aJoannes Aegidius, Zamorensis, $d1240 or 41-ca. 1316.

100 0#$aH. D. $q(Hilda Doolittle), $d1886-1961.

100 1#$aGresham, G. A. $q(Geoffrey Austin)

100 1#$aSmith, Elizabeth $q(Ann Elizabeth)

100 1#$aBeeton, $cMrs. $q(Isabella Mary), $d1836- 1865.

100 1#$a'Atthawimonbandit (To), $cPhra, $d1883- 1973.

100 1#$aBrown, B. F. $uChemistry Dept., American University.

100 3#$aFarquhar family.

100 1#$aMorgan, John Pierpont, $d1837-1913, $ecollector.

100 0#$aE.S., $cMeister, $d15th cent., $jFollower of

100 1#$aReynolds, Joshua, $cSir, $d1723-1792, $jPupil of

110 - MAIN ENTRY—CORPORATE NAME (NR)

Indicators

First - Type of corporate name entry element

0 - Inverted name

1 - Jurisdiction name

2 - Name in direct order

Second - Undefined

- Undefined

Second - Main entry/subject relationship (BK MU SE) [OBSOLETE]

Subfield Codes

$a - Corporate name or jurisdiction name as entry element (NR)

$b - Subordinate unit (R)

$c - Location of meeting (NR)

$d - Date of meeting or treaty signing (R)

$e - Relator term (R)

$f - Date of a work (NR)

$g - Miscellaneous information (NR)

$k - Form subheading (R)

$l - Language of a work (NR)

$n - Number of part/section/meeting (R)

$p - Name of part/section of a work (R)

$t - Title of a work (NR)

$u - Affiliation (NR)

$4 - Relator code (R)

$6 - Linkage (NR)

$8 - Field link and sequence number (R)

Examples:

110 0#$aNewman (Jean and Dorothy) Industrial Relations Library.

110 2#$aJ.C. Penney Co.

110 1#$aCyprus (Archdiocese)

110 1#$aPennsylvania. $bState Board of Examiners of Nursing Home Administrators.

110 1#$aJalisco (Mexico). $tLey que aprueba el plan regional urbano de Guadalajara, 1979- 1983.

110 1#$aUnited States. $bPresident (1981-1989 : Reagan)

110 2#$aPRONAPADE (Firm)

110 1#$aBirmingham (Ala.)

110 2#$aScientific Society of San Antonio (1892- 1894)

110 2#$aSt. James Church (Bronx, New York, N.Y.)

110 1#$aUnited States. $bCongress. $bJoint Committee on the Library.

110 1#$aParis. $bMontmartre.

110 2#$aCatholic Church. $bConcilium Plenarium Americae Latinae $d(1899 : $cRome, Italy)

110 2#$aInternational Labour Organisation. $bEuropean Regional Conference $n(2nd : $d1968 : $cGeneva, Switzerland)

110 2#$aEastman Kodak Company, $edefendant-appellant

110 1#$aMinnesota. $bConstitutional Convention $d(1857 : $gRepublican)

110 1#$aUnited States. $bCongress $n(97th, 2nd session : $d1982). $bHouse.

110 2#$aNew York Public Library. $kManuscript. $pAulendorf Codex.

110 1#$aUnited States. $bNational Technical Information Service. $u5205 Port Royal Road, Springfield, VA 22161.

110 2#$aJ.H. Bufford & Co. $4pop

110 1#$aUnited States. $bCourt of Appeals (2nd Circuit

110 1#$aUnited States. $kTreaties, etc. $gFrance. $dJan 28, 1967.

110 1#$aBombay. $kCourt rules. $gCivil Court

111 - MAIN ENTRY—MEETING NAME (NR)

Indicators

First - Type of meeting name entry element

0 - Inverted name

1 - Jurisdiction name

2 - Name in direct order

Second - Undefined

- Undefined

Second - Main entry/subject relationship (BK MU SE) [OBSOLETE]

Subfield Codes

$a - Meeting name or jurisdiction name as entry element (NR)

$b - Number (BK CF MP MU SE VM MX) [OBSOLETE]

$c - Location of meeting (NR)

$d - Date of meeting (NR)

$e - Subordinate unit (R)

$f - Date of a work (NR)

$g - Miscellaneous information (NR)

$k - Form subheading (R)

$l - Language of a work (NR)

$n - Number of part/section/meeting (R)

$p - Name of part/section of a work (R)

$q - Name of meeting following jurisdiction name entry element (NR)

$t - Title of a work (NR)

$u - Affiliation (NR)

$4 - Relator code (R)

$6 - Linkage (NR)

$8 - Field link and sequence number (R)

Examples:

111 2#$aSymposium Internacional "Manuel Pedroso" In Memoriam $d(1976 : $cGuanajuato, Mexico)

111 1#$aChicago. $qCartography Conference.

111 2#$aGovernor's Conference on Aging (N.Y.) $d(1982 : $cAlbany, N.Y.)

111 2#$aEsto '84 $d(1984 : $cToronto. Ont). $eRaamatunaituse Komitee.

111 2#$aWorld Peace Conference $n(1st : $d1949 $cParis. France and Prague. Czechoslovakia)

111 2#$aWhite House Conference on Library and Information Services $d(1979 : $cWashington, D.C.). $eOhio Conference Delegation.

111 2#$aInternational Symposium on Quality Control (1974-)

111 2#$aNational Conference on Physical Measurement of the Disabled. $n2nd. $cMayo Clinic, $d1981, $gProjected, not held

111 1#$aParis. $qPeace Conference. $d1919.

11 2#$aSymposium on the Underground Disposal of Radioactive Wastes $d(1979 $cOtaniemi, Finland) $4fnd

111 2#$aSobranie innostranykh prepodavatelei russkogo iazyka.

111 2#$aExpo '70 $c(Osaka, Japan)

130 - MAIN ENTRY—UNIFORM TITLE (NR)

Indicators

First - Nonfiling characters

0-9 - Number of nonfiling characters present

- Nonfiling characters not specified [OBSOLETE

Second - Undefined

- Undefined

Second - Main entry/subject relationship (BK MU SE) [OBSOLETE]

Subfield Codes

$a - Uniform title (NR)

$d - Date of treaty signing (R)

$f - Date of a work (NR)

$g - Miscellaneous information (NR)

$h - Medium (NR)

$k - Form subheading (R)

$l - Language of a work (NR)

$m - Medium of performance for music (R)

$n - Number of part/section of a work (R)

$o - Arranged statement for music (NR)

$p - Name of part/section of a work (R)

$r - Key for music (NR)

$s - Version (NR)

$t - Title of a work (NR)

$6 - Linkage (NR)

$8 - Field link and sequence number (R)

Examples:

130 0#$aElektroshlakovyi pereplav.

130 0#$aSiege d'Orleans (Mystery play)

130 0#$aBeowulf.

130 0#$aDialogue (Montreal, Quebec : 1962). $lEnglish.

130 0#$aTosefta. $lEnglish. $f1977.

130 0#$aKing Kong (1933)

130 0#$aGone with the wind (Motion picture). $hSound recording.

130 0#$aBible. $pO.T. $pFive Scrolls. $lHebrew. $sBiblioteca apostolica vaticana. $kManuscript. $nUrbiniti Hebraicus 1. $f1980.

130 0#$aConvention for the Protection of Human Rights and Fundamental Freedoms $d(1950). $kProtocols, etc., $d1963 Sept. 16.

130 0#$a Portrait and biographical album of Isabella County, Mich. $k Selections.

130 0#$aVedas. $pRgveda. $lItalian & Sanskrit. $kSelections.

130 0#$aConcertos. $mviolin, string orchestra, $rD major.

130 0#$aAnnale Universiteit van Stellenbosch. $nSerie A2. $pSoologie.

130 0#$aBible. $pN.T. $pPhilippians. $lEnglish. $sRevised Standard. $f1980.

130 0#$aKathy (Motion picture : 1981)

—Title and Title-Related Fields (20X-24X)—

Fields 20X-247 contain the title of the item described in the bibliographic record and variant titles that also apply to the item These fields may be used to generate access points and to display notes for the various titles.

210 - Abbreviated Key Title (NR)

222 - Key Title (R)

240 - Uniform Title (NR)

242 - Translation of Title by Cataloging Agency (R)

243 - Collective Uniform Title (NR)

245 - Title Statement (NR)

246 - Varying form of Title (R)

247 - Former Title or Title Variations (R)

210 - ABBREVIATED TITLE (R)

Abbreviations of the nouns and adjectives in the Key Title (field 222) that are determined by national centers under the auspices of the International Serials Data System in accordance with IS0 4, Documentation Rules for the Abbreviation of Title Words and Titles of Publications and List of Serial Title Word Abbreviations. (The abbreviated title is an agency-assigned data element.)

Indicators

First - Title added entry

0 - No added entry

1 - Added entry

Second - Type

- Abbreviated key title

0 - Other abbreviated title

Subfield Codes

$a - Abbreviated title (NR)

$b - Qualifying information (NR)

$2 - Source (R)

$6 - Linkage (NR)

$8 - Field link and sequence number (R)

Examples:

210 0#$aManage. improv. cost reduct. goals

210 0#$aSurg. clin. North Am.

210 0#$aPlant prot. bull. $b(Faridabad)

210 0#$aAnnu. rep. - Dep. Public Welfare $b(Chic.)

210 0#$aIssled. zhur. Inst. geofiz.

211 - ACRONYM OR SHORTENED TITLE (R) [OBSOLETE]

Indicators

First - Title added entry

0 - No title added entry

1 - Title added entry

Second - Nonfiling characters

0-9 - Number of nonfiling characters present

Subfield Codes

$a - Acronym or shortened title (NR)

$6 - Linkage (NR)

212 - VARIANT ACCESS TITLE (R) [OBSOLETE]

Indicators

First - Title added entry

0 - No title added entry

1 - Title added entry

Second - Undefined

- Undefined

Subfield Codes

$a - Variant access title (NR)

$6 - Linkage (NR)

214 - AUGMENTED TITLE (R) [OBSOLETE]

Indicators

First - Title added entry

0 - No title added entry

1 - Title added entry

Second - Nonfiling characters

0-9 - Number of nonfiling characters present

Subfield Codes

$a - Augmented title (NR)

$6 - Linkage (NR)

222 - KEY TITLE (R)

A unique title for a serial that is assigned in conjunction with an ISSN recorded in field 022 by national centers under the auspices of the International Serials Data System. (The key title is an agency-assigned data element.) A note formatted as ISSN [number] = [Key Title] (AACR 2) or Key title: [title], ISSN [number] (pre-AACR 2) is not carried in the MARC record. It may be generated from data in field 022 (International Standard Serial Number), field 222, and the value in Leader/18 (Descriptive cataloging form).

Indicators

First - Undefined

- Undefined

First - Specifies whether variant title and/or added entry is required

(CF SE) [OBSOLETE]

0 - No key title added entry; title proper same

1 - Key title added entry; title proper different

2 - Key title added entry; title proper same

3 - No key title added entry; title proper different

Second - Nonfiling characters

0-9 - Number of nonfiling characters

Subfield Codes

$a - Key title (NR)

$b - Qualifying information (NR)

$6 - Linkage (NR)

$8 - Field link and sequence number (R)

Examples:

222 #0$aViva $b(New York)

222 #0$aCauses of death

222 #5$aDer Offentliche Dienst $b(Koln)

222 #0$aJournal of polymer science. Part B. Polymer letters

222 #0$aEconomic education bulletin $b(Great Barrington)

222 #0$6880-02 $aMezhdunarodnaia zhizn`

240 - UNIFORM TITLE (NR)

The uniform title for an item when the bibliographic description is entered under a main entry that contains a personal (field 100), corporate (field 110), or meeting (field 111) name. The brackets that customarily enclose a uniform title are not carried in the MARC record. They may be generated based on the field tag.

Indicators

First - Uniform title printed or displayed

0 - Not printed or displayed

1 - Printed or displayed

2 - Not printed on card, title added entry (MU) [OBSOLETE]

3 - Printed on card, title added entry (MU) [OBSOLETE]

Second - Nonfiling characters

0-9 - Number of nonfiling characters

Subfield Codes

$a - Uniform title (NR)

$d - Date of treaty signing (R)

$f - Date of a work (NR)

$g - Miscellaneous information (NR)

$h - Medium (NR)

$k - Form subheading (R)

$l - Language of a work (NR)

$m - Medium of performance for music (R)

$n - Number of part/section of a work (R)

$o - Arranged statement for music (NR)

$p - Name of part/section of a work (R)

$r - Key for music (NR)

$s - Version (NR)

$6 - Linkage (NR)

$8 - Field link and sequence number (R)

Examples:

240 14$aThe Pickwick papers. $lFrench

240 10$aLaws, etc. (1969-1970)

240 10$aTreaties, etc. $gPoland, $d1948 Mar. 2. $kProtocols, etc., $d1951 Mar. 6

240 10$aPoems. $kSelections

240 10$aInstitutiones. $nLiber 2. $nCapitulum 5. $lEnglish

240 10$aFidelio $n(1814). $sLibretto. $lEnglish & German

240 00$aVariations, $mpiano, 4 hands, $nK. 501, $rG major

241 - ROMANIZED TITLE (BK AM CF MP MU VM) (NR) [OBSOLETE]

Indicators

First - Title added entry

0 - No title added entry

1 - Title added entry

Second - Nonfiling characters

0-9 - Number of nonfiling characters

Subfield Codes

$a - Romanized title (NR)

$h - Medium (NR)

242 - TRANSLATION OF TITLE BY CATALOGING AGENCY (R)

A translation of the title proper that is made by the cataloger when the translated title does not appear as a parallel title on the item. The introductory phrase Title translated: that customarily precedes the translation of the title is not carried in the MARC record. It may be generated based on the field tag.

Indicators

First - Title added entry

0 - No added entry

1 - Added entry

Second - Nonfiling characters

0-9 - Number of nonfiling characters

Subfield Codes

$a - Title (NR)

$b - Remainder of title (NR)

$c - Statement of responsibility, etc. (NR)

$d - Designation of section (BK AM MP MU VM SE) [OBSOLETE]

$e - Name of part/section (BK AM MP MU VM SE) [OBSOLETE]

$h - Medium (NR)

$n - Number of part/section of a work (R)

$p - Name of part/section of a work (R)

$y - Language code of translated title (NR)

$6 - Linkage (NR)

$8 - Field link and sequence number (R)

Examples:

242 10$aWorld of art. $yeng

242 04$aThe Arab East. $yeng

242 00$aLand surveying and agriculture equipment. $yeng

242 00$aAnnals of chemistry $nSeries C, $pOrganic chemistry and biochemistry. $yeng

243 - COLLECTIVE UNIFORM TITLE (NR)

A generic title that is constructed by the cataloger to collect works by prolific author. The brackets that customarily enclose a collective uniform title are not carried in the MARC record. They may be generated based on the field tag.

Indicators

First - Uniform title printed or displayed

0 - Not printed or displayed

1 - Printed or displayed

2 - Not printed on card, title added entry (MU) [OBSOLETE]

3 - Printed on card, title added entry (MU) [OBSOLETE]

Second - Nonfiling characters

0-9 - Number of nonfiling characters

Subfield Codes

$a - Uniform title (NR)

$d - Date of treaty signing (R)

$f - Date of a work (NR)

$g - Miscellaneous information (NR)

$h - Medium (NR)

$k - Form subheading (R)

$l - Language of a work (NR)

$m - Medium of performance for music (NR)

$n - Number of part/section of a work (R)

$o - Arranged statement for music (NR)

$p - Name of part/section of a work (R)

$r - Key for music (NR)

$s - Version (NR)

$6 - Linkage (NR)

$8 - Field link and sequence number (R)

Examples:

243 10$aWorks. $f1983

243 10$aSpeeches

243 00$aLaws, etc.

243 10$aOrchestra music. $kSelections

245 - TITLE STATEMENT (NR)

The title and statement of responsibility area of the bibliographic description of a work.

Indicators

First - Title added entry

0 - No added entry

1 - Added entry

Second - Nonfiling characters

0-9 - Number of nonfiling characters

Subfield Codes

$a - Title (NR)

$b - Remainder of title (NR)

$c - Statement of responsibility, etc. (NR)

$d - Designation of section (SE) [OBSOLETE]

$e - Name of part/section (SE) [OBSOLETE]

$f - Inclusive dates (NR)

$g - Bulk dates (NR)

$h - Medium (NR)

$k - Form (R)

$n - Number of part/section of a work (R)

$p - Name of part/section of a work (R)

$s - Version (NR)

$6 - Linkage (NR)

$8 - Field link and sequence number (R)

Examples:

245 00$a[Man smoking at window].

245 03$aLe Bureau $h[filmstrip] = $bLa Oficina = Das Buro.

245 10$aStatistics : $bfacts or fiction.

245 10$a—as others see us.

245 04$aThe Year book of medicine.

245 15$a"The eve that never sleeps ... "

245 18$aThe ... annual report to the Governor.

245 00$aProceedings / $c ...

245 10$aUnder the hill, or, The story of Venus and Tannhauser.

245 00$aHamlet ; $bRomeo and Juliette ; Othello ...

245 00$aOklahoma $h[sound recording] ; $bCarousel ; South Pacific ...

245 00$aLord Macaulay's essays ; $band, Lays of ancient Rome.

245 00$aMap of Nelson, Richmond, Motueka : $bscale 1:20000.

245 00$aJournal of the Faculty of Science, the University of Tokyo. $nSection IV, $pZoology = $bTokyo Daigaku Rigakubu kiyo. Dai 4-rui, Dobutseugaku.

245 00$aF.N.I.B. : $borgane de la Federation nationale des infirmieres belges = N.V.B.V. : tijdschrift van het Nationaal Verbond van Belgische Verpleegsters.

245 04$aThe plays of Oscar Wilde / $cAlan Bird.

245 10$aHow to play chess / $cKevin Wicker ; with a foreword by David Pritchard ; illustrated by Karel Feuerstein.

245 10$aProject directory / $cTDC = Repertoire des projets / CDT.

245 14$aThe analysis of the law / $cSir Matthew Hale. The students companion / Giles Jacob.

245 00$aManagement report. $nPart I /$cU.S. Navy's Military Sealift Command.

245 00$aShort-Harrison-Symmes family papers, $f1760-1878.

245 00$kRecords, $f1939-1973 $g1965-1972.

245 00$a[Geode] $h[realia].

245 03$aLa mer $h[sound recording] ; $bKhamma ; Rhapsody for clarinet and orchestra / $cClaude Debussy.

245 10$aFour years at Yale : $kdiaries, $f1903 Sept. 16-1907 Oct. 5.

245 00$aPL 17 Hearing Files $kCase Files $f1974 $pDistrict 6 $hmicrofilm (jacketted in fiche).

245 14$aThe charity ball : $ba comedy in four acts : $ktypescript, $f1889 / $cby David Belasco and Henry C. DeMille.

245 00$aZentralblatt fur Bakteriologie, Parasitenkunde, Infektionkrankheiten und giene. $n1. Abt. Originale. $nReihe B, $pHygiene. Krankenhaushygiene. Betriebshygiene, praventive Medizin.

245 10$aDirector's report of the Association of Insurance Adjusters. $sMember release.

246 - VARYING FORM OF TITLE (R)

A form of the title appearing on different parts of an item or a portion of the title proper, or an alternative form of the title when the form differs significantly from the title contained in field 245.

Indicators

First - Note/added entry controller

0 - Note, no added entry

1 - Note, added entry

2 - No note, no title added entry

3 - No note, added entry

Second - Type of title

- No type specified

0 - Portion of title

1 - Parallel title

2 - Distinctive title

3 - Other title

4 - Cover title

5 - Added title page title

6 - Caption title

7 - Running title

8 - Spine title

Subfield Codes

$a - Title proper/short title (NR)

$b - Remainder of title (NR)

$d - Designation of section (SE) [OBSOLETE]

$e - Name of part/section (SE) [OBSOLETE]

$f - Date or sequential designation (NR)

$g - Miscellaneous information (NR)

$h - Medium (NR)

$i - Display text (NR)

$n - Number of part/section of a work (R)

$p - Name of part/section of a work (R)

$5 - Institution to which field applies (NR)

$6 - Linkage (NR)

$8 - Field link and sequence number (R)

Examples:

246 0#$iAdded title page title on some issues: $aAnnual report

246 13$aCalifornia State Assembly file analysis

246 3#$aFour corners power review

246 1#$iPanel title: $aWelcome to big Wyoming

246 1#$iAlso known as: $aCOMPENDEX

246 1#$iAugmented title: $aDevelopment of electro-optical laser velocimeter system for flame studies

246 30$aLRMP

246 31$aNihon

246 12$aCreating jobs $f1980

246 15$aMurshid al-Sudan $f1982- 1983

246 3#$aBEEC bulletin

246 17$aB.E.E.C. bulletin

246 04$a[variant title] $g(varies slightly)

246 1#$iAt head of title: $aScience and public affairs $fJan. 1970-Apr. 1974

246 1#$iTitle on container: $aNew Brunswick royal gazette

246 1#$iAlternate issues published with title: $aChicago daily telegraph

246 3#$a[title of reissue]; $5DLC

247 - FORMER TITLE (R)

A former title or title variation when one bibliographic record represents all issues of a serial that has changed title.

Indicators

First - Title added entry

0 - No added entry

1 - Added entry

Second - Note controller

0 - Display note

1 - Do not display note

Subfield Codes

$a - Title (NR)

$b - Remainder of title (NR)

$d - Designation of section (SE) [OBSOLETE]

$e - Name of part/section (SE) [OBSOLETE]

$f - Date or sequential designation (NR)

$g - Miscellaneous information (NR)

$h - Medium (NR)

$n - Number of part/section of a work (R)

$p - Name of part/section of a work (R)

$x - International Standard Serial Number (NR)

$6 - Linkage (NR)

$8 - Field link and sequence number (R)

Examples:

247 10$aEverywoman's magazine $fv 1-24. Jan 1948-57.

247 10$aJournalism bulletin $fMar. 1924-Nov 1927

247 01$a[former title] $g(varies slightly)

—Edition, Imprint, etc. Fields 250-270—

Fields 250-270 contain edition, imprint, address, and other publication source information, and data related to specific forms of material that apply to the item described in the bibliographic record.

250 - Edition Statement (NR)

254 - Musical Representation Statement (NR)

255 - Cartographic Mathematical Data (R)

256 - Computer File Characteristics (NR)

257 Country of Producing Entity for Archival Films (NR)

260 Publication, Distribution, Etc. (Imprint) (NR)

263 - Projected Publication Date (NR)

270 - Address (R)

250 - EDITION STATEMENT (NR)

Indicators

First - Undefined

- Undefined

Second - Undefined

- Undefined

Subfield Codes

$a - Edition statement (NR)

$b - Remainder of edition statement(NR)

$6 - Linkage (NR)

$8 - Field link and sequence number (R)

Examples:

250 ##$a2nd ed.

250 ##$aSpecial education ed.

250 ##$aMedium-high voice ed.

250 ##$aRev. as of Jan. 1, 1958.

250 ##$a4th ed. / $brevised by J.G. Le Mesurier and E. McIntosh, Repr. with corrections.

250 ##$aRev. ed. / $bwith revisions, an introduction, and a chapter on writing by E.B. White, 2nd ed. / with the assistance of Eleanor Gould Packard.

250 ##$aCanadian ed. = $bEd. canadienne.

254 - MUSICAL PRESENTATION STATEMENT (NR)

A description of the format of an edition of a work of printed or manuscript music that may differ from the format of another edition of the same work.

Indicators

First - Undefined

- Undefined

Second - Undefined

- Undefined

Subfield Codes

$a - Musical presentation statement (NR)

$6 - Linkage (NR)

$8 - Field link and sequence number (R)

Examples:

254 ##$aFull score.

254 ##$aComposer's facsimile study score.

254 ##$aScore and set of parts.

254 ##$aPartition, reproduction du manuscrit de l'auteur.

255 - CARTOGRAPHIC MATHEMATICAL DATA (R)

Mathematical data that is associated with map material, including celestial charts. This data may also be coded in field 034 (Coded Mathematical Data).

Indicators

First - Undefined

- Undefined

Second - Undefined

- Undefined

Subfield Codes

$a - Statement of scale (NR)

$b - Statement of projection (NR)

$c - Statement of coordinates (NR)

$d - Statement of zone (NR)

$e - Statement of equinox (NR)

$f - Outer G-ring coordinate pairs (NR)

$g - Exclusion G-ring coordinate pairs (NR)

$6 - Linkage (NR)

$8 - Field link and sequence number (R)

Examples:

255 ##$aScale not given.

255 ##$aScale [ca. 1:90,000].

255 ##$aScale [1:6,336,000]. 1" = 100 miles. Vertical scale [1:192,000]. 1/16" = approx. 1000'.

255 ##$aScale not given ; $bConic proj.

255 ##$aScale 1:22,000,000 ; $bConic proj. $c(E 72o—E 148o/N 13o—N 18o).

255 ##$aScale 1:250,000 $c(E 32o30'—E 34o30'/N 35o30'—N 35o00').

255 ##$aScales vary $d(Zones +90o to +81o to 63o, -81o to 98o ; $eeq. 1950).

255 ##$aScale not given $d(RA 0 hr. to 24 hr./Decl. +90o to -90o ; $eeq. 1980).

256 - COMPUTER FILE CHARACTERISTICS (NR)

Characteristics of a computer file, such as the type of file, the number of records or statements.

Indicators

First - Undefined

- Undefined

Second - Undefined

- Undefined

Subfield Codes

$a - Computer file characteristics (NR)

$6 - Linkage (NR)

$8 - Field link and sequence n

Examples:

256 ##$aComputer data (2 files : 876,000, 775,000 records)

256 ##$aComputer programs (2 files : 4300, 1250 bytes).

256 ##$aData (1 file : 350 records).umber (R)

257 - COUNTRY OF PRODUCING ENTITY FOR ARCHIVAL FILMS (NR)

The name or abbreviation of the name of the country where the principal offices of the producing entity of a moving image work are located.

Indicators

First - Undefined

- Undefined

Second - Undefined

- Undefined

Subfield Codes

$a - Country of producing entity (NR)

$6 - Linkage (NR)

$8 - Field link and sequence number (R)

Examples.

257 ##$aU.S.

257 ##$a[S.l.].

57 ##$aItaly ; France.

260 - PUBLICATION, DISTRIBUTION, ETC. (IMPRINT) (R)

Information relating to the publication, printing, distribution, issue, release, or production of a work.

Indicators

First - Sequence of publishing statements

- Not applicable/No information provided/Earliest available publisher

2 - Intervening publisher

3 - Current/latest publisher

Second - Undefined

- Undefined

First - Presence of publisher in imprint (BK MP MU SE) [OBSOLETE]

0 - Publisher, distributor, etc. is present

1 - Publisher, distributor, etc. is not present

Second - Added entry/publisher relationship (SE) [OBSOLETE]

0 - Publisher, distributor, etc. not same as issuing body in added entry

1 - Publisher, distributor, etc. same as issuing body in added entry

Subfield Codes

$a - Place of publication, distribution, etc. (R)

$b - Name of publisher, distributor, etc. (R)

$c - Date of publication, distribution, etc. (R)

$d - Plates of publisher's number for music (Pre-AACR 2) (R) [LOCAL]

$e - Place of manufacture (NR)

$f - Manufacturer (NR)

$g - Date of manufacture (NR)

$3 - Materials specified (NR)

$6 - Linkage (NR)

$8 - Field link and sequence number (R)

Examples:

260 ##$aNew York, N.Y. : $bElsevier, $c1984.

260 ##$a[S.l.] : $bInsight Press, $c1981.

260 ##$aWashington, D.C. (1649 K St., N.W., Washington 20006) : $bWider Opportunities for Women, $c1979 printing, c1975.

260 ##$aBelfast [i.e. Dublin] : $b[s.n.], $c1946 [reprinted 1965]

260 ##$a[S.l. : $bs.n., $c15—?]

260 ##$aNew York ; $aBerlin : $bSpringer Verlag, $c1977.

260 ##$aReston, Va.? : $bU.S. Geological Survey ; $aWashington, D.C. : $bFor sale by the Supt. of Docs., U.S. G.P.O., $c1986-

260 ##$aParis : $bGauthier-Villars ; $aChicago : $bUniversity of Chicago Press, $c1955.

260 ##$aLondon : $bMacmillan, $c1971 $g(1973 printing)

260 ##$c1908-1924.

260 ##$a[S.l. : $bs.n.], $c1970 $e(London : $fHigh Fidelity Sound Studios)

260 ##$aParis : $bImpr. Vincent, $c1798 $a[i.e. Bruxelles : $bMoens, $c1883]

260 ##$aChicago, etc. : $bTime Inc.,

260 ##$aLeipzig, $bBreitkopf & Hartel $c[1888 or 9] $dPl. no. 18315

260 ##$aLondon : $bArts Council of Great Britain, $c1976 $e(Twickenham : $fCTD Printers, $g1974)

260 ##$aHarmondsworth : $bPenguin, $c1949 $g(1963 printing)

261 - IMPRINT STATEMENT FOR FILMS (Pre-AACR 1 Revised) (NR) [LOCAL]

Indicators

First - Undefined

- Undefined

Second - Undefined

- Undefined

Subfield Codes

$a - Producing company (R)

$b - Releasing company (primary distributor) (R)

$d - Date of production, release, etc. (R)

$e - Contractual producer (R)

$f - Place of production, release, etc. (R)

$6 - Linkage (NR)

$8 - Field link and sequence number (R)

262 - IMPRINT STATEMENT FOR SOUND RECORDINGS (Pre-AACR 2) (NR) [LOCAL]

Indicators

First - Undefined

- Undefined

Second - Undefined

- Undefined

Subfield Codes

$a - Place of production, release, etc. (NR)

$b - Publisher or trade name (NR)

$c - Date of production, release, etc. (NR)

$k - Serial identification (NR)

$l - Matrix and/or take number (NR)

$6 - Linkage (NR)

$8 - Field link and sequence number (R)

263 - PROJECTED PUBLICATION DATE (NR)

The projected date of publication used in bibliographic records for works that have not yet been published.

Indicators

First - Undefined

- Undefined

Second - Undefined

- Undefined

Subfield Code

$a - Projected publication date (NR)

$6 - Linkage (NR)

$8 - Field link and sequence number (R)

Examples:

263 ##$a199412

263 ##$a1998—

263 ##$a200102

265 - SOURCE FOR ACQUISITION/SUBSCRIPTION ADDRESS (NR) [OBSOLETE]

Indicators

First - Undefined

- Undefined

Second - Undefined

- Undefined

Subfield Codes

$a - Source for acquisition/subscription address (R)

$6 - Linkage (NR)

270 - ADDRESS (R)

Contains an address (as well as electronic access data such as telephone, fax, TTY, etc. numbers) associated with a bibliographic item. Multiple addresses, such as mailing addresses and addresses corresponding to the physical location of an item or facilities, are recorded in separate occurrences of field 270.

The styles used for identifying the portions of telephone, fax, and related numbers (i.e., country code, city/area code, exchange/ line number, and any extension) varies greatly. In field 270, periods, spaces, and parentheses used to divide the portions of a number are replaced with hyphens. The portions of numbers recorded in subfields $j, $k, $l, and $n are recorded in the order [country code]- [area/city code]- [exchange/line number] The exchange/line number portion often includes internal separators which are replaced by hyphens. If an extension is also given, it is appended to the telephone number preceded by a space and " x".

Indicators

First - Level

- No level specified

1 - Primary

2 - Secondary

Second - Type of address

- No type specified

0 - Mailing

7 - Type specified in subfield $i

Subfield Codes

$a - Address (R)

$b - City (NR)

$c - State or province (NR)

$d - Country (NR)

$e - Postal code (NR)

$f - Terms preceding attention name (NR)

$g - Attention name (NR)

$h - Attention position (NR)

$i - Type of address (NR)

$j - Specialized telephone number (R)

$k - Telephone number (R)

$l - Fax number (R)

$m - Electronic mail address (R)

$n - TDD or TTY number (R)

$p - Contact person (R)

$q - Title of contact person (R)

$r - Hours (R)

$z - Public note (R)

$4 - Relator code (R)

$6 - Linkage (NR)

$8 - Field link and sequence number (R)

—Physical Description, etc. Fields (3XX)—

300 - PHYSICAL DESCRIPTION (R)

A physical description of the described item, including its extent, dimensions, and such other physical details as a description of any accompanying materials and unit type and size.

Indicators

First - Undefined

- Undefined

Second - Undefined

- Undefined

Subfield Codes

$a - Extent (R)

$b - Other physical details (NR)

$c - Dimensions (R)

$e - Accompanying material (NR)

$f - Type of unit (R)

$g - Size of unit (R)

$3 - Materials specified (NR)

$6 - Linkage (NR)

$8 - Field link and sequence number (R)

Examples

300 ##$a149 p. ; $c23 cm.

300 ##$a1 score (16 p.) ; $c29 cm.

300 ##$a11 v. : $bill. ; $c24 cm.

300 ##$a1 sound disc (20 min.) : $banalog, 33 1/3 rpm, stereo. ; $c12 in.

300 ##$a160 slides : $bcol. ; $c2 x 2 in.

300 ##$a8 reels of 8 (7557 ft.) : $bsd., col. ; $c35 mm. $3dupe neg nitrate (copy 2).

300 ##$a1 videocassette of 1 (Beta) (30 min.) : $bsd., col. ; $c1/2 in. $3(2 copies)

300 ##$a1 computer disk : $bsd., col. ; $c3 1/2 in.

300 ##$a42 $fcu. ft.

300 ##$3poems $a1 $fpage : $c108 cm. x 34.5 cm.

300 ##$adiary $a1 $fvolume $a(463 $fpages) : $c17 cm. x 34.5 cm.

300 ##$a17 $fboxes $a(7 $flinear ft.)

300 ##$a1 reel (312 ft.) : $bsi., b&w ; $c16 mm. $3ref print.

300 ##$a65 prints : $brelief process ; $c29 x 22 cm.

300 ##$a1 score (30 p.) ; $c20 cm. + $a16 parts ; $c32 cm.

300 ##$a1 globe : $bcol., wood, mounted on brass stand : $c12 cm. in diam.

300 ##$a1 sound disc (56 min.) : $bdigital, stereo : $c4 3/4 in.

300 ##$a271 p. : $bill. ; $c21 cm. + $eatlas (37 p., 19 leaves of plates : 19 col. maps ; 37 cm.)

300 ##$a40 p. : $bill. (woodcuts) ; $c20 cm. (8vo)

300 ##$a1 computer disk ; $c3 1/2 in. + $ereference manual.

300 ##$a24 $ffile drawers.

301 - PHYSICAL DESCRIPTION FOR FILMS (PRE-AACR 2) (VM) [OBSOLETE]

Indicators

First - Undefined

- Undefined

Second - Undefined

- Undefined

Subfield Codes

$a - Extent of item (NR)

$b - Sound characteristics (NR)

$c - Color characteristics (NR)

$d - Dimensions (NR)

$e - Accompanying material (NR)

$f - Speed (NR)

302 - PAGE OR ITEM COUNT (BK AM) [OBSOLETE]

Indicators

First - Undefined

- Undefined

Second - Undefined

- Undefined

Subfield Codes

$a - Page count (NR)

303 - UNIT COUNT (AM) [OBSOLETE]

Indicators

First - Undefined

- Undefined

Second - Undefined

- Undefined

Subfield Codes

$a - Unit count (NR)

304 - LINEAR FOOTAGE (AM) [OBSOLETE]

Indicators

First - Undefined

- Undefined

Second - Undefined

- Undefined

Subfield Codes

$a - Linear footage (NR)

305 - PHYSICAL DESCRIPTION FOR SOUND RECORDINGS (Pre-AACR 2) (MU) [OBSOLETE]

Indicators

First - Undefined

- Undefined

Second - Undefined

- Undefined

Subfield Codes

$a - Extent (NR)

$b - Other physical details (NR)

$c - Dimensions (NR)

$d - Microgroove or standard (NR)

$e - Stereophonic, monaural (NR)

$f - Number of tracks (NR)

$m - Serial identification (NR)

$n - Matrix and/or take number (NR)

$6 - Linkage (NR)

306 - PLAYING TIME (NR)

Six numeric characters, in the pattern hhmmss, that represent the playing time for a sound recording or the stated duration of performance of printed or manuscript music. If the playing time is less than 1 hour, the hour (hh) is recorded as two zeroes; if less than a minute, the minute (mm) is also recorded as two zeroes.

Indicators

First - Undefined

- Undefined

Second - Undefined

- Undefined

Subfield Code

$a - Playing time (R)

$6 - Linkage (NR)

$8 - Field link and sequence number (R)

Examples

306 ##$a002016

306 ##$a003100 $a001839

307 - HOURS, ETC. (R)

Contains chronological information identifying the days and/or times an item is available or accessible. It is used primarily in records for electronic resources.

Indicators

First - Display constant controller

- Hours

8 - No display constant generated

Second - Undefined

- Undefined

Subfield Codes

$a - Hours (NR)

$b - Additional information (NR)

$6 - Linkage (NR)

$8 - Field link and sequence number (R)

Examples

307 ##$aM-F, 9:30am-3:30pm, USA EST.

307 8#$aDate: Dec. 1, 1993, 2:00 p.m.

307 ##$aM-F, 6:30am-9:00pm (EST); $bwith brief interruptions for periodic update/backup of data.

307 ##$aDaily, 7am-7pm; $btext files only.

308

308 - PHYSICAL DESCRIPTION FOR FILMS (ARCHIVAL) (VM) [OBSOLETE]

Indicators

First - Undefined

- Undefined

Second - Undefined

- Undefined

Subfield Codes

$a - Number of reels (NR)

$b - Footage (NR)

$c - Sound characteristics (NR)

$d - Color characteristics (NR)

$e - Width (NR)

$f - Presentation format (NR)

$6 - Linkage (NR)

310 - CURRENT PUBLICATION FREQUENCY (NR)

The current stated frequency of an item. Dates are included when the beginning date of the current frequency is not the same as the beginning date of publication. These data are related to coded data in field 008/18 (Frequency) and 008/19 (Regularity).

Indicators

First - Undefined

- Undefined

Second - Undefined

- Undefined

Subfield Codes

$a - Current publication frequency (NR)

$b - Date of current publication frequency (NR)

$6 - Linkage (NR)

$8 - Field link and sequence number (R)

Examples

310 ##$aMonthly

310 ##$aMonthly, including annual cumulation

310 ##$aBimonthly (monthly June-July)

310 ##$aAnnual, $b1983-

310 ##$aMonthly, $bJan. 1984

310 ##$a5 no. a year, $b1946-1948

315 - FREQUENCY (NR) (CF MP) [OBSOLETE]

Indicators

First - Undefined

- Undefined

Second - Undefined

- Undefined

Subfield Codes

$a - Frequency (R)

$b - Dates of frequency (R)

$6 - Linkage (NR)

321 - FORMER PUBLICATION FREQUENCY (R)

Indicators

First - Undefined

- Undefined

Second - Undefined

- Undefined

Subfield Codes

$a - Former publication frequency (NR)

$b - Dates of former publication frequency (NR)

$6 - Linkage (NR)

$8 - Field link and sequence number (R)

340 - PHYSICAL MEDIUM (R)

Indicators Physical description information for an item that requires technical equipment for its use or an item that has special conservation or storage needs.

First - Undefined

- Undefined

Second - Undefined

- Undefined

Subfield Codes

$a - Material base and configuration (R)

$b - Dimensions (R)

$c - Materials applied to surface (R)

$d - Information recording technique (R)

$e - Support (R)

$f - Production rate/ratio (R)

$h - Location within medium (R)

$i - Technical specifications of medium (R)

$3 - Materials specified (NR)

$6 - Linkage (NR)

$8 - Field link and sequence number (R)

Examples

340 ##$amarble.

340 ##$aparchment $b20 cm. folded to 10 x 12 cm.

340 ##$3self-portrait $arice paper $b7" x 9" $ccolored inks $enone $hbetween entry for April 7 and April 19, 1843.

340 ##$dhandwritten $dtyped.

340 ##$acanvas $b30 x 57 cm. $ccolored oil-base paints $ewood.

340 ##$3case files $aaperture cards $b9 x 19 cm. $dmicrofilm $f48x.

342 - GEOSPATIAL REFERENCE DATA (R)

IndicatorsContains a description of the frame of reference for the coordinates in a data set. To work with a data set a user must be able to identify how location accuracy has been affected through the application of a geospatial reference method, thus enabling the user to manipulate the data set to recover location accuracy. This field is used in conjunction with the Federal Geographic Data Committee's Content Standards for Digital Geospatial Metadata.

First - Geospatial reference dimension

0 - Horizontal coordinate system

1 - Vertical coordinate system

Second - Geospatial reference method

0 - Geographic

1 - Map projection

2 - Grid coordinate system

3 - Local planar

4 - Local

5 - Geodetic model

6 - Altitude

7 - Method specified in $2

8 - Depth

Subfield Codes

$a - Name (NR)

$b - Coordinate or distance units (NR)

$c - Latitude resolution (NR)

$d - Longitude resolution (NR)

$e - Standard parallel or oblique line latitude (R)

$f - Oblique line longitude (R)

$g - Longitude of central meridian or projection center (NR)

$h - Latitude of projection origin or projection center (NR)

$i - False easting (NR)

$j - False northing (NR)

$k - Scale factor (NR)

$l - Height of perspective point above surface (NR)

$m - Azimuthal angle (NR)

$n - Azimuth measure point longitude or straight vertical longitude from pole (NR)

$o - Landsat number and path number (NR)

$p - Zone identifier (NR)

$q - Ellipsoid name (NR)

$r - Semi-major axis (NR)

$s - Denominator of flattening ratio (NR)

$t - Vertical resolution (NR)

$u - Vertical encoding method (NR)

$v - Local planar, local, or other projection or grid description NR)

$w - Local planar or local georeference information (NR)

$2 - Reference method used (NR)

$6 - Linkage (NR)

$8 - Field link and sequence number (R)

Examples

342 01$aPolyconic $g0.9996 $h0 $i500,000 $j0

342 16$aNational geodetic vertical datum of 1929 $v1 $bmeters $wImplicit coordinates.

342 00$c0.0004 $d0.0004 $bDecimal degrees

342 05$sWorld geodetic system 72 $t6378135 $u298.26

342 18$aLowest astronomical tide

342 05$aWorld Geodetic System 1984 (WGS-84) $c0.0000001 $d0.0000001 $bDegrees, Minutes, and Decimal seconds $qWorld Geodetic System 1984 (WGS-84) $r6378137.0 $s298.257223563

342 02$aUniversal Transverse Mercator $p13 $k0.9996 $g-105.00 $h0.00 $i500,000 $j0.0

342 02$aState Plane Coordinate System 27, Lambert Conformal Conic $p0405 $g-69.0 $h0.0 $i500000.0 $j0.0

342 03$vMissouri East State Plane NAD27 $qClarke 1866 $r6378206.4 M $s294.97869821

342 18$aNGVD 1929 $t0.01 $bfeet $uExplicit depth coordinate included with horizontal coordinates

343 - PLANAR COORDINATE DATA (R)

Contains information about the coordinate system developed on a planar surface. The information is provided to allow the user of a geospatial data set to identify the quantities of distances, or distances and angles. These define the position of a point on a reference plane onto which the surface of the Earth has been projected. This field is used in conjunction with the Federal Geographic Data Committee's Content Standards for Digital Geospatial Metadata.

Indicators

First - Undefined

- Undefined

Second - Undefined

- Undefined

Subfield Codes

$a - Planar coordinate encoding method (NR)

$b - Planar distance units (NR)

$c - Abscissa resolution (NR)

$d - Ordinate resolution (NR)

$e - Distance resolution (NR)

$f - Bearing resolution (NR)

$g - Bearing units (NR)

$h - Bearing reference direction (NR)

$i - Bearing reference meridian (NR)

$6 - Linkage (NR)

$8 - Field link and sequence number (R)

Examples

343 ##$aDistance and bearing

343 ##$aCoordinate pair; $bmeters; $c22; $d22.

343 ##$aCoordinate pair $e30.0 $f0.0001 $gDegrees, minutes and decimal seconds $hNorth $bU.S. feet

343 ##$iMagnetic

344

350 - PRICE (NR) (BK AM CF MU VM SE) [OBSOLETE]

Indicators

First - Undefined

- Undefined

Second - Undefined

- Undefined

Subfield Codes

$a - Price (R)

$b - Form of issue (R)

$6 - Linkage (NR)

351 - ORGANIZATION AND ARRANGEMENT OF MATERIALS (R)

Contains information about the coordinate system developed

on a planar surface. The information is provided to allow the user of a geospatial data set to identify the quantities of distances, or distances and angles. These define the position of a point on a reference plane onto which the surface of the Earth has been projected. This field is used in conjunction with the Federal Geographic Data Committee's Content Standards for Digital Geospatial Metadata.

Indicators

First - Undefined

- Undefined

Second - Undefined

- Undefined

Subfield Codes

$a - Organization (R)

$b - Arrangement (R)

$c - Hierarchical level (NR)

$3 - Materials specified (NR)

$6 - Linkage (NR)

$8 - Field link and sequence number (R)

Examples

343 ##$aDistance and bearing

343 ##$aCoordinate pair; $bmeters; $c22; $d22.

343 ##$aCoordinate pair $e30.0 $f0.0001 $gDegrees, minutes and decimal seconds $hNorth $bU.S. feet

343 ##$iMagnetic

352 - DIGITAL GRAPHIC REPRESENTATION (R)

Contains a description of the method of referencing and the mechanism used to represent graphic information in a data set. This information consists of the type of storage technique used and the number of items in the data set.

Indicators

First - Undefined

- Undefined

Second - Undefined

- Undefined

Subfield Codes

$a - Direct reference method (NR)

$b - Object type (R)

$c - Object count (R)

$d - Row count (NR)

$e - Column count (NR)

$f - Vertical count (NR)

$g - VPF topology level (NR)

$i - Indirect reference description (NR)

$6 - Linkage (NR)

$8 - Field link and sequence number (R)

Examples

352 ##$aVector

352 ##$aPoint $bEntity point

352 ##$aRaster $bpixel

352 ##$aVector $bGT-polygon composed of chains. $c70

352 ##$avector $i100 year floodplain boundary. 500 year floodplain boundary

355 - SECURITY CLASSIFICATION CONTROL (R)

Contains specifics pertaining to the security classification associated with the document, title, abstract, contents note, and/or the author. In addition, it can contain handling instructions and external dissemination information pertaining to the dissemination of the document, title, abstract, contents note, and author. The field may also contain downgrading or declassification data, the name of the classification system, and a country of origin code. The source of the code is the MARC Code List for Countries maintained by the Library of Congress.

Indicators

First - Controlled element

0 - Document

1 - Title

2 - Abstract

3 - Contents note

4 - Author

5 - Record

8 - Other element

Second - Undefined

- Undefined

Subfield Codes

$a - Security classification (NR)

$b - Handling instructions (R)

$c - External dissemination information (R)

$d - Downgrading or declassification event (NR)

$e - Classification system (NR)

$f - Country of origin code (NR)

$g - Downgrading date (NR)

$h - Declassification date (NR)

$j - Authorization (R)

$6 - Linkage (NR)

$8 - Field link and sequence number (R)

Examples

355 0#$aUnclassified $bFOUO

355 2#$aConfidential $bNOFORN

355 3#$aSecret

355 1#$aSecret $bNOFORN $bNOCONTRACT

355 0#$aSecret $bFRD $cAS $d010101

355 0#$aConfidential $bNOCONTRACT $cUK $d990101

355 0#$aSecret $bNOFORN $bWNINTEL $bNOCONTRACT $dOADR

355 0#$aTop Secret $cUS $cCA $fxxk

355 0#$aSecret $bNOFORN $h20230301

355 0#$aSecret $bNOFORN $h20230301 $j[agency identifier]

357 - ORIGINATOR DISSEMINATION CONTROL (NR)

Contains specifics pertaining to originator (i.e., author, producer) control of dissemination of the material in hand. Subfield $a contains a specific term denoting that the originator has control over the material.

Indicators

First - Undefined

- Undefined

Second - Undefined

- Undefined

Subfields

$a - Originator control term (NR)

$b - Originating agency (R)

$c - Authorized recipients of material (R)

$g - Other restrictions (R)

$6 - Linkage (NR)

$8 - Field link and sequence number (R)

Examples

357 ##$aPROPIN $bLockport Aviation $cNorthfield Avionics Project 11234 $cAir Frames Inc., Project 11234 Support Team

357 ##$aORCON $bITAC $cCIA $cDIA $cUKIA

357 ##$aORCON $bITAC $c313 th MIB $cDistribution List B-32-91 $gMust be returned to originator after 30 days

359 - RENTAL PRICE (VM) [OBSOLETE]

Indicators

First - Undefined

- Undefined

Second - Undefined

- Undefined

Subfield Code

$a - Rental price (NR)

362 - DATES OF PUBLICATION AND/OR SEQUENTIAL DESIGNATION (R)

Contains the beginning/ending date(s) of an item and/or the sequential designations used on each part. Dates to be used in this field are chronological designations that identify individual issues of the serial. The sequential designations are usually numeric but can be alphabetic as well. The information may be formatted or unformatted. If the date information has been obtained from a source other than the first and/or last issue of the item published. the information is given in an unformatted note and the source of the information is usually cited.

Indicators

First - Format of date

0 - Formatted style

1 - Unformatted note

Second - Undefined

- Undefined

Subfield Codes

$a - Dates of publication and/or sequential designation (NR)

$z - Source of information (NR)

$6 - Linkage (NR)

$8 - Field link and sequence number (R)

Examples

362 0#$aVol. 1, no. 1 (Apr. 1981)-

362 0#$a1968-

362 0#$aVol. 1, no. 1 (Apr. 1983)-v. 1, no. 3 (June 1983)

362 1#$aBegan with 1930 issue. $zCf. Letter from Ak. State Highway Dept., Aug. 6, 1975.

362 1#$aCeased with 2 (1964).

362 0#$aVol. 77, num. 1 (enero-abr. 1981)-

—Series Statement Fields (4XX)—

Fields 440 and 490 contain series statements. Field 440 also provides an added entry for the series. A series statement is recorded in field 490 when either it is given no added entry in the record (an untraced series) or is given an added entry in a form that differs from the series statement appearing on the item. One of fields 800-830 (Series added entries) is used in conjunction with field 490 when the series is to be traced differently.

The parentheses that customarily enclose a series statement and the tracing Series., preceded by a roman numeral, in some displays for field 440 are not carried in the MARC record. They may be generated based on the field tag.

440 - Series Statement—Added Entry—Title (R)

490 - Series Statement (R)

400 - SERIES STATEMENT/ADDED ENTRY—PERSONAL NAME (R) [US-LOCAL]

A series statement consisting of a series title alone.

Indicators

First - Type of personal name entry element

0 - Forename

1 - Surname

2 - Multiple surname [OBSOLETE]

3 - Family name

Second - Pronoun represents main entry

0 - Main entry not represented by pronoun

1 - Main entry represented by pronoun

Subfield Codes

$a - Personal name (NR)

$b - Numeration (NR)

$c - Titles and other words associated with a name (R)

$d - Dates associated with a name (NR)

$e - Relator term (R)

$f - Date of a work (NR)

$g - Miscellaneous information (NR)

$k - Form subheading (R)

$l - Language of a work (NR)

$n - Number of part/section of a work (R)

$p - Name of part/section of a work (R)

$q - Fuller form of name (NR) [OBSOLETE]

$t - Title of a work (NR)

$u - Affiliation (NR)

$v - Volume number/sequential designation (NR)

$x - International Standard Serial Number (NR)

$4 - Relator code (R)

$6 - Linkage (NR)

$8 - Field link and sequence number (R)

Examples

440 #0$aCollection africaine

440 #0$aOkonomische Studien ; $vBd. 22

440 #4$aThe Pediatric clinics of North America ; $vv. 2, no. 4

440 #0$aJournal of polymer science. $nPart C, $pPolymer symposia ; $vno. 39

440 #4$aThe Rare book tapes. $nSeries 1 ; $v5

440 #0$aJanua linguarum. $pSeries maior, $x0075-3114 ; $v100

440 #0$aRomanica Gothoburgensia, $x0080-3863 ; $v12. 16

410 - SERIES STATEMENT/ADDED ENTRY—CORPORATE NAME (R) [US-LOCAL]

Indicators

First - Type of corporate name entry element

0 - Inverted name

1 - Jurisdiction name

2 - Name in direct order

Second - Pronoun represents main entry

0 - Main entry not represented by pronoun

1 - Main entry represented by pronoun

Subfield Codes

$a - Corporate name or jurisdiction name as entry element (NR)

$b - Subordinate unit (R)

$c - Location of meeting (NR)

$d - Date of meeting or treaty signing (R)

$e - Relator term (R)

$f - Date of a work (NR)

$g - Miscellaneous information (NR)

$k - Form subheading (R)

$l - Language of a work (NR)

$n - Number of part/section/meeting (R)

$p - Name of part/section of a work (R)

$t - Title of a work (NR)

$u - Affiliation (NR)

$v - Volume number/sequential designation (NR)

$x - International Standard Serial Number (NR)

$4 - Relator code (R)

$6 - Linkage (NR)

$8 - Field link and sequence number (R)

411 - SERIES STATEMENT/ADDED ENTRY—MEETING NAME (R) [US-LOCAL]

Indicators

First - Type of meeting name entry element

0 - Inverted name

1 - Jurisdiction name

2 - Name in direct order

Second - Pronoun represents main entry

0 - Main entry not represented by pronoun

1 - Main entry represented by pronoun

Subfield Codes

$a - Meeting name or jurisdiction name as entry element (NR)

$b - Number [OBSOLETE]

$c - Location of meeting (NR)

$d - Date of meeting (NR)

$e - Subordinate unit (R)

$f - Date of a work (NR)

$g - Miscellaneous information (NR)

$k - Form subheading (R)

$l - Language of a work (NR)

$n - Number of part/section/meeting (R)

$p - Name of part/section of a work (R)

$q - Name of meeting following jurisdiction name entry element (NR)

$t - Title of a work (NR)

$u - Affiliation (NR)

$v - Volume number/sequential designation (NR)

$x - International Standard Serial Number (NR)

$4 - Relator code (R)

$6 - Linkage (NR)

$8 - Field link and sequence number (R)

440 - SERIES STATEMENT/ADDED ENTRY—TITLE (R)

Indicators

First - Undefined

- Undefined

Second - Nonfiling characters

0-9 - Number of nonfiling characters

Subfield Codes

$a - Title (NR)

$n - Number of part/section of a work (R)

$p - Name of part/section of a work (R)

$v - Volume number/sequential designation (NR)

$x - International Standard Serial Number (NR)

$6 - Linkage (NR)

$8 - Field link and sequence number (R)

490 - SERIES STATEMENT (R)

A series statement for which no series added entry is traced or for which the added entry is traced in one of the 800-830 fields in a form different from the form contained in field 490.

Indicators

First - Specifies whether series is traced

0 - Series not traced

1 - Series traced differently

Second - Undefined

- Undefined

Subfield Codes

$a - Series statement (R)

$l - Library of Congress call number (NR)

$v - Volume number/sequential designation (R)

$x - International Standard Serial Number (NR)

$6 - Linkage (NR)

$8 - Field link and sequence number (R)

Examples

490 0#$aPelican books

490 1#$aUniform crime reports

490 1#$aDepartment of the Army pamphlet : $v27-50

490 1#$a[1981-]: Reference works

490 1#$aDepartment of State publication ; $v7846. $aDepartment and Foreign Service series ; $v128

490 1#$aBulletin / U.S. Department of Labor, Bureau of Labor Statistics

490 1#$av. 9-[10]: MPCHT art and anthropological monographs ; $vno. 35

490 1#$aAnnual census of manufactures = $aRecensement des manufactures. $x0315-5587

490 1#$aBulletin / Engineering Experiment Station ; $vno. 50 $l(TA7.O74)

490 1#$aMap / Geological Survey of Alabama ; $v158, plate 3

490 1#$aWest Virginia University bulletin ; $vser. 74, no. 11-3. $aBulletin / Experiment Station, West Virginia University ; $v111

—Note Fields (Part 1: 50X-53X)—

Fields 500-535 contain notes relating to aspects of bibliographic items that are not specific to any particular type of material or control (e.g., archival control). Specialized note fields are used when access to the data is needed and/or the note is introduced by a distinctive word or phrase. Field 500 is used for all other note information.

500 - General Note (R)

501 - With Note (R)

502 - Dissertation Note (R)

504 - Bibliography, Etc. Note (R)

505 - Formatted Contents Note (NR)

506 - Restrictions on Access Note (R)

507 - Scale Note for Graphic Material (NR)

508 - Creation/Production Credits Note (NR)

510 - Citation/References Note (R)

511 - Participant or Performer Note (R)

513 - Type of Report and Period Covered Note (R)

514 - Data Quality Note (NR)

515 - Numbering Peculiarities Note (R)

516 - Type of Computer File or Data Note (R)

518 - Date/Time and Place of an Event Note (R)

520 - Summary, Etc. (R)

521 - Target Audience Note (R)

522 - Geographic Coverage Note (R)

524 - Preferred Citation of Described Materials Note (NR)

525 - Supplement Note (R)

526 - Study Program Information Note (R)

530 - Additional Physical Form Available Note (R)

533 - Reproduction Note (R)

534 - Original Version Note (R)

535 - Location of Originals/Duplicates Note (R)

500 - GENERAL NOTE (R)

General information for which a specialized 5XX note field has not been defined.

Indicators

First - Undefined

- Undefined

Second - Undefined

- Undefined

Subfield Codes

$a - General note (NR)

$l - Library of Congress call number (SE) [OBSOLETE]

$x - International Standard Serial Number (SE) [OBSOLETE]

$z - Source of note information (AM SE) [OBSOLETE]

$3 - Materials specified (NR)

$5 - Institution to which field applies (NR)

$6 - Linkage (NR)

$8 - Field link and sequence number (R)

Examples

500 ##$aRecast in bronze from artist's plaster original of 1903.

500 ##$aCaption title.

500 ##$aProgram notes by Phillip Ramey on album.

500 ##$aBased on a play which originally appeared in France as "Un peu plus tard, un peu plus tot."

500 ##$aImprint stamped on verso of t.p.

500 ##$aThree-dimensional film: Natural vision.

500 ##$aSlides in pocket.

500 ##$aIncludes index.

500 ##$a"The first American Jewish weekly of its kind"—The Jewish encyclopedia, v. 8.

500 ##$aSubsequent publishers: William M. Swain & Co., 1857-64; George W. Childs, 1864. Cf. Pa. Hist. Commission. A checklist of Pa. newspapers.

500 ##$aFrom the papers of the Chase family. $5DLC

501 - WITH NOTE (R)

A note that is used when more than one bibliographic work is contained in a physical item at the time of publishing, release, issue, or execution. The works usually have distinctive titles and lack a collective title.

Indicators

First - Undefined

- Undefined

Second - Undefined

- Undefined

Subfield Codes

$a - With note (NR)

$5 - Institution to which field applies (NR)

$6 - Linkage (NR)

$8 - Field link and sequence number (R)

Examples

501 ##$aWith: The reformed school / John Dury. London : Printed for R. Wasnothe, [1850]

501 ##$aWith: Peer Gynt (Suite) no. 1-2 / Edvard Grieg — Till Eulenspiegels lustige Streiche / Richard Strauss.

501 ##$aWith (on verso): Motor road map of south- east England.

501 ##$aMounted on a wooden stand to form a pair with: Bale's New celestial globe, 1845.

501 ##$aIn cassette with: Dissection of the brain stem: inferior and superior cerebellar peduncle — Dissection of the hemispheres: long association bundles — Dissection of the hemispheres: extreme and external capsules and related structures.

501 ##$aOn reel with: They're in the Army now.

502 - DISSERTATION NOTE (R)

Indicators

First - Undefined

- Undefined

Second - Undefined

- Undefined

Subfield Codes

$a - Dissertation note (NR)

$6 - Linkage (NR)

$8 - Field link and sequence number (R)

504 - BIBLIOGRAPHY, ETC. NOTE (R)

Information on the presence of one or more bibliographies, discographies, filmographies, and/or other bibliographic references in a described item or in accompanying material.

Indicators

First - Undefined

- Undefined

Second - Undefined

- Undefined

Subfield Codes

$a - Bibliography, etc. note (NR)

$b - Number of references (NR)

$6 - Linkage (NR)

$8 - Field link and sequence number (R)

Examples

504 ##$aBibliography: p. 238-239.

504 ##$aSources: p. 125-152.

504 ##$aIncludes bibliographical references.

504 ##$aDiscography: p. 105-111.

504 ##$aFilmography: v. 2, p. 344- 360.

504 ##$aIncludes bibliographies and index.

504 ##$aChronological list of the author's works: p. 469-475.

504 ##$a"Literature cited": p. 67-68. $b19

504 ##$a"Spisok izdannikh knig": p. 277.

505 - FORMATTED CONTENTS NOTE (R)

The titles of separate works or parts of an item or the table of contents of a finding aid for materials under archival control. The field may also contain statements of responsibility and volume numbers or other sequential designations.

Indicators

First - Display constant controller

0 - Contents

1 - Incomplete contents

2 - Partial contents

8 - No display constant generated

Second - Level of content designation

- Basic

0 - Enhanced

Subfield Codes

$a - Formatted contents note (NR)

$g - Miscellaneous information (R)

$r - Statement of responsibility (R)

$t - Title (R)

$u - Uniform Resource Identifier (R)

$6 - Linkage (NR)

$8 - Field link and sequence number (R)

Examples

505 0#$aHow these records were discovered — A short sketch of the Talmuds — Constantine's letter.

505 00$gvol. 1. $tThe history of Anne Arundel County.— $gvol. 2. $tThe history of ... [intermediate volumes omitted from example] — $gvol. 23. $tThe history of Prince Georges County —

505 80$gvol. 24.$tThe history of Washington County beginning in 1884 — $gvol. 25. $tState manifest and birth record (1764- 1977).

505 8#$aContents on sound disk: A suitable tone : Left hand colouring : Rhythm and accent : Tempo : Flexibility : Ornaments — Sonata in D major, op V, no. 1 / Corelli — Sonata in G minor / Purcell (with Robert Donington, gamba) — Forlane from Concert royal no. 3 / Couperin.

505 00$tQuark models / $rJ. Rosner — $tIntroduction to gauge theories of the strong, weak, and electromagnetic interactions / $rC. Quigg — $tDeep inelastic leptognnucleon scattering / $rD.H. Perkins — $tJet phenomena / $rM. Jacob — $tAn accelerator design study / $rR.R. Wilson — $tLectures in accelerator theory / $rM. Month.

505 00$tQuatrain II $g(16:35) — $tWater ways $g(1:57) — $tWaves $g(10:49).

505 20$tBaptisms, 1816-1872 — $tChurch members, 1816-1831 — $tHistory of the Second Presbyterian Church of West Durham / $rby L. H. Fellows.

505 0#$uhttp://lcweb.loc.gov/catdir/toc/99176484.html

506 - RESTRICTIONS ON ACCESS NOTE (R)

Information on the restrictions that govern access to or the limited distribution of the described materials.

Indicators

First - Undefined

- Undefined

Second - Undefined

- Undefined

Subfield Codes

$a - Terms governing access (NR)

$b - Jurisdiction (R)

$c - Physical access provisions (R)

$d - Authorized users (R)

$e - Authorization (R)

$u - Uniform Resource Identifier (R)

$3 - Materials specified (NR)

$5 - Institution to which field applies (NR)

$6 - Linkage (NR)

$8 - Field link and sequence number (R)

Examples

506 ##$aClassified.

506 ##$aFor official use only.

506 ##$3Office files of Under Secretary $aNo one may examine these records or obtain information from them or copies of them except by written permission $bSecretary of the Treasury or his duly authorized representative; $cKept in remote storage. access requires 24 hours advance notice.

506 ##$aRestricted access; $cWritten permission required. $bDonor.

506 ##$aRestricted: cannot be viewed until 2010. $dMembers of donor's family.

506 ##$aClassified under national security provisions. $bDepartment of Defense; $eTitle 50, chapter 401. U.S.C.

507 - SCALE NOTE FOR GRAPHIC MATERIAL (NR)

In the VM specifications, this field contains the scale of architectural drawings or three-dimensional artifacts. In the MP specifications, the scale of an item is contained in this field only in pre-AACR 2 cataloging records. Scale information is contained in field 255 (Mathematical Data Area) in AACR 2 formulated records.

Indicators

First - Undefined

- Undefined

Second - Undefined

- Undefined

Subfield Codes

$a - Representative fraction of scale note (NR)

$b - Remainder of scale note (NR)

$6 - Linkage (NR)

$8 - Field link and sequence number (R)

Examples

507 ##$aScale 1:10 of the original.

507 ##$aScale 1/16 in. to 1 ft.

507 ##$aScale 1:500,000; $b1 in. equals 8 miles.

507 ##$bPerspective map not drawn to scale.

508 - CREATION/PRODUCTION CREDITS NOTE (R)

The names of the persons (other than members of the cast) or organizations who participated in the artistic or technical production of the work. The introductory term Credits: that customarily precedes the names is not carried in the MARC record. It may be generated based on the field tag.

Indicators

First - Undefined

- Undefined

Second - Undefined

- Undefined

Subfield Codes

$a - Creation/production credits note (NR)

$6 - Linkage (NR)

$8 - Field link and sequence number (R)

510 - CITATION/REFERENCES NOTE (R)

Citations or references to published bibliographic descriptions, reviews, abstracts, or indexes of the content of the described item.

Indicators

First - Coverage/location in source

0 - Coverage unknown

1 - Coverage complete

2 - Coverage is selective

3 - Location in source not given

4 - Location in source given

Second - Undefined

- Undefined

Subfield Codes

$a - Name of source (NR)

$b - Coverage of source (NR)

$c - Location within source (NR)

$x - International Standard Serial Number (NR)

$3 - Materials specified (NR)

$6 - Linkage (NR)

$8 - Field link and sequence number (R)

Examples

510 1#$aEducation index, $b1966-, $x0013- 1385

510 2#$aMoving picture world, $b1975-

510 4#$aAlgae abstracts, $cv. 3, W73-11952

510 4#$aGoff, $cA- 970

510 2#$aChemical abstracts, $x0009-2258

510 4#$331911 Arctic field notebook $aDay, Harold. "Statistical Methods for Population Transport Estimation," Journal of Ecological Studies, $cvol. 7, 1974, p. 187

511 - PARTICIPANT OR PERFORMER NOTE (R)

Indicators

First - Display constant controller

- No information provided (VM MU) [OBSOLETE]

0 - No display constant generated

1 - Cast

2 - Presenter (VM MU) [OBSOLETE]

3 - Narrator (VM MU) [OBSOLETE]

Second - Undefined

- Undefined

Subfield Codes

$a - Participant or performer note (NR)

$6 - Linkage (NR)

$8 - Field link and sequence number (R)

512 - EARLIER OR LATER VOLUMES SEPARATELY CATALOGED NOTE (SE) (R) [OBSOLETE]

Indicators

First - Undefined

- Undefined

Second - Undefined

- Undefined

Subfield Codes

$a - Earlier or later volumes separately cataloged note (NR)

$6 - Linkage (NR)

513 - TYPE OF REPORT AND PERIOD COVERED NOTE (R)

Indicators

First - Undefined

- Undefined

Second - Undefined

- Undefined

Subfield Codes

$a - Type of report (NR)

$b - Period covered (NR)

$6 - Linkage (NR)

$8 - Field link and sequence number (R)

514 - DATA QUALITY NOTE (NR)

Indicators

First - Undefined

- Undefined

Second - Undefined

- Undefined

Subfield Codes

$a - Attribute accuracy report (NR)

$b - Attribute accuracy value (R)

$c - Attribute accuracy explanation (R)

$d - Logical consistency report (R)

$e - Completeness report (NR)

$f - Horizontal position accuracy report (NR)

$g - Horizontal position accuracy value (R)

$h - Horizontal position accuracy explanation (R)

$i - Vertical positional accuracy report (NR)

$j - Vertical positional accuracy value (R)

$k - Vertical positional accuracy explanation (R)

$m - Cloud cover (NR)

$u - Uniform Resource Identifier (R)

$z - Display note (R)

$6 - Linkage (NR)

$8 - Field link and sequence number (R)

515 - NUMBERING PECULIARITIES NOTE (R)

Indicators

First - Undefined

- Undefined

Second - Undefined

- Undefined

Subfield Codes

$a - Numbering peculiarities note (NR)

$z - Source of note information (NR) (SE) [OBSOLETE]

$6 - Linkage (NR)

$8 - Field link and sequence number (R)

516 - TYPE OF COMPUTER FILE OR DATA NOTE (R)

A general descriptor that characterizes a file (e.g., text, computer program, numeric). Specific information such as the form or genre of textual material (e.g., biography, indexes) also may be included. The general type of file is coded in field 008/26 (Type of computer file).

Indicators

First - Display constant controller

- Type of file

8 - No display constant generated

Second - Undefined

- Undefined

Subfield Codes

$a - Type of computer file or data note (NR)

$6 - Linkage (NR)

$8 - Field link and sequence number (R)

Examples

516 ##$aComputer programs

516 ##$aNumeric (Summary statistics)

516 ##$aNumeric (Spatial data: Point)

516 ##$aText (Law reports and digests)

517 - CATEGORIES OF FILMS NOTE (ARCHIVAL) (VM) (NR) [OBSOLETE]

Indicators

First - Fiction specification

0 - Nonfiction

1 - Fiction

First - Undefined

- Undefined

Second - Undefined

- Undefined

Subfield Codes

$a - Different formats (NR)

$b - Content descriptors (R)

$c - Additional animation techniques (R)

518 - DATE/TIME AND PLACE OF AN EVENT NOTE (R)

Textual information on the date/time and/or place of creation, capture, or broadcast, associated with an event or the finding of a naturally occurring object. This information in coded form is contained in field 033 (Date/Time and Place of an Event).

Indicators

Indicators

First - Undefined

- Undefined

Second - Undefined

- Undefined

Subfield Codes

$a - Date/time and place of an event note (NR)

$3 - Materials specified (NR)

$6 - Linkage (NR)

$8 - Field link and sequence number (R)

Examples

518 ##$aRecorded in Vienna in 1961, previously released as WST 17035.

518 ##$aFound on March 5, 1975, in Richmond, Tex.

518 ##$aFilmed on location in Rome and Venice from January through June 1976.

518 ##$aRecorded Aug. 29-31, 1977, Smetana Hall, Prague (the 1st work) and Nov. 21-23, 1966, "Stadion" Studio, Brno (the 2nd).

518 ##$aBroadcast October 17, 1954 at 7:30 p.m. (PST).

518 ##$3Horse $aCast in 1925.

520 - SUMMARY, ETC. (R)

Contains unformatted information that describes the scope and general contents of the materials. This could be a summary, abstract, annotation, review, or only a phrase describing the material.

The level of detail appropriate in a summary may vary depending on the audience for a particular product. When a distinction between levels of detail is required, a brief summary is given in subfield $a and a fuller annotation is given in subfield $b.

The text is sometimes displayed and/or printed with an introductory term that is generated as a display constant based on the first indicator value.

Indicators

Indicators

First - Display constant controller

- Summary

0 - Subject

1 - Review

2 - Scope and content

3 - Abstract

8 - No display constant generated

Second - Undefined

- Undefined

Subfield Codes

$a - Summary, etc. note (NR)

$b - Expansion of summary note (NR)

$u - Uniform Resource Identifier (R)

$z - Source of note information (NR) [OBSOLETE]

$3 - Materials specified (NR)

$6 - Linkage (NR)

$8 - Field link and sequence number (R)

Examples

520 ##$aAn illustrated collection of nursery rhymes set to music.

520 0#$aTwo head-and-shoulder portraits in separate ornamental oval frames, one frame held by eagle.

520 ##$aDescribes associations made between different animal species for temporary gain or convenience as well as more permanent alliances formed for mutual survival.

520 ##$aMiscellaneous cartographic records with an emphasis on biogeography of the United States and Alaska, 1872- 1941. $bIncludes published and photoprocessed maps of Alaska and coastal waters, 1888-90, many of which were compiled from surveys made on the "Albatross";- maps, 1908-19, annotated by the Alaskan Fisheries Division ...

520 ##$aPublic release motion pictures, 1915- 37. $bIncludes films on control of rats, prairie dogs and porcupines; fish culture in the United States and pearl culture in Japan; inspection trip to Alaska by Service officials; life in a Boy Scout camp and Air Service bombing techniques in 1921.

520 1#$a"Combines the most frequently asked questions regarding AIDS with the most prominent US physician, former Surgeon General C. Everett Koop, resulting in an informative 38-minute production"—Cf. Video rating guide for libraries, winter 1990.

520 ##$aPapers "originally commissioned as course material for a series of continuing legal education seminars"— Pref., v. 1.

520 2#$aFonds consists of minutes of meetings. research files relating to the delivery of health case services in

Nova Scotia, recorded...

520 3#$uhttp://www.ojp.usdoj.gov/bjs/abstract/cchrie98.htm

521 - TARGET AUDIENCE NOTE (R)

Information that identifies the specific audience or intellectual level for which the content of the described item is considered appropriate.

Indicators

First - Display constant controller

- Audience

0 - Reading grade level

1 - Interest age level

2 - Interest grade level

3 - Special audience characteristics

4 - Motivation interest level

8 - No display constant generated

Second - Undefined

- Undefined

Subfield Codes

$a - Target audience note (R)

$b - Source (NR)

$3 - Materials specified (NR)

$6 - Linkage (NR)

$8 - Field link and sequence number (R)

Examples

521 0#$a3.1.

521 1#$a008-012.

521 2#$a7 & up.

521 3#$aVision impaired $afine motor skills impaired $aaudio learner $bLENOCA.

521 4#$aHighly motivated $ahigh interst $bLENOCA.

521 ##$aProgram designed for geographers, planners, geologists, meteorologists and others who have a professional interest in analyzing spatial data.

521 8#$a"Roman Catholics."

521 8#$aMPAA rating: R.

521 0#$a5.

521 3#$3Puzzles $aTactile learner.

522 - GEOGRAPHIC COVERAGE NOTE (R)

Information on the geographic coverage of the described material (usually survey material). This information in coded form may be contained in field 052 (Geographic Classification).

Indicators

First - Display constant controller

- Geographic coverage

8 - No display constant generated

Second - Undefined

- Undefined

Subfield Codes

$a - Geographic coverage note (NR)

$6 - Linkage (NR)

$8 - Field link and sequence number (R)

Examples

522 8#$aCounty-level data from four Northwestern states (Idaho, Montana, Oregon, Washington).

522 ##$aCanada.

523 - TIME PERIOD OF CONTENT NOTE (NR) (CF) [OBSOLETE]

Indicators

First - Undefined

- Undefined

Second - Undefined

- Undefined

Subfield Codes

$a - Time period of content note (NR)

$b - Dates of data collection note (NR)

$6 - Linkage (NR)

524 - PREFERRED CITATION OF DESCRIBED MATERIALS NOTE (R)

Information on the geographic coverage of the described material (usually survey material). This information in coded form may be contained in field 052 (Geographic Classification).

Indicators

First - Display constant controller

- Cite as

8 - No display constant generated

Second - Undefined

- Undefined

Subfield Codes

$a - Preferred citation of described materials note (NR)

$2 - Source of schema used (NR)

$3 - Materials specified (NR)

$6 - Linkage (NR)

$8 - Field link and sequence number (R)

525 - SUPPLEMENT NOTE (R)

Information on the existence of supplements or special issues (usually unnamed) that are neither cataloged as separate records nor recorded in field 770 (Supplement/Special Issue Entry).

Indicators

First - Undefined

- Undefined

Second - Undefined

- Undefined

Subfield Codes

$a - Supplement note (NR)

$z - Source of note information (NR) (SE) [OBSOLETE]

$6 - Linkage (NR)

$8 - Field link and sequence number (R)

Examples

525 ##$aSupplements accompany some issues.

525 ##$aSeparately paged supplement accompanies v. 5.

525 ##$aVols. for 1961- - kept up to date by midyear supplements. Cf. New serial titles.

526 - STUDY PROGRAM INFORMATION NOTE (R)

Indicators

First - Display constant controller

0 - Reading program

8 - No display constant generated

Second - Undefined

- Undefined

Subfield Codes

$a - Program name (NR)

$b - Interest level (NR)

$c - Reading level (NR)

$d - Title point value (NR)

$i - Display text (NR)

$x - Nonpublic note (R)

$z - Public note (R)

$5 - Institution to which field applies (NR)

$6 - Linkage (NR)

$8 - Field link and sequence number (R)

527 - CENSORSHIP NOTE (VM) (R) [OBSOLETE]

Indicators

First - Undefined

- Undefined

Second - Undefined

- Undefined

Subfield Codes

$a - Censorship note (NR)

$6 - Linkage (NR)

530 - ADDITIONAL PHYSICAL FORM AVAILABLE NOTE (R)

Indicators

First - Undefined

- Undefined

Second - Undefined

- Undefined

Subfield Codes

$a - Additional physical form available note (NR)

$b - Availability source (NR)

$c - Availability conditions (NR)

$d - Order number (NR)

$u - Uniform Resource Identifier (R)

$z - Source of note information (NR) (AM CF VM SE) [OBSOLETE]

$3 - Materials specified (NR)

$6 - Linkage (NR)

$8 - Field link and sequence number (R)

533 - REPRODUCTION NOTE (R)

Indicators

First - Undefined

- Undefined

Second - Undefined

- Undefined

Subfield Codes

$a - Type of reproduction (NR)

$b - Place of reproduction (R)

$c - Agency responsible for reproduction (R)

$d - Date of reproduction (NR)

$e - Physical description of reproduction (NR)

$f - Series statement of reproduction (R)

$m - Dates and/or sequential designation of issues reproduced (R)

$n - Note about reproduction (R)

$3 - Materials specified (NR)

$6 - Linkage (NR)

$7 - Fixed-length data elements of reproduction (NR)

0 - Type of date/Publication status

1-4 - Date 1

5-8 - Date 2

9-11 - Place of publication, production, or execution

12 - Frequency

n - Not applicable

13 - Regularity

- Not applicable

14 - Form of item

$8 - Field link and sequence number (R)

534 - ORIGINAL VERSION NOTE (R)

Descriptive data for an original item when the main portion of the bibliographic record describes a reproduction of that item and the data differ.

Indicators

First - Undefined

- Undefined

Second - Undefined

- Undefined

First - Specifies presence of series statement on original (BK MP MU VM SE) [OBSOLETE]

0 - Note excludes series of original

1 - Note includes series of original

Subfield Codes

$a - Main entry of original (NR)

$b - Edition statement of original (NR)

$c - Publication, distribution, etc. of original (NR)

$e - Physical description, etc. of original (NR)

$f - Series statement of original (R)

$k - Key title of original (R)

$l - Location of original (NR)

$m - Material specific details (NR)

$n - Note about original (R)

$p - Introductory phrase (NR)

$t - Title statement of original (NR)

$x - International Standard Serial Number (R)

$z - International Standard Book Number (R)

$6 - Linkage (NR)

$8 - Field link and sequence number (R)

535 - LOCATION OF ORIGINALS/DUPLICATES NOTE (R)

The name and address of the repository that has custody of the original or a duplicate copy of the described material when either is housed in a repository different from that of the material being described.

Indicators

First - Additional information about custodian

0 - Repository (AM) [OBSOLETE]

1 - Holder of originals

2 - Holder of duplicates

3 - Holder of oral tapes (AM) [OBSOLETE]

Second - Undefined

- Undefined

Subfield Codes

$a - Custodian (NR)

$b - Postal address (R)

$c - Country (R)

$d - Telecommunications address (R)

$g - Repository location code (NR)

$3 - Materials specified (NR)

$6 - Linkage (NR)

$8 - Field link and sequence number (R)

Examples

535 1#$3Coal reports $aAmerican Mining Congress; $b1920 N St., NW, Washington, D.C. 20036; $d202-861-2800

535 2#$3Harrison papers $aNeils Bohr Library, Center for History of Physics, American Institute of Physics; $b335 East 45th Street, New York, NY 10017

535 2#$3Duplicate transcripts $aPennsylvania State University Archives; $bUniversity Park, PA

—Note Fields (Part 2: 53X-58X)—

Fields 536-586 contain bibliographic notes which are more specific in nature. A significant number of these note fields are used to record information relating to the archival or serial control of the bibliographic item.

536 - Funding Information Note (R)

538 - System Details Note (R)

540 - Terms Governing Use and Reproduction Note (R)

541 - Immediate Source of Acquisition Note (R)

544 - Location of Other Archival Materials Note (R)

545 - Biographical or Historical Data (R)

546 - Language Note (R)

547 - Former Title Complexity Note (R)

550 - Issuing Body Note (R)

552 - Entity and Attribute Information Note (R)

555 - Cumulative Index/Finding Aids Note (R)

556 - Information About Documentation Note (R)

561 - Ownership and Custodial History (R)

562 - Copy and Version Identification Note (R)

565 - Case File Characteristics Note (R)

567 - Methodology Note (R)

580 - Linking Entry and Complexity Note (R)

581 - Publications About Described Materials Note (R)

583 - Action Note (R)

584 - Accumulation and Frequency of Use Note (R)

585 - Exhibitions Note (R)

586 - Awards Note (R)

59X - Local Notes

536 - FUNDING INFORMATION NOTE (R)

Contract, grant, and/or project numbers when the described material is the result of a funded project. Information concerning the sponsor or funding agency also may be included.

Indicators

First - Undefined

- Undefined

Second - Undefined

- Undefined

Subfield Codes

$a - Text of note (NR)

$b - Contract number (R)

$c - Grant number (R)

$d - Undifferentiated number (R)

$e - Program element number (R)

$f - Project number (R)

$g - Task number (R)

$h - Work unit number (R)

$6 - Linkage (NR)

$8 - Field link and sequence number (R)

Examples

536 ##$aSponsored by the World Health Organization

536 ##$aSponsored by the Advanced Research Projects Agency through the Office of Naval Research. $bN00014-68-A-0245-0007 $cARPA Order No. 2616

536 ##$cEF-77-C-01-2556

536 ##$aSponsored by the U.S. Energy Research and Development Administration. $d9103450

536 ##$aSponsored by the U.S. Air Force ##$e601101F ##$f1LIR ##$g5H ##$hWUAFGLILIR5H01

536 ##$aSponsored by the U.S. Dept. of the Army ##$e61102A ##$f1D161102B710 ##$g00 ##$hWU425

536 ##$aSponsored by the U.S. Dept. of the Navy ##$e62711N ##$fF11121 ##$gRF11121806 ##$hWUNR004105

536 ##$aSponsored by the U.S. Defense Nuclear Agency ##$ePE62715H ##$fX88QAXV ##$gX000 ##$hWU08

537 - SOURCE OF DATA NOTE (NR) (CF) [OBSOLETE]

Indicators

First - Display constant controller

- No information provided

8 - No display constant generated

Second - Undefined

- Undefined

Subfield Codes

$a - Source of data note (NR)

$6 - Linkage (NR)

538 - SYSTEM DETAILS NOTE (R)

Indicators Technical information about an item, such as the presence or absence of certain kinds of codes, recording densities, parity, blocking factors, software programming language, computer requirements, peripheral requirements, trade name or recording systems, number of lines of resolution, and modulation frequency. For sound and videorecordings, information about the trade name or recording system(s) (e.g., VHS), modulation frequency and number of lines of resolution may be included.

First - Undefined

- Undefined

Second - Undefined

- Undefined

Subfield Codes

$a - System details note (NR)

$6 - Linkage (NR)

$8 - Field link and sequence number (R)

540 - TERMS GOVERNING USE AND REPRODUCTION NOTE (R)

Indicators

First - Undefined

- Undefined

Second - Undefined

- Undefined

Subfield Codes

$a - Terms governing use and reproduction (NR)

$b - Jurisdiction (NR)

$c - Authorization (NR)

$d - Authorized users (NR)

$u - Uniform Resource Identifier (R)

$3 - Materials specified (NR)

$5 - Institution to which field applies (NR)

$6 - Linkage (NR)

$8 - Field link and sequence number (R)

541 - IMMEDIATE SOURCE OF ACQUISITION NOTE (R)

Indicators

First - Undefined

- Undefined

Second - Undefined

- Undefined

Subfield Codes

$a - Source of acquisition (NR)

$b - Address (NR)

$c - Method of acquisition (NR)

$d - Date of acquisition (NR)

$e - Accession number (NR)

$f - Owner (NR)

$h - Purchase price (NR)

$n - Extent (R)

$o - Type of unit (R)

$3 - Materials specified (NR)

$5 - Institution to which field applies (NR)

$6 - Linkage (NR)

$8 - Field link and sequence number (R)

543 - SOLICITATION INFORMATION NOTE (AM) (R) [OBSOLETE]

Indicators

First - Undefined

- Undefined

Second - Undefined

- Undefined

Subfield Codes

$a - Solicitation information note (NR)

$6 - Linkage (NR)

544 - LOCATION OF OTHER ARCHIVAL MATERIALS NOTE (R)

The name and address of the custodian of materials that, at a previous time, have been part of the same collection or record group as the described materials.

Examples

544 ##$dBurt Barnes papers; $eAlso located at; $aArchives of American Art, Smithsonian Institution.

544 ##$dWilliam Fords Provenance; $eFreen College; $b727 Prologue Blvd., History City, MA, $cUSA.

544 $dSeries 462 (Register of criminal actions, 1929-1942); $eNot included in the initial transfer, accessioned as a separate series.

544 1#$nOther records relating to the delivery of health care services can be found in the Health Care Services Division files of the Dept. of Health Fonds.

Indicators

First - Relationship

- No information provided

0 - Associated materials

1 - Related materials

Second - Undefined

- Undefined

Subfield Codes

$a - Custodian (R)

$b - Address (R)

$c - Country (R)

$d - Title (R)

$e - Provenance (R)

$n - Note (R)

$3 - Materials specified (NR)

$6 - Linkage (NR)

$8 - Field link and sequence number (R)

545 - BIOGRAPHICAL OR HISTORICAL DATA (R)

Biographical information about an individual or historical information about an institution or an event used as the main entry of the bibliographic record for the described materials. When a distinction between levels of detail is required, a brief summary is given in subfield $a and a fuller annotation is given in subfield $b.

Indicators

First - Type of data

- No information provided

0 - Biographical sketch

1 - Administrative history

Second - Undefined

- Undefined

Subfield Codes

$a - Biographical or historical note (NR)

$b - Expansion (NR)

$u - Uniform Resource Identifier (R)

$6 - Linkage (NR)

$8 - Field link and sequence number (R)

Examples

545 ##$aActive from March 15, 1905 until April 17, 1989.

545 ##$aBorn Kingston, N.Y., April 4, 1856; worked at J.J. Bufford's Lith. in Boston, 1890-1895.

545 ##$aAuthor and reformer. Born Harriet Elizabeth Beecher. Married (1836) Calvin Ellis Stowe (1802-1886).

545 ##$aThe Faribault State School and Hospital provided care, treatment, training, and a variety of other services to mentally retarded individuals and their families. It was operated by the State of Minnesota from 1879 to 1998 under different administrative structures and with different names. A more detailed history of the Hospital may be found at $uhttp://www.mnhsorg/library/findaids/80881.html

546 - LANGUAGE NOTE (R)

Textual information on the language of the described materials. A description of the alphabet, script, or other symbol system (e.g., arabic alphabet, ASCII, musical notation system, bar code, logarithmic graphing) may also be included. Coded language information is contained in fields 008/35- 37 and/or 041.

Indicators

First - Undefined

- Undefined

Second - Undefined

- Undefined

Subfield Codes

$a - Language note (NR)

$b - Information code or alphabet (R)

$z - Source of note information (NR) (SE) [OBSOLETE]

$3 - Materials specified (NR)

$6 - Linkage (NR)

$8 - Field link and sequence number (R)

Examples

546 ##$aIn Hungarian; summaries in French, German, or Russian.

546 ##$aEnglish, French, or German.

546 ##$3John P. Harrington field notebooks $aApache; $bPhonetic alphabet.

546 ##$3Marriage certificate $aGerman; $bFraktur.

546 ##$aLatin; $bRoman alphabet.

547 - FORMER TITLE COMPLEXITY NOTE (R)

Indicators A description of the complex relationship between former titles when an intelligible note cannot be generated from the data in field 247 (Former Title or Title Variations).

First - Undefined

- Undefined

Second - Undefined

- Undefined

Subfield Codes

$a - Former title complexity note (NR)

$z - Source of note information (NR) (SE) [OBSOLETE]

$6 - Linkage (NR)

$8 - Field link and sequence number (R)

Examples

547 ##$aTitle varies: 1716?-1858, Notizie del mundo—1860-71, 1912- - Annuario pontificio (1872-1911, Gerarchia cattolica).

547 ##$aEdition varies: 1916, New York edition.

550 - ISSUING BODY NOTE (R)

Indicators

First - Undefined

- Undefined

Second - Undefined

- Undefined

First - Existence of additional information (SE) [OBSOLETE]

0 - Repetitious

1 - Not repetitious

Subfield Codes

$a - Issuing body note (NR)

$z - Source of note information (NR) (SE) [OBSOLETE]

$6 - Linkage (NR)

$8 - Field link and sequence number (R)

552 - ENTITY AND ATTRIBUTE INFORMATION NOTE (R)

Indicators

First - Undefined

- Undefined

Second - Undefined

- Undefined

Subfield Codes

$a - Entity type label (NR)

$b - Entity type definition and source (NR)

$c - Attribute label (NR)

$d - Attribute definition and source (NR)

$e - Enumerated domain value (R)

$f - Enumerated domain value definition and source (R)

$g - Range domain minimum and maximum (NR)

$h - Codeset name and source (NR)

$i - Unrepresentable domain (NR)

$j - Attribute units of measurement and resolution (NR)

$k - Beginning date and ending date of attribute values (NR)

$l - Attribute value accuracy (NR)

$m - Attribute value accuracy explanation (NR)

$n - Attribute measurement frequency (NR)

$o - Entity and attribute overview (R)

$p - Entity and attribute detail citation (R)

$u - Uniform Resource Identifier (R)

$z - Display note (R)

$6 - Linkage (NR)

$8 - Field link and sequence number (R)

555 - CUMULATIVE INDEX/FINDING AIDS NOTE (R)

Indicators

First - Display constant controller

- Indexes

0 - Finding aids

8 - No display constant generated

Second - Undefined

- Undefined

Subfield Codes

$a - Cumulative index/finding aids note (NR)

$b - Availability source (R)

$c - Degree of control (NR)

$d - Bibliographic reference (NR)

$u - Uniform Resource Identifier (R)

$3 - Materials specified (NR)

$6 - Linkage (NR)

$8 - Field link and sequence number (R)

556 - INFORMATION ABOUT DOCUMENTATION NOTE (R)

Indicators

First - Display constant controller

- Documentation

8 - No display constant generated

Second - Undefined

- Undefined

Subfield Codes

$a - Information about documentation note (NR)

$z - International Standard Book Number (R)

$6 - Linkage (NR)

$8 - Field link and sequence number (R)

561 - OWNERSHIP AND CUSTODIAL HISTORY (R)

Indicators

First - Undefined

- Undefined

Second - Undefined

- Undefined

Subfield Codes

$a - History (NR)

$b - Time of collation (NR) [OBSOLETE]

$3 - Materials specified (NR)

$5 - Institution to which field applies (NR)

$6 - Linkage (NR)

$8 - Field link and sequence number (R)

562 - COPY AND VERSION IDENTIFICATION NOTE (R)

Indicators

First - Undefined

- Undefined

Second - Undefined

- Undefined

Subfield Codes

$a - Identifying markings (R)

$b - Copy identification (R)

$c - Version identification (R)

$d - Presentation format (R)

$e - Number of copies (R)

$3 - Materials specified (NR)

$5 - Institution to which field applies (NR)

$6 - Linkage (NR)

$8 - Field link and sequence number (R)

563 - BINDING INFORMATION (R)

Indicators

First - Undefined

- Undefined

Second - Undefined

- Undefined

Subfield Codes

$a - Binding note (NR)

$u - Uniform Resource Identifier (R)

$3 - Materials specified (NR)

$5 - Institution to which field applies (NR)

$6 - Linkage (NR)

$8 - Field link and sequence number (R)

565 - CASE FILE CHARACTERISTICS NOTE (R)

Indicators

First - Display constant controller

- File size

0 - Case file characteristics

8 - No display constant generated

Second - Undefined

- Undefined

Subfield Codes

$a - Number of cases/variables (NR)

$b - Name of variable (R)

$c - Unit of analysis (R)

$d - Universe of data (R)

$e - Filing scheme or code (R)

$3 - Materials specified (NR)

$6 - Linkage (NR)

$8 - Field link and sequence number (R)

567 - METHODOLOGY NOTE (R)

Indicators

First - Display constant controller

- Methodology

8 - No display constant generated

Second - Undefined

- Undefined

Subfield Codes

$a - Methodology note (NR)

$6 - Linkage (NR)

$8 - Field link and sequence number (R)

570 - EDITOR NOTE (SE) (R) [OBSOLETE]

Indicators

First - Undefined

- Undefined

Second - Undefined

- Undefined

Subfield Codes

$a - Editor note (NR)

$z - Source of note information (NR)

$6 - Linkage (NR)

580 - LINKING ENTRY COMPLEXITY NOTE (R)

A description of the complex relationship between the described item and other items when an intelligible note cannot be generated from data in the linking entry fields 760-787.

Indicators

First - Undefined

- Undefined

Second - Undefined

- Undefined

Subfield Codes

$a - Linking entry complexity note (NR)

$z - Source of note information (NR) [OBSOLETE]

$6 - Linkage (NR)

$8 - Field link and sequence number (R)

Examples

580 ##$aContinued in 1982 by: U.S. exports. Schedule E commodity groupings by world area and country.

580 ##$aMerged with: Index chemicus (Philadelphia, Pa : 1977), to form: Current abstracts of chemistry and index chemicus (Philadelphia, Pa : 1978).

785 17$tCurrent abstracts of chemistry and index chemicus (Philadelphia, Pa : 1978)$x0161-455X$w(DLC)###83642299

580 ##$aCumulates: Deutsche Bibliographie. Wochentliches Verzeichnis.

580 ##$aContinued by: Ionospheric predictions issued by the laboratory under its later name: Institute for Telecommunication Sciences and Aeronomy.

581 - PUBLICATIONS ABOUT DESCRIBED MATERIALS NOTE (R)

Indicators

First - Display constant controller

- Publications

8 - No display constant generated

Second - Undefined

- Undefined

Subfield Codes

$a - Publications about described materials note (NR)

$z - International Standard Book Number (R)

$3 - Materials specified (NR)

$6 - Linkage (NR)

$8 - Field link and sequence number (R)

582 - RELATED COMPUTER FILES NOTE (R) (CF) [OBSOLETE]

Indicators

First - Display constant controller

- No information provided

8 - No display constant generated

Second - Undefined

- Undefined

Subfield Codes

$a - Related computer files note (NR)

$6 - Linkage (NR)

583 - ACTION NOTE (R)

Indicators

First - Undefined

- Undefined

Second - Undefined

- Undefined

Subfield Codes

$a - Action (NR)

$b - Action identification (R)

$c - Time/date of action (R)

$d - Action interval (R)

$e - Contingency for action (R)

$f - Authorization (R)

$h - Jurisdiction (R)

$i - Method of action (R)

$j - Site of action (R)

$k - Action agent (R)

$l - Status (R)

$n - Extent (R)

$o - Type of unit (R)

$u - Uniform Resource Identifier (R)

$x - Nonpublic note (R)

$z - Public note (R)

$2 - Source of term (NR)

$3 - Materials specified (NR)

$5 - Institution to which field applies (NR)

$6 - Linkage (NR)

$8 - Field link and sequence number (R)

584 - ACCUMULATION AND FREQUENCY OF USE NOTE (R)

Indicators

First - Undefined

- Undefined

Second - Undefined

- Undefined

Subfield Codes

$a - Accumulation (R)

$b - Frequency of use (R)

$3 - Materials specified (NR)

$5 - Institution to which field applies (NR)

$6 - Linkage (NR)

$8 - Field link and sequence number (R)

585 - EXHIBITIONS NOTE (R)

Indicators

First - Undefined

- Undefined

Second - Undefined

- Undefined

Subfield Codes

$a - Exhibitions note (NR)

$3 - Materials specified (NR)

$5 - Institution to which field applies (NR)

$6 - Linkage (NR)

$8 - Field link and sequence number (R)

586 - AWARDS NOTE (R)

Indicators

First - Display constant controller

- Awards

8 - No display constant generated

Second - Undefined

- Undefined

Subfield Codes

$a - Awards note (NR)

$3 - Materials specified (NR)

$6 - Linkage (NR)

$8 - Field link and sequence number (R)

59X - LOCAL NOTES

590 - LOCAL NOTE (BK CF MP MU SE VM MX) [OBSOLETE]

Indicators

First - Undefined

- Undefined

Second - Undefined

- Undefined

Subfield Codes

$a - Local note (NR)

590 - RECEIPT DATE NOTE (VM) [OBSOLETE]

Indicators

First - Undefined

- Undefined

Second - Undefined

- Undefined

Subfield Codes

$a - Receipt date (NR)

$b - Provenance (NR)

$d - Condition of individual reels (NR)

$d - Origin of safety copy (NR)

—Subject Access Fields (6XX)—

Fields 600-658 (with the exception of field 653 that is used for uncontrolled index terms) contain subject headings or access terms that provide additional access to a bibliographic record through a heading or term that is constructed according to established subject cataloging or thesaurus- building principles and guidelines. The standard list or authority file used is identified by the value in the second indicator position or by the MARC source code contained in subfield $2 that is used in conjunction with value 7.

The Arabic number that precedes a subject access field in some displays is not carried in the MARC record. It may be generated based on the field tag. The dash (-) that precedes a general subject subdivision is not carried in the MARC record; it may be generated based on the presence of subfields $v, $x, $y, and $z.

600 - Subject Added Entry—Personal Name (R)

610 - Subject Added Entry—Corporate Name (R)

630 - Subject Added Entry—Uniform Title (R)

650 - Subject Added Entry—Topical Term (R)

651 - Subject Added Entry—Geographic Name (R)

653 - Index Term—Uncontrolled (R)

654 - Subject Added Entry—Faceted Topical Terms (R)

655 - Index Term—Genre/Form (R)

656 - Index Term—Occupation (R)

657 - Index Term—Function (R)

658 - Index Term—Curriculum Objective (R)

600 - SUBJECT ADDED ENTRY—PERSONAL NAME (R)

A subject added entry in which the entry element is a personal name.

Indicators

First - Type of personal name entry element

0 - Forename

1 - Surname

2 - Multiple surname [OBSOLETE]

3 - Family name

Second - Thesaurus

0 - Library of Congress Subject Headings

1 - LC subject headings for children's literature

2 - Medical Subject Headings

3 - National Agricultural Library subject authority file

4 - Source not specified

5 - Canadian Subject Headings

6 - Répertoire de vedettes-matière

7 - Source specified in subfield $2

Subfield Codes

$a - Personal name (NR)

$b - Numeration (NR)

$c - Titles and other words associated with a name (R)

$d - Dates associated with a name (NR)

$e - Relator term (R)

$f - Date of a work (NR)

$g - Miscellaneous information (NR)

$h - Medium (NR)

$k - Form subheading (R)

$j - Attribution qualifier (R)

$l - Language of a work (NR)

$m - Medium of performance for music (R)

$n - Number of part/section of a work (R)

$o - Arranged statement for music (NR)

$p - Name of part/section of a work (R)

$q - Fuller form of name (NR)

$r - Key for music (NR)

$s - Version (NR)

$t - Title of a work (NR)

$u - Affiliation (NR)

$v - Form subdivision (R)

$x - General subdivision (R)

$y - Chronological subdivision (R)

$z - Geographic subdivision (R)

$2 - Source of heading or term (NR)

$3 - Materials specified (NR)

$4 - Relator code (R)

$6 - Linkage (NR)

$8 - Field link and sequence number (R)

Examples

600 00$aNorodom Sihanouk, $cPrince, $d1922-

600 10$aSmith, $dfl. 1641.

600 30$aDunlop family.

600 30$aPremyslid dynasty.

600 30$aMorton family.

600 00$aMoses $c(Biblical leader)

600 10$aDrake, Francis, $cSir, $d1540?- 1596.

600 10$aGarcia Lorca, Federico, $d1898-1936, $kin fiction, drama, poetry, etc.

600 10$aShakespeare, William, $d1564-1616. $tHamlet.

600 00$aGautama Buddha $vBiography $vEarly works to 1800.

600 10$aShakespeare, William, $d1564-1616 $xCriticism and interpretation $xHistory $y18th century.

600 10$aReagan, Ronald $xAssassination attempt, 1981.

610 - SUBJECT ADDED ENTRY—CORPORATE NAME (R)

A subject added entry in which the entry element is a corporate name.

Indicators

First - Type of corporate name entry element

0 - Inverted name

1 - Jurisdiction name

2 - Name in direct order

Second - Thesaurus

0 - Library of Congress Subject Headings

1 - LC subject headings for children's literature

2 - Medical Subject Headings

3 - National Agricultural Library subject authority file

4 - Source not specified

5 - Canadian Subject Headings

6 - Répertoire de vedettes-matière

7 - Source specified in subfield $2

Subfield Codes

$a - Corporate name or jurisdiction name as entry element (NR)

$b - Subordinate unit (R)

$c - Location of meeting (NR)

$d - Date of meeting or treaty signing (R)

$e - Relator term (R)

$f - Date of a work (NR)

$g - Miscellaneous information (NR)

$h - Medium (NR)

$k - Form subheading (R)

$l - Language of a work (NR)

$m - Medium of performance for music (R)

$n - Number of part/section/meeting (R)

$o - Arranged statement for music (NR)

$p - Name of part/section of a work (R)

$r - Key for music (NR)

$s - Version (NR)

$t - Title of a work (NR)

$u - Affiliation (NR)

$v - Form subdivision (R)

$x - General subdivision (R)

$y - Chronological subdivision (R)

$z - Geographic subdivision (R)

$2 - Source of heading or term (NR)

$3 - Materials specified (NR)

$4 - Relator code (R)

$6 - Linkage (NR)

$8 - Field link and sequence number (R)

Examples:

610 20$aBenjamin F. Packard (Sailing ship)

610 20$aEmpire State Building (New York, N.Y.)

610 10$aFrance. $tConstitution (1946)

610 10$aGreat Britain. $tTreaties, etc. $gIreland, $d1985 Nov. 15.

610 20$aBritish Library. $kManuscript. $nArundel 384.

610 10$aUruguay. $tTreaties, etc. $gArgentina, $d1974 Aug. 20. $kProtocols, etc. $d1982 Dec. 20.

610 20$aDaughters of the American Revolution. $bMary Clap Wooster Chapter (New Haven, Conn.). $kCharters and regulations.

610 20$aUnited States Strategic Bombing Survey $tReports. $pPacific war $vIndexes.

610 10$aUnited States. $bArmy. $bCavalry $xHistory $yCivil War, 1861-1865 $vMaps.

610 20$aCatholic Church. $bProvince of Baltimore (Md.)

610 20$aUnited Nations $zAfrica.

611 - SUBJECT ADDED ENTRY—MEETING NAME (R)

Indicators

First - Type of meeting name entry element

0 - Inverted name

1 - Jurisdiction name

2 - Name in direct order

Second - Thesaurus

0 - Library of Congress Subject Headings

1 - LC subject headings for children's literature

2 - Medical Subject Headings

3 - National Agricultural Library subject authority file

4 - Source not specified

5 - Canadian Subject Headings

6 - Répertoire de vedettes-matière

7 - Source specified in subfield $2

Subfield Codes

$a - Meeting name or jurisdiction name as entry element (NR)

$b - Number (BK CF MP MU SE VM MX) [OBSOLETE]

$c - Location of meeting (NR)

$d - Date of meeting (NR)

$e - Subordinate unit (R)

$f - Date of a work (NR)

$g - Miscellaneous information (NR)

$h - Medium (NR)

$k - Form subheading (R)

$l - Language of a work (NR)

$n - Number of part/section/meeting (R)

$p - Name of part/section of a work (R)

$q - Name of meeting following jurisdiction name entry element (NR)

$s - Version (NR)

$t - Title of a work (NR)

$u - Affiliation (NR)

$v - Form subdivision (R)

$x - General subdivision (R)

$y - Chronological subdivision (R)

$z - Geographic subdivision (R)

$2 - Source of heading or term (NR)

$3 - Materials specified (NR)

$4 - Relator code (R)

$6 - Linkage (NR)

$8 - Field link and sequence number (R)

630 - SUBJECT ADDED ENTRY—UNIFORM TITLE (R)

A subject added entry in which the entry element is a uniform title.

Indicators

First - Nonfiling characters

0-9 - Number of nonfiling characters

- Nonfiling characters not specified [OBSOLETE]

Second - Thesaurus

0 - Library of Congress Subject Headings

1 - LC subject headings for children's literature

2 - Medical Subject Headings

3 - National Agricultural Library subject authority file

4 - Source not specified

5 - Canadian Subject Headings

6 - Répertoire de vedettes-matière

7 - Source specified in subfield $2

Subfield Codes

$a - Uniform title (NR)

$d - Date of treaty signing (R)

$f - Date of a work (NR)

$g - Miscellaneous information (NR)

$h - Medium (NR)

$k - Form subheading (R)

$l - Language of a work (NR)

$m - Medium of performance for music (R)

$n - Number of part/section of a work (R)

$o - Arranged statement for music (NR)

$p - Name of part/section of a work (R)

$r - Key for music (NR)

$s - Version (NR)

$t - Title of a work (NR)

$v - Form subdivision (R)

$x - General subdivision (R)

$y - Chronological subdivision (R)

$z - Geographic subdivision (R)

$2 - Source of heading or term (NR)

$3 - Materials specified (NR)

$6 - Linkage (NR)

$8 - Field link and sequence number (R)

Examples:

630 00$aDead Sea scrolls.

630 00$aFour seasons (Motion picture 1981)

630 00$aInter-American Treaty of Reciprocal Assistance $d(1947)

630 00$aNew York times $vIndexes.

630 00$aKoran $xCriticism, interpretation, etc $xHistory $y19th century.

630 05$aStudio magazine. $pContemporary paintings $vPeriodicals.

630 00$aBible. $pN.T. $pRomans $xGeography $vMaps.

630 00$aSilent running (Motion picture)

648 - SUBJECT ADDED ENTRY—CHRONOLOGICAL TERM (R)

Indicators

First - Undefined

- Undefined

Second - Thesaurus

0 - Library of Congress Subject Headings

1 - LC subject headings for children's literature

2 - Medical Subject Headings

3 - National Agricultural Library subject authority file

4 - Source not specified

5 - Canadian Subject Headings

6 - Répertoire de vedettes-matière

7 - Source specified in subfield $2

Subfield Codes

$a - Chronological term (NR)

$v - Form subdivision (R)

$x - General subdivision (R)

$y - Chronological subdivision (R)

$z - Geographic subdivision (R)

$2 - Source of heading or term (NR)

$3 - Materials specified (NR)

$6 - Linkage (NR)

$8 - Field link and sequence number (R)

650 - SUBJECT ADDED ENTRY—TOPICAL TERM (R)

A subject added entry in which the entry element is a topical term.

Indicators

First - Level of subject

- No information provided

0 - No level specified

1 - Primary

2 - Secondary

Second - Thesaurus

0 - Library of Congress Subject Headings

1 - LC subject headings for children's literature

2 - Medical Subject Headings

3 - National Agricultural Library subject authority file

4 - Source not specified

5 - Canadian Subject Headings

6 - Répertoire de vedettes-matière

7 - Source specified in subfield $2

Subfield Codes

$a - Topical term or geographic name as entry element (NR)

$b - Topical term following geographic name as entry element (NR)

$c - Location of event (NR)

$d - Active dates (NR)

$e - Relator term (NR)

$v - Form subdivision (R)

$x - General subdivision (R)

$y - Chronological subdivision (R)

$z - Geographic subdivision (R)

$2 - Source of heading or term (NR)

$3 - Materials specified (NR)

$6 - Linkage (NR)

$8 - Field link and sequence number (R)

Examples

650 #0$aArchitecture, Modern $y19th century.

650 00$aFlour and feed trade $vPeriodicals.

650 17$aCareer Exploration. $2ericd

650 #0$aConcertos (String orchestra)

650 #0$aVocal music $zFrance $y18th century.

650 #0$aDentistry $vJuvenile films.

650 #0$aReal property $zMississippi $zTippah County $vMaps.

650 #7$aEducational buildings $zWashington (D.C.) $y1890- 1910. $2lctgm

651 - SUBJECT ADDED ENTRY—GEOGRAPHIC NAME (R)

A subject added entry in which the entry element is a geographic name.

Indicators

First - Undefined

- Undefined

Second - Thesaurus

0 - Library of Congress Subject Headings

1 - LC subject headings for children's literature

2 - Medical Subject Headings

3 - National Agricultural Library subject authority file

4 - Source not specified

5 - Canadian Subject Headings

6 - Répertoire de vedettes-matière

7 - Source specified in subfield $2

Subfield Codes

$a - Geographic name (NR)

$b - Geographic name following place entry element (R) [OBSOLETE]

$v - Form subdivision (R)

$x - General subdivision (R)

$y - Chronological subdivision (R)

$z - Geographic subdivision (R)

$2 - Source of heading or term (NR)

$3 - Materials specified (NR)

$6 - Linkage (NR)

$8 - Field link and sequence number (R)

Examples

651 #0$aAmazon River.

651 #0$aAltamira Cave (Spain)

651 #0$aPompeii (Ancient city)

651 #0$aAntietam National Battlefield (Md.)

651 #0$aKing Ranch (Tex.)

651 #0$aMing Tombs (China)

651 #0$aChelsea (London, England)

651 #0$aRussia $xHistory $vMaps.

651 #0$aTexas $xGovernors $xStaff.

651 #0$aUnited States $xBoundaries $zCanada

651 #0$3Psychiatric admission records $aPennsylvania $xNuclear reactor safety $y1975-1985 $zUnited States

652 - SUBJECT ADDED ENTRY—REVERSED GEOGRAPHIC (BK MP SE) [OBSOLETE]

Indicators

First - Undefined

- Undefined

Second - Undefined

- Undefined

Subfield Codes

$a - Geographic name of place element (NR)

$x - General subdivision (R)

$y - Chronological subdivision (R)

$z - Geographic subdivision (R)

653 - INDEX TERM—UNCONTROLLED (R)

An index term added entry that is not constructed by standard subject heading/thesaurus-building conventions.

Indicators

First - Level of index term

- No information provided

0 - No level specified

1 - Primary

2 - Secondary

Second - Undefined

- Undefined

Subfield Codes

$a - Uncontrolled term (R)

$6 - Linkage (NR)

$8 - Field link and sequence number (R)

Examples

653 1#$afuel cells $amolten carbonate $apower generation

653 ##$aMan $aEyes $aDiseases

654 - SUBJECT ADDED ENTRY—FACETED TOPICAL TERMS (R)

Indicators

First - Level of subject

- No information provided

0 - No level specified

1 - Primary

2 - Secondary

Second - Undefined

- Undefined

Subfield Codes

$a - Focus term (NR)

$b - Non-focus term (R)

$c - Facet/hierarchy designation (R)

$v - Form subdivision (R)

$y - Chronological subdivision (R)

$z - Geographic subdivision (R)

$2 - Source of heading or term (NR)

$3 - Materials specified (NR)

$6 - Linkage (NR)

$8 - Field link and sequence number (R)

655 - INDEX TERM—GENRE/FORM (R)

Indicators655 - Index Term—Genre/Form (R)

Contains terms indicating the genre, form, and/or physical characteristics of the materials being described. A genre term designates the style or technique of the intellectual content of textual materials or, for graphic materials, aspects such as vantage point, intended purpose, or method of representation. A form term designates historically and functionally specific kinds of materials distinguished by their physical character, the subject of their intellectual content, or the order of information within them. Physical characteristic terms designate historically and functionally specific kinds of materials as distinguished by an examination of their physical character, subject of their intellectual content, or the order of information with them.

First - Type of heading

- Basic

0 - Faceted

Second - Thesaurus

0 - Library of Congress Subject Headings

1 - LC subject headings for children's literature

2 - Medical Subject Headings

3 - National Agricultural Library subject authority file

4 - Source not specified

5 - Canadian Subject Headings

6 - Répertoire de vedettes-matière

7 - Source specified in subfield $2

Subfield Codes

$a - Genre/form data or focus term (NR)

$b - Non-focus term (R)

$c - Facet/hierarchy designation (R)

$v - Form subdivision (R)

$x - General subdivision (R)

$y - Chronological subdivision (R)

$z - Geographic subdivision (R)

$2 - Source of term (NR)

$3 - Materials specified (NR)

$5 - Institution to which field applies (NR)

$6 - Linkage (NR)

$8 - Field link and sequence number (R)

Examples

655 #7$aBird's-eye views $y1874. $2gmgpc

655 07$ck $bLaminated $cm $bmarblewood $cv $abust. $2aat

655 #7$aDictionaries $xFrench $y18th century. $2rbgenr

655 ##$aSigning patterns (Printing) $zGermany $y18th century. $2rbpri

655 #7$3Municipal Fire Station records $aFire reports $zAtlanta, Georgia $y1978. $2[thesaurus code]

655 ##$aAnnotations (Provenance) $zSweden $y18th century. $2rbprov $5MH-H

656 - INDEX TERM—OCCUPATION (R)

An index term that is descriptive of the occupation reflected in the contents of the described materials.

Indicators

First - Undefined

- Undefined

Second - Source of term

7 - Source specified in subfield $2

Subfield Codes

$a - Occupation (NR)

$k - Form (NR)

$v - Form subdivision (R)

$x - General subdivision (R)

$y - Chronological subdivision (R)

$z - Geographic subdivision (R)

$2 - Source of term (NR)

$3 - Materials specified (NR)

$6 - Linkage (NR)

$8 - Field link and sequence number (R)

Examples

656 #7$aAnthropologists. $2[thesaurus code]

656 #7$aEducators. $2[thesaurus code]

656 #7$aMigrant laborers. $kSchool district case files $2[thesaurus code>]

657 - INDEX TERM—FUNCTION (R)

Indicators

First - Undefined

- Undefined

Second - Source of term

7 - Source specified in subfield $2

Subfield Codes

$a - Function (NR)

$v - Form subdivision (R)

$x - General subdivision (R)

$y - Chronological subdivision (R)

$z - Geographic subdivision (R)

$2 - Source of term (NR)

$3 - Materials specified (NR)

$6 - Linkage (NR)

$8 - Field link and sequence number (R)

658 - INDEX TERM—CURRICULUM OBJECTIVE (R)

Contains index terms denoting curriculum or course-of-study objectives applicable to the content ofthe described materials. The field may also contain correlation factors indicating the degree to which the described materials meet an objective. Codes assigned to specific objectives in published lists are also recorded in this field.

Indicators

First - Undefined

- Undefined

Second - Undefined

- Undefined

Subfield Codes

$a - Main curriculum objective (NR)

$b - Subordinate curriculum objective (R)

$c - Curriculum code (NR)

$d - Correlation factor (NR)

$2 - Source of term or code (NR)

$6 - Linkage (NR)

$8 - Field link and sequence number (R)

Examples

658 ##$aReading objective 1 (fictional) $bunderstanding language, elements of plots, themes, motives, characters, setting by responding to the multiple-meaning word $cNRPO2-1991 $dhighly correlated. $2ohco

658 ##$aMath manipulatives $dhighly correlated. $2[source code]

658 ##$aDrug abuse awareness $bpeer pressure $bunderstanding the law. $2local

658 ##$aHealth objective 1 $bhandicapped awareness $cNHP01-1991 $dhighly correlated. $2ohco

658 ##$aReading objective 1 $bidentify, locate, and use information $cNRP01-1991. $2accssd

—Added Entry Fields (70X-75X)—

Fields 700-754 contain a name and/or title or a term that provides access to a bibliographic record that is not provided through main entry (1XX), subject access (6XX), series statement (4XX), series added entry (8XX), or title (20X-24X) fields. The roman numeral and the word Title: that precede an added entry field in some displays are not carried in the MARC record. They may be generated based on the field tag.

700 - Added Entry—Personal Name (R)

710 - Added Entry—Corporate Name (R)

711 - Added Entry—Meeting Name (R)

720 - Added Entry—Uncontrolled Name (R)

730 - Added Entry—Uniform Title (R)

740 - Added Entry—Uncontrolled Related/Analytical Title (R)

752 - Added Entry—Hierarchical Place Name (R)

753 - System Details—Access to Computer Files (R)

754 - Added Entry—Taxonomic Identification (R)

700 - ADDED ENTRY—PERSONAL NAME (R)

Indicators

First - Type of personal name entry element

0 - Forename

1 - Surname

2 - Multiple surname [OBSOLETE]

3 - Family name

Second - Type of added entry

- No information provided

0 - Alternative entry (BK CF MP MU SE MX) [OBSOLETE]

1 - Secondary entry (BK CF MP MU SE MX) [OBSOLETE]

1 - Printed on card (VM) [OBSOLETE]

2 - Analytical entry

3 - Not printed on card (VM) [OBSOLETE]

Subfield Codes

$a - Personal name (NR)

$b - Numeration (NR)

$c - Titles and other words associated with a name (R)

$d - Dates associated with a name (NR)

$e - Relator term (R)

$f - Date of a work (NR)

$g - Miscellaneous information (NR)

$h - Medium (NR)

$j - Attribution qualifier (R)

$k - Form subheading (R)

$l - Language of a work (NR)

$m - Medium of performance for music (R)

$n - Number of part/section of a work (R)

$o - Arranged statement for music (NR)

$p - Name of part/section of a work (R)

$q - Fuller form of name (NR)

$r - Key for music (NR)

$s - Version (NR)

$t - Title of a work (NR)

$u - Affiliation (NR)

$x - International Standard Serial Number (NR)

$3 - Materials specified (NR)

$4 - Relator code (R)

$5 - Institution to which field applies (NR)

$6 - Linkage (NR)

$8 - Field link and sequence number (R)

Examples:

700 0#$aFather Divine.

700 0#$aR. M. B.

700 1#$aVerez Peraza, Elena, $d1919-

700 1#$aSalamin C., Marcel A.

700 1#$aIbn al-Mu'tazz, 'Abd Allah, $d861-908.

700 0#$aSpagna $c(Artist), $dca. 1450-1528.

700 0#$aCharles Edward, $cPrince, grandson of James II, King of England, $d1720-1788.

700 1#$aHecht, Ben, $d1893-1964, $ewriting, $edirection, $eproduction.

700 1#$aE , Sheila. $q(Escovedo). $d1959- $tDawn, the beginning. $hSound recording

700 12$aShakespeare, William. $d1564-1616 $tSelections $lGerman. $f1982.

700 1#$aRies, Ferdinand, $d1784-1838 $tOctets. $mpiano, winds, strings, $nop. 128. $rAb major

700 1#$aHarrison, Tinsley Randolph. $d1900- $tPrinciples of internal medicine. $s9th ed.

700 1#$aHerrman, Egbert. $4org

700 1#$aGalway, James. $4prf $4cnd

700 1#$a Jefferson, Thomas, $d1743-1826. $eformer owner. $5MH

700 1#$aFord, John, $d1894-1973, $edirection.

705 - ADDED ENTRY—PERSONAL NAME (PERFORMER) (MU) [OBSOLETE]

Indicators

First - Type of personal name entry element

0 - Forename

1 - Single surname

2 - Multiple surname

3 - Family name

Second - Type of added entry

0 - Alternative entry

1 - Secondary entry

2 - Analytical entry

Subfield Codes

$a - Personal name (NR)

$b - Numeration (NR)

$c - Titles and other words associated with a name (R)

$d - Dates associated with a name (NR)

$e - Relator term (R)

$f - Date of a work (NR)

$g - Miscellaneous information (NR)

$h - Medium (NR)

$k - Form subheading (R)

$l - Language of a work (NR)

$m - Medium of performance for music (R)

$n - Number of part/section of a work (R)

$o - Arranged statement for music (NR)

$p - Name of part/section of a work (R)

$r - Key for music (NR)

$s - Version (NR)

$t - Title of a work (NR)

710 - ADDED ENTRY—CORPORATE NAME (R)

Indicators

First - Type of corporate name entry element

0 - Inverted name

1 - Jurisdiction name

2 - Name in direct order

Second - Type of added entry

- No information provided

0 - Alternative entry (BK CF MP MU SE MX) [OBSOLETE]

1 - Secondary entry (BK CF MP MU SE MX) [OBSOLETE]

1 - Printed on card (VM) [OBSOLETE]

2 - Analytical entry

3 - Not printed on card (VM) [OBSOLETE]

Subfield Codes

$a - Corporate name or jurisdiction name as entry element (NR)

$b - Subordinate unit (R)

$c - Location of meeting (NR)

$d - Date of meeting or treaty signing (R)

$e - Relator term (R)

$f - Date of a work (NR)

$g - Miscellaneous information (NR)

$h - Medium (NR)

$k - Form subheading (R)

$l - Language of a work (NR)

$m - Medium of performance for music (R)

$n - Number of part/section/meeting (R)

$o - Arranged statement for music (NR)

$p - Name of part/section of a work (R)

$r - Key for music (NR)

$s - Version (NR)

$t - Title of a work (NR)

$u - Affiliation (NR)

$x - International Standard Serial Number (NR)

$3 - Materials specified (NR)

$4 - Relator code (R)

$5 - Institution to which field applies (NR)

$6 - Linkage (NR)

$8 - Field link and sequence number (R)

Examples:

710 1#$aAlgeria. $tTreaties, etc. $gEngland and Wales, $d1682 Apr. 20.

710 22$aCatholic Church. $tMass, 33rd Sunday of ordinary time (Chant). $f1979.

710 22$aCatholic Church. $bPope (1958-1963 : John XXIII). $tMater et magistra. $lFrench. $kSelections $f1963.

710 1#$aUnited States. $tConstitution. $p13th Amendment

710 1#$aEcuador. $tPlan Nacional de Desarrollo, 1980

1984. $nParte 1, $pGrandes objetivos nacionales $lEnglish.

710 2#$aBridgewater Library, $eformer owner. $5NjP

710 1#$aMinnesota. $bConstitutional Convention $d(1857 : $gRepublican)

710 2#$aHerbert E. Budek Films and Slides (Firm)

710 1#$aUnited States. $bArmy Map Service. $tEastern United States 1:250,000.

710 2#$aNew Orleans Blue Serenaders. $4prf

710 2#$aWGBH (Television station : Boston, Mass.)

710 2#$aHallmark Collection (Library of Congress) $5DLC

711 - ADDED ENTRY—MEETING NAME (R)

Indicators

First - Type of meeting name entry element

0 - Inverted name

1 - Jurisdiction name

2 - Name in direct order

Second - Type of added entry

- No information provided

0 - Alternative entry (BK CF MP MU SE MX) [OBSOLETE]

1 - Secondary entry (BK CF MP MU SE MX) [OBSOLETE]

1 - Printed on card (VM) [OBSOLETE]

2 - Analytical entry

3 - Not printed on card (VM) [OBSOLETE]

Subfield Codes

$a - Meeting name or jurisdiction name as entry element (NR)

$b - Number (BK CF MP MU SE VM MX) [OBSOLETE]

$c - Location of meeting (NR)

$d - Date of meeting (NR)

$e - Subordinate unit (R)

$f - Date of a work (NR)

$g - Miscellaneous information (NR)

$h - Medium (NR)

$k - Form subheading (R)

$l - Language of a work (NR)

$n - Number of part/section/meeting (R)

$p - Name of part/section of a work (R)

$q - Name of meeting following jurisdiction name entry element (NR)

$s - Version (NR)

$t - Title of a work (NR)

$u - Affiliation (NR)

$x - International Standard Serial Number (NR)

$3 - Materials specified (NR)

$4 - Relator code (R)

$5 - Institution to which field applies (NR)

$6 - Linkage (NR)

$8 - Field link and sequence number (R)

715 - ADDED ENTRY—CORPORATE NAME (PERFORMING GROUP) (MU) [OBSOLETE]

Indicators

First - Type of corporate name entry element

0 - Inverted name

1 - Jurisdiction name

2 - Name in direct order

Second - Type of added entry

0 - Alternative entry

1 - Secondary entry

2 - Analytical entry

Subfield Codes

$a - Corporate name or jurisdiction name (NR)

$b - Subordinate unit (R)

$e - Relator term (R)

$f - Date of a work (NR)

$g - Miscellaneous information (NR)

$h - Medium (NR)

$k - Form subheading (R)

$l - Language of a work (NR)

$m - Medium of performance for music (R)

$n - Number of part/section/meeting (R)

$o - Arranged statement for music (NR)

$p - Name of part/section of a work (R)

$r - Key for music (NR)

$s - Version (NR)

$t - Title of a work (NR)

$u - Nonprinting information (NR)

720 - ADDED ENTRY—UNCONTROLLED NAME (R)

IndicatorsContains an added entry in which the name is not controlled in an authority file or list. It is also used for names that have not been formulated according to cataloging rules. Names may be of any type (e.g., personal, corporate, meeting).

First - Type of name

- Not specified

1 - Personal

2 - Other

Second - Undefined

- Undefined

Subfield Codes

$a - Name (NR)

$e - Relator term (R)

$4 - Relator code (R)

$6 - Linkage (NR)

$8 - Field link and sequence number (R)

Examples:

720 1#$aBlacklock, Joseph

720 ##$aVonderrohe, Robert, 1934- $eeditor

720 2#$aCAPCON Library Network $eauthor

720 ##$aU.S. Energy Information Administration. Coal Statistics Division

720 1#$aTheodore K. Hepburn $einventor

730 - ADDED ENTRY—UNIFORM TITLE (R)

Indicators

First - Nonfiling characters

0-9 - Number of nonfiling characters

- Nonfiling characters not specified [OBSOLETE]

Second - Type of added entry

- No information provided

0 - Alternative entry (BK CF MP MU SE MX) [OBSOLETE]

1 - Secondary entry (BK CF MP MU SE MX) [OBSOLETE]

1 - Printed on card (VM) [OBSOLETE]

2 - Analytical entry

3 - Not printed on card (VM) [OBSOLETE]

Subfield Codes

$a - Uniform title (NR)

$d - Date of treaty signing (R)

$f - Date of a work (NR)

$g - Miscellaneous information (NR)

$h - Medium (NR)

$k - Form subheading (R)

$l - Language of a work (NR)

$m - Medium of performance for music (R)

$n - Number of part/section of a work (R)

$o - Arranged statement for music (NR)

$p - Name of part/section of a work (R)

$r - Key for music (NR)

$s - Version (NR)

$t - Title of a work (NR)

$x - International Standard Serial Number (NR)

$3 - Materials specified (NR)

$5 - Institution to which field applies (NR)

$6 - Linkage (NR)

$8 - Field link and sequence number (R)

Examples:

730 0#$a60 minutes (Television program)

730 02$aBonn Convention $d(1952). $f1980.

730 0#$aEconomics library selections. $nSeries I, $pNew books in economics.

730 02$aGod save the king; $oarr. $f1982.

730 0#$aBible. $pN.T. $pLuke. $lGreek. $sCodex Sinaiticus.

730 0#$aGone with the wind (Motion picture)

730 0#$aPeople speak (Radio program)

730 02$aAutomatic heat and air conditioning.

730 02$aTarski's world. $f1993

740 - ADDED ENTRY—UNCONTROLLED RELATED/ ANALYTICAL TITLE (R)

Indicators

First - Nonfiling characters

0-9 - Number of nonfiling characters

- Nonfiling characters not specified [OBSOLETE]

Second - Type of added entry

- No information provided

0 - Alternative entry (BK AM CF MP MU) [OBSOLETE]

1 - Secondary entry (BK AM CF MP MU) [OBSOLETE]

1 - Printed on card (VM) [OBSOLETE]

2 - Analytical entry

3 - Not printed on card (VM) [OBSOLETE]

Subfield Codes

$a - Uncontrolled related/analytical title (NR)

$h - Medium (NR)

$n - Number of part/section of a work (R)

$p - Name of part/section of a work (R)

$5 - Institution to which field applies (NR)

$6 - Linkage (NR)

$8 - Field link and sequence number (R)

An added entry in which the entry element is a title that is different from the title proper portion (subfields $a, $n, and $p) of field 245 (Title Statement) but that is not the uniform title for the item.

752 - ADDED ENTRY—HIERARCHICAL PLACE NAME (R)

Indicators

First - Undefined

- Undefined

Second - Undefined

- Undefined

Subfield Codes

$a - Country (NR)

$b - State, province, territory (NR)

$c - County, region, islands area (NR)

$d - City (NR)

$6 - Linkage (NR)

$8 - Field link and sequence number (R)

753 - SYSTEM DETAILS ACCESS TO COMPUTER FILES (R)

Information on the technical aspects of a computer file and any accompanying material that may be used to select and arrange the record with other records in a printed index.

Indicators

First - Undefined

- Undefined

Second - Undefined

- Undefined

Subfield Codes

$a - Make and model of machine (NR)

$b - Programming language (NR)

$c - Operating system (NR)

$6 - Linkage (NR)

$8 - Field link and sequence number (R)

Examples:

753 ##$aIBM PC $bPascal $cDOS 1.1

753 ##$aCompaq $bBasic $cDOS 3.2

753 ##$aApple II $cDOS 3.3

754 - ADDED ENTRY—TAXONOMIC IDENTIFICATION (R)

An added entry in which the entry element is the taxonomic name or category associated with the described item.

Indicators

First - Undefined

- Undefined

Second - Undefined

- Undefined

Subfield Codes

$a - Taxonomic name (R)

$c - Taxonomic category (R)

$d - Common or alternative name (R)

$x - Non-public note (R)

$z - Public note (R)

$2 - Source of taxonomic identification (NR)

$6 - Linkage (NR)

$8 - Field link and sequence number (R)

Example:

754 ##$aPlantae (Kingdom) $aSpermatophyta (Phylum) $aAngiospermae (Class) $aDicotyledoneae (Subclass) $aRosales (Order) $aRosaceae (Family) $aRosa (Genus) $asetigera (Species) $atomentosa (Variety). $2[code for Lyman David Benson's Plant Classification]

755 - ADDED ENTRY—PHYSICAL CHARACTERISTICS (R) [OBSOLETE]

Indicators

First - Undefined

- Undefined

Second - Undefined

- Undefined

Subfield Codes

$a - Access term (NR)

$x - General subdivision (R)

$y - Chronological subdivision (R)

$z - Geographic subdivision (R)

$2 - Source of term (NR)

$3 - Materials specified (NR)

$6 - Linkage (NR)

$8 - Field link and sequence number (R)

—Linking Entry Fields (76X-78X)—

Fields 760-787 contain information that identifies other bibliographic items. Each of the linking entry fields specifies a different relationship between the target item described by the record and a related item. These relationships fall into three categories: 1) related items that assist the user in continuing to search but are not physically required to obtain the target item (e.g., former entries for serials, translations of the target item); 2) related items that have to be obtained physically in order to use the target item (e.g., the host item for a component part: a journal issue containing a specific article); 3) related items that are constituent units of a larger whole (e.g., the individual photographs contained in a visual material collection). The linking entry fields are designed to generate a note in the record in they appear. They can also provide machine linkage between the bibliographic record for the target item and the bibliographic record for the related item, if the related item is covered by a separate record.

Definitions of Terms Used in the Linking Entry Field

Record Links and Notes—General Information

760 - Main Series Entry (R)

762 - Subseries Entry (R)

765 - Original Language Entry (R)

767 - Translation Entry (R)

770 - Supplement/Special Issue Entry (R)

772 - Supplement Parent Record Entry (R)

773 - Host Item Entry (R)

774 - Constituent Unit Entry (R)

775 - Other Edition Entry (R)

776 - Additional Physical Form Entry (R)

777 - Issued with Entry (R)

780 - Preceding Entry (R)

785 - Succeeding Entry (R)

786 - Data Source Entry (R)

787 - Nonspecific Relationship Entry (R)

Definitions of Terms Used in the Linking Entry Field

Target Item

A bibliographic item that is the principal or primary unit for the description of which the record was constructed. The target item is the item to which the data in Leader/06 (Type of record) and /07 (Bibliographic level) apply.

Related Item

A bibliographic item that has either a chronological, horizontal, or vertical relationship with a target item, and for which the linking entry field is formulated.

Component Part

A bibliographic item that is physically part of another bibliographic item such that the retrieval of the part is dependent on the physical identification and location of the host item (e.g., a chapter in a book, an article in a journal).

Constituent Unit

A bibliographic item that is part of another item. The constituent unit is physically separate from the item of which it is consider a part.

Host Item

A bibliographic item that either physically contains (as in the case of the component part), or bibliographically includes, (as in the case of a constituent unit), the subpart that is the target item for the record. For example: if a record describes a journal article, the host is the journal; if a record describes one digital item in a set, the host is the set.

Chronological Relationship

The relationship in time between bibliographic items (e.g., the relation of a serial to its predecessors and successors).

Horizontal Relationship

The relationship between versions of a bibliographic item in different languages, format, media, etc.

Vertical Relationship

The hierarchical relationship of the whole to its parts and the parts to the whole (e.g., a journal article to the journal, subseries to main entry series).

RECORD LINKS AND NOTES—GENERAL INFORMATION

The record-linking technique in MARC is described below.

Linking Entry Fields (fields 760-787)

These fields carry descriptive data concerning the related item, the control number for the record of the related item, or both. Minimal content designation is provided for the data concerning the related item that is used in the linking entry fields. For data operations requiring fuller content designation, such as indexing and sorting, subfield $w (the record control number for the related item) allows the system to follow that link to the related record to obtain fully content-designated data. Moreover, the coded data in control subfield $7 allows some types of indexing without reference to the actual related record. The value used in the first indicator position of a linking entry field determines whether a note is to be generated from the field.

Linking Entry Complexity Note (field 580)

The Linking Entry Fields are designed to support generation of a note concerning the related item in a display of the record for the target item. When the relationship is too complex to be expressed using a display constant and the data from the linking entry field or the linked record, the note is recorded in the Linking Entry Complexity Note field. When used, this field appears in addition to any relevant 760-787 linking entry field, and no note is generated from the linking entry field.

Linked-Record Requirement (Leader/19)

This data element indicates whether sufficient information is present in the linking entry field to support generation of an eye-readable note that identifies the related item or whether only a related record number is recorded. If only a record number appears, the system will need to obtain the appropriate information from the related record to construct a standard display.

The following subfields or subfield combinations are considered sufficient for display purposes:

Subfield $a + $t (Main entry heading + Title)

Subfield $a + $s (Main entry heading + Uniform title)

Subfield $a (Main entry heading

Subfield $t (Title)

Subfield $s (Uniform title)

Subfield $u (Standard Technical Report Number)

Subfield $r (Report number)

Added Entries (fields 700-730)

When an added entry is needed for a title used in a linking field, the added entry is recorded in the appropriate 700-730 field. Linking fields are not intended take the place of added entries. Likewise, an added entry in field 700-730 does not take the place of a linking field, as it cannot cause a note to be generated or carry a record link.

Component Parts

The linking entry field 773 (Host Item Entry) is used to link a target item that is an integral part of another item to the record for the other item. For example, in records for journal articles it contains the identification of the journal. In subfield $g of field 773, the exact location of the article in the journal is recorded.

760 - MAIN SERIES ENTRY (R)

Information concerning the related main series when the target item is a subseries (vertical elationship). When a note is generated from this field, the introductory phrase Main series: or Subseries of: may be generated based on the field tag.

Indicators

First - Note controller

0 - Display note

1 - Do not display note

Second - Display constant controller

- Main series

8 - No display constant generated

Subfield Codes

$a - Main entry heading (NR)

$b - Edition (NR)

$c - Qualifying information (NR)

$d - Place, publisher, and date of publication (NR)

$g - Relationship information (R)

$h - Physical description (NR)

$i - Display text (NR)

$m - Material-specific details (NR)

$n - Note (R)

$o - Other item identifier (R)

$q - Parallel title (NR) (BK SE) [OBSOLETE]

$s - Uniform title (NR)

$t - Title (NR)

$w - Record control number (R)

$x - International Standard Serial Number (NR)

$y - CODEN designation (NR)

$6 - Linkage (NR)

$7 - Control subfield (NR)

0 - Type of main entry heading

1 - Form of name

2 - Type of record

- Bibliographic level

$8 - Field link and sequence number (R)

Example

760 0#$7c1as $aUnited States. Geological Survey $tWater supply papers

762 - SUBSERIES ENTRY (R)

Information concerning a related subseries when the target item is a main series or a parent subseries (vertical relationship) When a note is generated from this field, the introductory phrase Has subseries: may be generated based on the field tag.

Indicators

First - Note controller

0 - Display note

1 - Do not display note

Second - Display constant controller

- Has subseries

8 - No display constant generated

Subfield Codes

$a - Main entry heading (NR)

$b - Edition (NR)

$c - Qualifying information (NR)

$d - Place, publisher, and date of publication (NR)

$g - Relationship information (R)

$h - Physical description (NR)

$i - Display text (NR)

$m - Material-specific details (NR)

$n - Note (R)

$o - Other item identifier (R)

$q - Parallel title (NR) (BK SE) [OBSOLETE]

$s - Uniform title (NR)

$t - Title (NR)

$w - Record control number (R)

$x - International Standard Serial Number (NR)

$y - CODEN designation (NR)

$6 - Linkage (NR)

$7 - Control subfield (NR)

0 - Type of main entry heading

1 - Form of name

2 - Type of record

3 - Bibliographic level

$8 - Field link and sequence number (R)

Examples:

762 0#$tQuality of surface waters of the United States

762 0#$tEvaporation control research

765 - ORIGINAL LANGUAGE ENTRY (R)

Information concerning the publication in its original language when the target item is a translation (horizontal relationship). When a note is generated from this field, the introductory phrase Translation of: may be generated based on the field tag.

Indicators

First - Note controller

0 - Display note

1 - Do not display note

Second - Display constant controller

- Translation of

8 - No display constant generated

Subfield Codes

$a - Main entry heading (NR)

$b - Edition (NR)

$c - Qualifying information (NR)

$d - Place, publisher, and date of publication (NR)

$g - Relationship information (R)

$h - Physical description (NR)
$i - Display text (NR)
$k - Series data for related item (R)
$m - Material-specific details (NR)
$n - Note (R)
$o - Other item identifier (R)
$q - Parallel title (NR) (BK SE) [OBSOLETE]
$r - Report number (R)
$s - Uniform title (NR)
$t - Title (NR)
$u - Standard Technical Report Number (NR)
$w - Record control number (R)
$x - International Standard Serial Number (NR)
$y - CODEN designation (NR)
$z - International Standard Book Number (R)
$6 - Linkage (NR)
$7 - Control subfield (NR)
0 - Type of main entry heading
1 - Form of name
2 - Type of record
3 - Bibliographic level
$8 - Field link and sequence number (R)

Examples:

765 0#$tAstrofizicheskie issledovaniia $w(DLC)###78648457 $w(OCoLC)4798581

765 1#$tMashinovedenie $w(DLC)###90646274 $w(OCoLC)6258868

767 - TRANSLATION ENTRY (R)

Information concerning the publication in some other language other than the original when the target item is in the original language or is another translation (horizontal relationship). When a note is generated from this field, the introductory phrase Translated as: may be generated based on the field tag.

Indicators

First - Note controller

0 - Display note

1 - Do not display note

Second - Display constant controller

- Translated as

8 - No display constant generated

Subfield Codes

$a - Main entry heading (NR)

$b - Edition (NR)

$c - Qualifying information (NR)

$d - Place, publisher, and date of publication (NR)

$g - Relationship information (R)

$h - Physical description (NR)

$i - Display text (NR)

$k - Series data for related item (R)

$m - Material-specific details (NR)

$n - Note (R)

$o - Other item identifier (R)

$q - Parallel title (NR) (BK SE) [OBSOLETE]

$r - Report number (R)

$s - Uniform title (NR)

$t - Title (NR)

$u - Standard Technical Report Number (NR)

$w - Record control number (R)

$x - International Standard Serial Number (NR)

$y - CODEN designation (NR)

$z - International Standard Book Number (R)

$6 - Linkage (NR)

$7 - Control subfield (NR)

0 - Type of main entry heading

1 - Form of name

2 - Type of record

3 - Bibliographic level

$8 - Field link and sequence number (R)

Examples:

767 0#$aAstrofizicheskie issledovaniia. English. $tBulletin of the Special Astrophysical Observatory North Caucasus $x0190-2709 $w(DLC)86649325 $w(OCoLC)4698159

767 1#$tFinance & development. Arabic. Tamwil wa-al-tanmiyah $x0250-7455

767 1#$tFinance & development. French. Finances et developpement $x0430-473X

767 1#$tFinance & development. German. Finanzierung & Entwicklung $x0250- 7439

767 1#$tFinance & development. Spanish. Finanzas y desarrollo $x0250-7447

767 1#$tFinance & development. Portuguese. Financas & desenvolvimento $x0250- 7404

770 - SUPPLEMENT/SPECIAL ISSUE ENTRY (R)

IndicatorsInformation concerning the supplement or special issue associated with the target item but cataloged and/or input as a separate record (vertical relationship). When a note is generated from this field, the introductory phrase Has supplement: may be generated based on the field tag.

First - Note controller

0 - Display note

1 - Do not display note

Second - Display constant controller

- Has supplement

8 - No display constant generated

Subfield Codes

$a - Main entry heading (NR)

$b - Edition (NR)

$c - Qualifying information (NR)

$d - Place, publisher, and date of publication (NR)

$g - Relationship information (R)

$h - Physical description (NR)

$i - Display text (NR)

$k - Series data for related item (R)

$m - Material-specific details (NR)

$n - Note (R)

$o - Other item identifier (R)

$q - Parallel title (NR) (BK SE) [OBSOLETE]

$r - Report number (R)

$s - Uniform title (NR)

$t - Title (NR)

$u - Standard Technical Report Number (NR)

$w - Record control number (R)

$x - International Standard Serial Number (NR)

$y - CODEN designation (NR)

$z - International Standard Book Number (R)

$6 - Linkage (NR)

$7 - Control subfield (NR)

0 - Type of main entry heading

1 - Form of name

2 - Type of record

3 - Bibliographic level

$8 - Field link and sequence number (R)

Examples:

770 0#$tDirectory: United States, territories, and Canada $w(DLC)###78646712 $w(OCoLC)4579783

770 0#$tJournal of cellular biochemistry. Supplement $x0733-1959

772 - SUPPLEMENT PARENT ENTRY (R)

Information concerning the related parent record when the target item is a single issue, supplement or special issue (vertical relationship) of the parent item. When a note is generated from this field, the introductory phrase Supplement to: may be generated based on the field tag

Indicators

First - Note controller

0 - Display note

1 - Do not display note

Second - Display constant controller

- Supplement to

0 - Parent

8 - No display constant generated

Subfield Codes

$a - Main entry heading (NR)

$b - Edition (NR)

$c - Qualifying information (NR)

$d - Place, publisher, and date of publication (NR)

$g - Relationship information (R)

$h - Physical description (NR)

$i - Display text (NR)

$k - Series data for related item (R)

$m - Material-specific details (NR)

$n - Note (R)

$o - Other item identifier (R)

$q - Parallel title (NR) (BK SE) [OBSOLETE]

$r - Report number (R)

$s - Uniform title (NR)

$t - Title (NR)

$u - Standard Technical Report Number (NR)

$w - Record control number (R)

$x - International Standard Serial Number (NR)

$y - CODEN designation (NR)

$z - International Stan dard Book Number (R)

$6 - Linkage (NR)

$7 - Control subfield (NR)

0 - Type of main entry heading

1 - Form of name

2 - Type of record

3 - Bibliographic level

$8 - Field link and sequence number (R)

Examples:

772 0#$aWorld agricultural situation (Washington, D.C. : 1970) $x0084-1358 $w(DLC)sf#81008035

772 1#$tStatistiques pour l'economie normande $g1979- $w(OCoLC)6260766

772 1#$tAval $g[1982-]

772 1#$7unas $aPost boy (London, England) $w(OCoLC)1234567

772 1#$7plas $aSilence, Timothy. $tFoundling hospital for wit. $w(DLC)###85014367

773 - HOST ITEM ENTRY (R)

Information concerning the host item for the component part/ subunit (Leader/07, Bibliographic level, code a, b, or d) that is described in the record (vertical relationship). When a note is generated from this field, the introductory term In may be generated based on the field tag.

Indicators

First - Note controller

0 - Display note

1 - Do not display note

Second - Display constant controller

- In

8 - No display constant generated

Subfield Codes

$a - Main entry heading (NR)

$b - Edition (NR)

$d - Place, publisher, and date of publication (NR)

$g - Relationship information (R)

$h - Physical description (NR)

$i - Display text (NR)

$k - Series data for related item (R)

$m - Material-specific details (NR)

$n - Note (R)

$o - Other item identifier (R)

$p - Abbreviated title (NR)

$r - Report number (R)

$s - Uniform title (NR)

$t - Title (NR)

$u - Standard Technical Report Number (NR)

$w - Record control number (R)

$x - International Standard Serial Number (NR)

$y - CODEN designation (NR)

$z - International Standard Book Number (R)

$3 - Materials specified (NR)

$6 - Linkage (NR)

$7 - Control subfield (NR)

0 - Type of main entry heading

1 - Form of name

2 - Type of record

3 - Bibliographic level

$8 - Field link and sequence number (R)

Examples

773 0#$tHorizon $gVol. 17, no. 98 (Feb 1948). p. 78-159

773 0#$gVol. 2, no. 2 (Feb. 1976), p. 195-230 $w(DLC)###75001234#

773 0#$tNetworks for networkers : critical issues in cooperative library development $w(DLC)###79024054# $w(Uk)8040016

773 0#$7p1am $aDesio. Ardito, 1897- $tGeographical features of the Karakorum. $dMilano : ISMEO, 1991

773 0#$7p1am $aHamilton. Milton W. (Milton Wheaton), 1901- $tSir William Johnson and the Indians of New York. $d[Albany] : University of the State of New York, State Education Dept., Office of State History, 1967 $w(DLC)###68066801#

773 0#$tGilbert H. Grosvenor Collection of Photographs of the Alexander Graham Bell family

773 0#$tEntomologists' monthly magazine $pENTOMOL MON MAG $dWallingford : Gem Publishing Company $x0013-8908 $yFNMMA

773 0#$7c2bc $aMassachusetts. Commission on Consumer Affairs $tRecords $w(MaRG)170

774 - CONSTITUENT UNIT ENTRY (R)

Information concerning a constituent unit associated with a larger bibliographic unit. When a note is generated from this field. the introductory term Constituent unit: may be generated based on the field tag.

Indicators

First - Note controller

0 - Display note

1 - Do not display note

Second - Display constant controller

- Constituent unit

8 - No display constant generated

Subfield Codes

$a - Main entry heading (NR)

$b - Edition (NR)

$c - Qualifying information (NR)

$d - Place, publisher, and date of publication (NR)

$g - Relationship information (R)

$h - Physical description (NR)

$i - Display text (NR)

$k - Series data for related item (R)

$m - Material-specific details (NR)

$n - Note (R)

$o - Other item identifier (R)

$r - Report number (R)

$s - Uniform title (NR)

$t - Title (NR)

$u - Standard Technical Report Number (NR)

$w - Record control number (R)

$x - International Standard Serial Number (NR)

$y - CODEN designation (NR)

$z - International Standard Book Number (R)

$6 - Linkage (NR)

$7 - Control subfield (NR)

0 - Type of main entry heading

1 - Form of name

2 - Type of record

3 - Bibliographic level

$8 - Field link and sequence number (R)

Examples:

774 00$81\c $oNYDA.1993.010.00130. $n[DIAPimage] $tMap of area with highlighted street

774 00$82\c $oNYDA.1993.010.00131. $n[DIAPimage] $tView of Mill Brook Houses from one of the houses $d89/05

774 00$83\c $oNYDA 1993.010.00132. $n[DIAPimage] $tView SE from Mill Brook Houses on rooftop on Cypress Ave. Between 136th St. and 137th St., $d93/05

774 00$84\c $oNYDA.1993.010.00133. $n[DIAPimage] $tView N from 136th St. roof top area between Bruckner Expressway and Cypress Ave., $d93/06

774 00$85\c $oNYDA.1993.010.00134. $n[DIAPimage] $tView E from rooftop of garden bounded by Bruckner Expressway, 136th St. and 135th St. $d93/06

775 - OTHER EDITION ENTRY (R)

The entry for another available edition of the target item (horizontal relationship). When a note is generated from this field, the introductory phrase Other editions available: may be generated based on the field tag.

Indicators

First - Note controller

0 - Display note

1 - Do not display note

Second - Display constant controller

- Other edition available

8 - No display constant generated

Second - Edition entry same as main entry or title (SE) [OBSOLETE]

0 - Entry not the same

1 - Entry is the same as title

2 - Entry is the same as main entry and title

Subfield Codes

$a - Main entry heading (NR)

$b - Edition (NR)

$c - Qualifying information (NR)

$d - Place, publisher, and date of publication (NR)

$e - Language code (NR)

$f - Country code (NR)

$g - Relationship information (R)

$h - Physical description (NR)

$i - Display text (NR)

$k - Series data for related item (R)

$m - Material-specific details (NR)

$n - Note (R)

$o - Other item identifier (R)

$q - Parallel title (NR) (BK SE) [OBSOLETE]

$r - Report number (R)

$s - Uniform title (NR)

$t - Title (NR)

$u - Standard Technical Report Number (NR)

$w - Record control number (R)

$x - International Standard Serial Number (NR)

$y - CODEN designation (NR)

$z - International Standard Book Number (R)

$6 - Linkage (NR)

$7 - Control subfield (NR)

0 - Type of main entry heading

1 - Form of name

2 - Type of record

3 - Bibliographic level

$8 - Field link and sequence number (R)

Examples:

775 1#$tCuba economic news $x0590-2932 $eeng $w(OCoLC)2259984

775 1#$tModern maturity $x0026-8046 $w(DLC)###63047860 $w(OCoLC)1758471

775 1#$tCommunist $filu

775 1#$tModern maturity $bNRTA edition

775 1#$aHospital practice (Office ed.) $x8750-2836

776 - ADDITIONAL PHYSICAL FORM ENTRY (R)

Information concerning another available physical form of the target item (horizontal relationship). When a note is generated from this field, the introductory phrase Available in other form: may be generated based on the field tag.

Indicators

First - Note controller

0 - Display note

1 - Do not display note

Second - Display constant controller

- Available in another form

8 - No display constant generated

Subfield Codes

$a - Main entry heading (NR)

$b - Edition (NR)

$c - Qualifying information (NR)

$d - Place, publisher, and date of publication (NR)

$g - Relationship information (R)

$h - Physical description (NR)

$i - Display text (NR)

$k - Series data for related item (R)

$m - Material-specific details (NR)

$n - Note (R)

$o - Other item identifier (R)

$q - Parallel title (NR) (BK SE) [OBSOLETE]

$r - Report number (R)

$s - Uniform title (NR)

$t - Title (NR)

$u - Standard Technical Report Number (NR)

$w - Record control number (R)

$x - International Standard Serial Number (NR)

$y - CODEN designation (NR)

$z - International Standard Book Number (R)

$6 - Linkage (NR)

$7 - Control subfield (NR)

0 - Type of main entry heading

1 - Form of name

2 - Type of record

3 - Bibliographic level

$8 - Field link and sequence number (R)

Examples:

776 1#$tCollege English $x0010-0994 $w(DLC)sc#84007753 $w(OCoLC)3546316

776 1#$tCollege English $x0010-0994 $w(DLC)###41006180 $w(OCoLC)1564053

776 1#$tAmericas $x0003-1615 $w(OCoLC)8370205

776 1#$cOriginal $w(DLC)###24020326

777 - ISSUED WITH ENTRY (R)

Information concerning the publication that is separately cataloged but that is issued with or included in the target item (horizontal relationship). When a note is generated from this field, the introductory phrase Issued with: may be generated based on the field tag.

Indicators

First - Note controller

0 - Display note

1 - Do not display note

Second - Display constant controller

- Issued with

8 - No display constant generated

Subfield Codes

$a - Main entry heading (NR)

$b - Edition (NR)

$c - Qualifying information (NR)

$d - Place, publisher, and date of publication (NR)

$g - Relationship information (R)

$h - Physical description (NR)

$i - Display text (NR)

$k - Series data for related item (R)

$m - Material-specific details (NR)

$n - Note (R)

$o - Other item identifier (R)

$q - Parallel title (NR) (BK SE) [OBSOLETE]

$s - Uniform title (NR)

$t - Title (NR)

$w - Record control number (R)

$x - International Standard Serial Number (NR)

$y - CODEN designation (NR)

$6 - Linkage (NR)

$7 - Control subfield (NR)

0 - Type of main entry heading

1 - Form of name

2 - Type of record

3 - Bibliographic level

$8 - Field link and sequence number (R)

Examples:

777 1#$tMythprint $x0146- 9347

777 1#$tCurrent drug handbook $g1962- $x0070-1939 $w(DLC)###58006390 $w(OCoLC)1565622

777 1#$tDrug, the nurse, the patient $w(DLC)###66015620 $w(OCoLC)3995456

780 - PRECEDING ENTRY (R)

Information concerning the immediate predecessor of the target item (chronological relationship). When a note is generated from this field, the introductory term or phrase may be generated based on the value in the second indicator position.

Indicators

First - Note controller

0 - Display note

1 - Do not display note

Second - Type of relationship

0 - Continues

1 - Continues in part

2 - Supersedes

3 - Supersedes in part

4 - Formed by the union of ... and ...

5 - Absorbed

6 - Absorbed in part

7 - Separated from

Subfield Codes

$a - Main entry heading (NR)

$b - Edition (NR)

$c - Qualifying information (NR)

$d - Place, publisher, and date of publication (NR)

$g - Relationship information (R)

$h - Physical description (NR)

$i - Display text (NR)

$k - Series data for related item (R)

$m - Material-specific details (NR)

$n - Note (R)

$o - Other item identifier (R)

$q - Parallel title (NR) (BK SE) [OBSOLETE]

$r - Report number (R)

$s - Uniform title (NR)

$t - Title (NR)

$u - Standard Technical Report Number (NR)

$w - Record control number (R)

$x - International Standard Serial Number (NR)

$y - CODEN designation (NR)

$z - International Standard Book Number (R)

$6 - Linkage (NR)

$7 - Control subfield (NR)

0 - Type of main entry heading

1 - Form of name

2 - Type of record

3 - Bibliographic level

$8 - Field link and sequence number (R)

Examples:

780 00$aAmerican Hospital Association. $tBulletin of the American Hospital Association $w(OCoLC)1777831

780 01$tAnnales scientifiques de l'Universite de Besancon $w(OCoLC)6179013

780 03$tElevage

780 14$tAnnales de geophysique $x0003-4029 $w(OCoLC)1481255 $w(DLC)###52016346

780 14$tAnnali de geofisica $w(OCoLC)1847060 $w(DLC)gs#49000041

780 05$aAmerican Society of International Law. $tProceedings $g1971

780 06$tGraphic notices and supplemental data $w(OCoLC)4276671

780 07$aBritish Columbia. Ministry of Provincial Secretary and Government Services. $tAnnual report $x0226-0883 $w(OCoLC)6270433 $w(DLC)###80649039

785 - SUCCEEDING ENTRY (R)

Information concerning the immediate successor to the target item (chronological relationship). When a note is generated from this field, the introductory phrase may be generated based on the value in the second indicator position.

Indicators

First - Note controller

0 - Display note

1 - Do not display note

Second - Type of relationship

0 - Continued by

1 - Continued in part by

2 - Superseded by

3 - Superseded in part by

4 - Absorbed by

5 - Absorbed in part by

6 - Split into ... and ...

7 - Merged with ... to form ...

8 - Changed back to

Subfield Codes

$a - Main entry heading (NR)

$b - Edition (NR)

$c - Qualifying information (NR)

$d - Place, publisher, and date of publication (NR)

$g - Relationship information (R)

$h - Physical description (NR)

$i - Display text (NR)

$k - Series data for related item (R)

$m - Material-specific details (NR)

$n - Note (R)

$o - Other item identifier (R)

$q - Parallel title (NR) (BK SE) [OBSOLETE]

$r - Report number (R)

$s - Uniform title (NR)

$t - Title (NR)

$u - Standa rd Technical Report Number (NR)

$w - Record control number (R)

$x - International Standard Serial Number (NR)

$y - CODEN designation (NR)

$z - International Standard Book Number (R)

$6 - Linkage (NR)

$7 - Control subfield (NR)

0 - Type of main entry heading

1 - Form of name

2 - Type of record

3 - Bibliographic level

$8 - Field link and sequence number (R)

Examples:

785 00$tTEIC quarterly seismological bulletin $x0741-1898 $w(OCoLC)8978559 $w(DLC)sc#83007721

785 10$tLearning in New York (University of the State of New York) $g1983 $w(OCoLC)10120612

785 01$aSoutheastern College Art Conference. $tSECAC newsletter $w(OCoL- C)4973820

785 02$tBritish Columbia medical journal. $x0007-0556

785 04$tBusiness week $gOct. 1940 $x0007-7135 $w(DLC)###31006225 $w(OCoLC)1537921

785 05$tSheet metal worker $x0096-9249 $w(OCoLC)2054610

785 16$aHospital practice (Hospital ed.) $x8755-4542 $w(DLC)sn#84001694

785 16$aHospital practice (Office ed.) $x8750-2836 $w(OCoLC)10716242

785 17$tServices correctionnels au Canada. $x0711-6810

785 17$tAdult correctional services in Canada. $x0715-2973

785 08$aLos Angeles (Calif.). Dept. of City Planning. $tAnnual report of the Department of City Planning (1966) $w(DLC)sn#86032686

786 - DATA SOURCE ENTRY (R)

Information pertaining to a data source to which the described item is related. It may contain information about other files, printed sources, or collection procedures.

Indicators

First - Note controller

0 - Display note

1 - Do not display note

Second - Display constant controller

- Data source

8 - No display constant generated

Subfield Codes

$a - Main entry heading (NR)

$b - Edition (NR)

$c - Qualifying information (NR)

$d - Place, publisher, and date of publication (NR)

$g - Relationship information (R)

$h - Physical description (NR)

$i - Display text (NR)

$j - Period of content (NR)

$k - Series data for related item (R)

$m - Material-specific details (NR)

$n - Note (R)

$o - Other item identifier (R)

$p - Abbreviated title (NR)

$r - Report number (R)

$s - Uniform title (NR)

$t - Title (NR)

$u - Standard Technical Report Number (NR)

$v - Source Contribution (NR)

$w - Record control number (R)

$x - International Standard Serial Number (NR)

$y - CODEN designation (NR)

$z - International Standard Book Number (R)

$6 - Linkage (NR)

$7 - Control subfield (NR)

0 - Type of main entry heading

1 - Form of name

2 - Type of record

3 - Bibliographic level

$8 - Field link and sequence number (R)

Examples:

786 0#$aUnited States. Defense Mapping Agency. $tReno, NV-CA west digital terrain elevation data $vData for reformatting to DEM format

787 - NONSPECIFIC RELATIONSHIP ENTRY (R)

Information concerning the work related to the target item when the relationship does not fit any of those defined in fields 760-785.

Indicators

First - Note controller

0 - Display note

1 - Do not display note

Second - Display constant controller

- Related item

8 - No display constant generated

Subfield Codes

$a - Main entry heading (NR)

$b - Edition (NR)

$c - Qualifying information (NR)

$d - Place, publisher, and date of publication (NR)

$g - Relationship information (R)

$h - Physical description (NR)

$i - Display text (NR)

$k - Series data for related item (R)

$m - Material-specific details (NR)

$n - Note (R)

$o - Other item identifier (R)

$r - Report number (R)

$s - Uniform title (NR)

$t - Title (NR)

$u - Standard Technical Report Number (NR)

$w - Record control number (R)

$x - International Standard Serial Number (NR)

$y - CODEN designation (NR)

$z - International Standard Book Number (R)

$6 - Linkage (NR)

$7 - Control subfield (NR)

0 - Type of main entry heading

1 - Form of name

2 - Type of record

3 - Bibliographic level

$8 - Field link and sequence number (R)

Examples:

787 1#$aEmpire State report (1982) $x0747-0711 $w(DLC)###84647292 $w(OCoLC)8541622

787 1#$tEmpire State report weekly $x0745-8622 $w(DLC)###84647299 $w(OCoLC)9403759

—Series Added Entry Fields (80X-830)—

Fields 800-840 contain a name/title or a title used as a series added entry when the series statement is contained in field 490 (Series Statement) or field 500 (General Note) and a series added entry is required for the bibliographic record. No 8XX series added entry field is used in conjunction with a series statement in the 400-440 fields because each of these fields functions both as part of the bibliographic description and as a series added entry.

The roman numeral and the word Series: that precede a series added entry field in some displays are not carried in the MARC record. They may be generated based on the field tag.

800 - Series Added Entry—Personal Name (R)

810 - Series Added Entry—Corporate Name (R)

811 - Series Added Entry—Meeting Name (R)

830 - Series Added Entry—Uniform Title (R)

800 - SERIES ADDED ENTRY—PERSONAL NAME (R)

IndicatorsAn author/title series added entry in which the author portion is a personal name.

First - Type of personal name entry element

0 - Forename

1 - Surname

3 - Family name

Second - Undefined

- Undefined

Subfield Codes

$a - Personal name (NR)

$b - Numeration (NR)

$c - Titles and other words associated with a name (R)

$d - Dates associated with a name (NR)

$e - Relator term (R)

$f - Date of a work (NR)

$g - Miscellaneous information (NR)

$h - Medium (NR)

$j - Attribution qualifier (R)

$k - Form subheading (R)

$l - Language of a work (NR)

$m - Medium of performance for music (R)

$n - Number of part/section of a work (R)

$o - Arranged statement for music (NR)

$p - Name of part/section of a work (R)

$q - Fuller form of name (NR)

$r - Key for music (NR)

$s - Version (NR)

$t - Title of a work (NR)

$u - Affiliation (NR)

$v - Volume/sequential designation (NR)

$4 - Relator code (R)

$6 - Linkage (NR)

$8 - Field link and sequence number (R)

Examples:

800 1#$aBerenholtz, Jim, $d1957- $tTeachings of the feathered serpent ; $vbk. 1

800 1#$aPoe, Edgar Allan, $d1809-1849. $tWorks. $lGerman. $f1922. $sRosl ; $v1. Bd.

800 1#$aJoyce, James, $d1882- 1941. $tJames Joyce archive.

800 1#$aDarnell, Jack. $tEdible wild plants of the planet earth.

800 1#$aArmstrong, Louis, $d1900-1971. $4prf $tLouie Armstrong (Universal City Studios) ; $v6.

810 - SERIES ADDED ENTRY—CORPORATE NAME (R)

An author/title series added entry in which the author portion is a corporate name.

Indicators

First - Type of corporate name entry element

0 - Inverted name

1 - Jurisdiction name

2 - Name in direct order

Second - Undefined

- Undefined

Subfield Codes

$a - Corporate name or jurisdiction name as entry element (NR)

$b - Subordinate unit (R)

$c - Location of meeting (NR)

$d - Date of meeting or treaty signing (R)

$e - Relator term (R)

$f - Date of a work (NR)

$g - Miscellaneous information (NR)

$h - Medium (NR)

$k - Form subheading (R)

$l - Language of a work (NR)

$m - Medium of performance for music (R)

$n - Number of part/section/meeting (R)

$o - Arranged statement for music (NR)

$p - Name of part/section of a work (R)

$r - Key for music (NR)

$s - Version (NR)

$t - Title of a work (NR)

$u - Affiliation (NR)

$v - Volume/sequential designation (NR)

$4 - Relator code (R)

$6 - Linkage (NR)

$8 - Field link and sequence number (R)

Examples:

810 2#$aJohn Bartholomew and Son. $tBartholomew world travel series ; $v10.

810 2#$aCentral Institute of Indian Languages. $tCIIL linguistic atlas series ; $v1.

810 2#$aEuropean Court of Human Rights. $tPublications de la Cour europeenne des droits de l'homme. $nSerie A, $pArrets et decisions ; $vvol. 48.

810 1#$aUnited States. $bArmy Map Service. $tA.M.S., $vZ201.

811 - SERIES ADDED ENTRY—MEETING NAME (R)

An author/title series added entry in which the author portion is a meeting name.

Indicators

First - Type of meeting name entry element

0 - Inverted name

1 - Jurisdiction name

2 - Name in direct order

Second - Undefined

- Undefined

Subfield Codes

$a - Meeting name or jurisdiction name as entry element (NR)

$c - Location of meeting (NR)

$d - Date of meeting (NR)

$e - Subordinate unit (R)

$f - Date of a work (NR)

$g - Miscellaneous information (NR)

$h - Medium (NR)

$k - Form subheading (R)

$l - Language of a work (NR)

$n - Number of part/section/meeting (R)

$p - Name of part/section of a work (R)

$q - Name of meeting following jurisdiction name entry element (NR)

$s - Version (NR)

$t - Title of a work (NR)

$u - Affiliation (NR)

$v - Volume/sequential designation (NR)

$4 - Relator code (R)

$6 - Linkage (NR)

$8 - Field link and sequence number (R)

Examples:

811 2#$aInternational Congress of Romance Linguistics and Philology $n(17th : $d1983 : $cAix-en-Provence, France). $tActes du XVIIeme Congres international de linguistique et philologie romanes ; $vvol. no. 5.

811 2#$aInternational Congress of Nutrition $n(11th : $d1978 : $cRio de Janeiro, Brazil). $tNutrition and food science ; $vv. 1.

811 2#$aDelaware Symposium on Language Studies. $tDelaware symposia on language studies ; $v4.

830 - SERIES ADDED ENTRY—UNIFORM TITLE (R)

A series added entry consisting of a series title alone.

Indicators

First - Undefined

- Undefined

Second - Nonfiling characters

0-9 - Number of nonfiling characters

Subfield Codes

$a - Uniform title (NR)

$d - Date of treaty signing (R)

$f - Date of a work (NR)

$g - Miscellaneous information (NR)

$h - Medium (NR)

$k - Form subheading (R)

$l - Language of a work (NR)

$m - Medium of performance for music (R)

$n - Number of part/section of a work (R)

$o - Arranged statement for music (NR)

$p - Name of part/section of a work (R)

$r - Key for music (NR)

$s - Version (NR)

$t - Title of a work (NR)

$v - Volume/sequential designation (NR)

$6 - Linkage (NR)

$8 - Field link and sequence number (R)

Examples:

830 #0$aResources information series.

830 #0$aImago (Series)

830 #0$aSerie Mariano Azvela ; $v2.

830 #0$aSport (International Union of Students. Physical Education and Sports Dept.) ; $vv. 10.

830 #0$aMonograph (University of California, Los Angeles. Dept. of Continuing Education in Health Sciences).

830 #0$aMusica da camera (Oxford University Press) ; $v72.

830 #0$aBasic nursing skills (Robert J. Brady Company) ; $vtape 14.

830 #0$aTeenage years. $h[Videorecording]

840 - SERIES ADDED ENTRY—TITLE (R) [OBSOLETE]

Indicators

First - Undefined

- Undefined

Second - Nonfiling characters

0-9 - Number of nonfiling characters

Subfield Codes

$a - Title (NR)

$h - Medium (NR)

$v - Volume/sequential designation (NR)

—Holdings, Location, Alternate Graphics, etc. Fields (841-88X)—

Fields 841-886 contain descriptions for data elements which are an integral part of the MARC 21 Format for Bibliographic Data and data elements which may appear either in bibliographic records or in separate MARC holdings records.

Field 850 is a bibliographic record field that contains minimal holdings location holdings location data. Field 852 contains more extensive location data. Field 856 covers information about the location of electronic resources. These fields are described in this document. Fields 841-845, 853-855, and 863-878 are only listed here. Fuller descriptions for them appear in the MARC 21 Concise Format for Holdings Data.

Fields 880 and 886 are special-use bibliographic data fields.

841 - Holdings Coded Data Values (NR)

842 - Textual Physical Form Designator (NR)

843 - Reproduction Note (R)

844 - Name of Unit (NR)

845 - Terms Governing Use and Reproduction (R)

850 - Holding Institution (R)

852 - Location (R)

853 - Captions and Pattern—Basic Bibliographic Unit (R)

854 - Captions and Pattern—Supplementary Material (R)

855 - Captions and Pattern—Indexes (R)

856 - Electronic Location and Access (R)

863 - Enumeration and Chronology—Basic Bibliographic Unit (R)

864 - Enumeration and Chronology—Supplementary Material (R)

865 - Enumeration and Chronology—Indexes (R)

866 - Textual Holdings—Basic Bibliographic Unit (R)

867 - Textual Holdings—Supplementary Material (R)

868 - Textual Holdings—Indexes (R)

876 - Item Information—Basic Bibliographic Unit (R)

877 - Item Information—Supplementary Material (R)

878 - Item Information—Indexes (R)

880 - Alternate Graphic Representation (R)

886 - Foreign MARC Information Field (R)

841 - HOLDINGS CODED DATA VALUES (NR)

842 - TEXTUAL PHYSICAL FORM DESIGNATOR (NR)

843 - REPRODUCTION NOTE (R)

844 - NAME OF UNIT (NR)

845 - TERMS GOVERNING USE AND REPRODUCTION NOTE (R)

850 - HOLDING INSTITUTION (R)

Indicators

First - Undefined

- Undefined

Second - Undefined

- Undefined

Subfield Codes

$a - Holding institution (R)

$b - Holdings (NR) (MU VM SE) [OBSOLETE]

$d - Inclusive dates (NR) (MU VM SE) [OBSOLETE]

$e - Retention statement (NR) (CF MU VM SE) [OBSOLETE]

$8 - Field link and sequence number (R)

851 - LOCATION (R) [OBSOLETE]

Indicators

First - Undefined

- Undefined

Second - Undefined

- Undefined

Subfield Codes

$a - Name (custodian or owner) (NR)

$b - Institutional division (NR)

$c - Street address (NR)

$d - Country (NR)

$e - Location of units (NR)

$f - Item number (NR)

$g - Repository location code (NR)

$3 - Materials specified (NR)

$6 - Linkage (NR)

852 - LOCATION (R)

Identifies the organization holding the item or from which it is available. This field may also contain detailed information about how to locate the item in a collection.

Indicators

First - Shelving scheme

- No information provided

0 - Library of Congress classification

1 - Dewey Decimal classification

2 - National Library of Medicine classification

3 - Superintendent of Documents classification

4 - Shelving control number

5 - Title

6 - Shelved separately

7 - Source specified in subfield $2

8 - Other scheme

Second - Shelving order

- No information provided

0 - Not enumeration

1 - Primary enumeration

2 - Alternative enumeration

Subfield Codes

$a - Location (NR)

$b - Sublocation or collection (R)

$c - Shelving location (R)

$e - Address (R)

$f - Coded location qualifier (R)

$g - Non-coded location qualifier (R)

$h - Classification part (NR)

$i - Item part (R)

$j - Shelving control number (NR)

$k - Call number prefix (R)

$l - Shelving form of title (NR)

$m - Call number suffix (R)

$n - Country code (NR)

$p - Piece designation (NR)

$q - Piece physical condition (NR)

$s - Copyright article-fee code (R)

$t - Copy number (NR)

$x - Nonpublic note (R)

$z - Public note (R)

$2 - Source of classification or shelving scheme (NR)

$3 - Materials specified (NR)

$6 - Linkage (NR)

$8 - Sequence number (NR)

Examples:

852 01$aCtY $bMain $hLB201 $i.M63

852 ##$aCLU

852 ##$aNational Archives and Records Service $bGenealogical Research Recording $ePennsylvania Ave. at 8th St., N.W., Washington, D.C. USA $ndcu

852 ##$aCSf $bSci $t1

852 ##$aNational Geographic Society $bPersonnel Dept. $e17th & M St., N.W., Washington, DC USA

852 81$a[location identifier] $bMain $cmezzanine stacks

852 81$aFrPALP $hPer $iREF

852 4#$aDLC $bMicRR $jMicrofilm 82/528 MicRR

852 ##$a[location identifier] $bMain $coversize shelving $qchild's graffiti on end papers

852 ##$aMH $cCurrent issues in R.R. $x1-54 on order in Mfiche

852 81$a[location identifier] $hM $iS:55 $p1100064014 $xaccession no.: 90/84370

852 #0$3Correspondence $a[location identifier] $bManuscript Division

853 - CAPTIONS AND PATTERN—BASIC BIBLIOGRAPHIC UNIT (R)

854 - CAPTIONS AND PATTERN—SUPPLEMENTARY MATERIAL (R)

855 - CAPTIONS AND PATTERN—INDEXES (R)

856 - ELECTRONIC LOCATION AND ACCESS (R)

This field contains the information needed to locate and access an electronic resource. The field may be used in a bibliographic record for a resource when that resource or a subset of it is available electronically. In addition, it may be used to locate and access an electronic version of a non-electronic resource described in the bibliographic record or a related electronic resource.

Field 856 is repeated when the location data elements vary (the URL in subfield $u or subfields $a, $b, $d, when used). It is also repeated when more than one access method is used, different portions of the item are available electronically, mirror sites are recorded, different formats/resolutions with different URLs are indicated, and related items are recorded.

Indicators

First - Access method

- No information provided

0 - Email

1 - FTP

2 - Remote login (Telnet)

3 - Dial-up

4 - HTTP

7 - Method specified in subfield $2

Second - Relationship

- No information provided

0 - Resource

1 - Version of resource

2 - Related resource

8 - No display constant generated

Subfield Codes

$a - Host name (R)

$b - Access number (R)

$c - Compression information (R)

$d - Path (R)

$f - Electronic name (R)

$g - Uniform Resource Name (R) [OBSOLETE]

$h - Processor of request (NR)

$i - Instruction (R)

$j - Bits per second (NR)

$k - Password (NR)

$l - Logon (NR)

$m - Contact for access assistance (R)

$n - Name of location of host (NR)

$o - Operating system (NR)

$p - Port (NR)

$q - Electronic format type (NR)

$r - Settings (NR)

$s - File size (R)

$t - Terminal emulation (R)

$u - Uniform Resource Identifier (R)

$v - Hours access method available (R)

$w - Record control number (R)

$x - Nonpublic note (R)

$y - Link text (R)

$z - Public note (R)

$2 - Access method (NR)

$3 - Materials specified (NR)

$6 - Linkage (NR)

$8 - Field link and sequence number (R)

Examples:

856 ##$gurn:doi:10.1000/100

856 0#$umailto:ejap@phil.indiana.edu $iejap subscription

856 1#$u ftp://path.net/pub/docs/urn2urc.ps

856 2#$utelnet://pucc.princeton.edu $nPrinceton University, Princeton, N.J.

856 3#$alocis.loc.gov $b140.147.254.3 $mlconline@loc.gov $t3270 $tline mode (e.g., vt100) $vM-F 06:00-21:30 USA EST, Sat. 08:30-17:00 USA EST, Sun. 13:00-17:00 USA EST

856 40$u http://jefferson.village.virginia.edu/pmc/contents.all.html

856 4#$uhttp://hdl.handle.net/loc.test/gotthome $gurn:hdl.loc.test/gotthome

856 7#$3b&w film neg. $ddag $f3d01926 $2file

856 42$3Finding aid $u http://lcweb2.loc.gov/ammem/ead/jackson.sgm

856 41$u http://www.jstor.org/journals/0277903x.html

856 40$uhttp://www.cdc.gov/ncidod/EID/eid.htm $qtext/html

856 41$u http://purl.oclc.org/OCLC/OLUC/34907403/1 $xhttp://export.uswest.com/

856 1#$uftp://harvarda.harvard.edu $kguest

856 42$3French version $u http://www.cgiar.org/ifpri/reports/0297rpt/0297-ft.htm

856 42$3Essays from annual reports $u http://woodrow.mpls.frb.fed.us/publs/ar/index.html

856 1#$uftp://wuarchive.wustl.edu/mirrors/info-mac/ut il/color-system-icons.hqx $s16874 ytes

856 2#$utelnet://maine.maine.edu $nUniversity of Maine $t3270

856 1#$uftp://wuarchive.wustl.edu/mirrors2/win3/games/atmoids.zip $cdecompress with PKUNZIP.exe $xcannot verify because of transfer difficulty

856 4#$zPart of the Ovid Mental Health Collection (MHC). Follow instructions on MedMenu page for Ovid login. $u http://info.med.yale.edu/medmenu/info%5Fcbc.html

856 40$u http://www.ref.oclc.org:2000 $zAddress for accessing the journal using authorization number and password through OCLC FirstSearch Electronic Collections Online. Subscription to online journal required for access to abstracts and full text

856 2#$aanthrax.micro.umn.edu $b128.101.95.23

856 1#$amaine.maine.edu $cMust be decompressed with PKUNZIP $fresource.zip

856 0#$akentvm.bitnet $facadlist file1 $facadlist file2 $facadlist file3

856 0#$auicvm.bitnet $fAN2 $hListserv

856 2#$amadlab.sprl.umich.edu $nUniversity of Michigan Weather Underground $p3000

856 10$zFTP access to PostScript version includes groups of article files with .pdf extension $aftp.cdc.gov $d/pub/EIS/vol*no*/adobe $f*.pdf $lanonymous $qapplication/pdf

863 - ENUMERATION AND CHRONOLOGY—BASIC BIBLIOGRAPHIC UNIT (R)

864 - ENUMERATION AND CHRONOLOGY—SUPPLEMENTARY MATERIAL (R)

865 - ENUMERATION AND CHRONOLOGY—INDEXES (R)

866 - TEXTUAL HOLDINGS—BASIC BIBLIOGRAPHIC UNIT (R)

867 - TEXTUAL HOLDINGS—SUPPLEMENTARY MATERIAL (R)

868 - TEXTUAL HOLDINGS—INDEXES (R)

870 - VARIANT PERSONAL NAME (SE) [OBSOLETE]

871 - VARIANT CORPORATE NAME (SE)[OBSOLETE]

872 - VARIANT CONFERENCE OR MEETING NAME (SE) [OBSOLETE]

873 - VARIANT UNIFORM TITLE HEADING (SE) [OBSOLETE]

876 - ITEM INFORMATION—BASIC BIBLIOGRAPHIC UNIT (R)

877 - ITEM INFORMATION—SUPPLEMENTARY MATERIAL (R)

878 - ITEM INFORMATION—INDEXES (R)

880 - ALTERNATE GRAPHIC REPRESENTATION (R)

The fully content-designated representation in a different script of another field in the same record. Field 880 is linked to the associated regular field by subfield $6 (Linkage). The first and second indicator positions in field 880 have the same definition and values as the indicators in the associated field. The subfield codes in field 880 are the same as those defined in the associated field except for subfield $6. The data in field 880 may be in more than one script.

Indicators

First - Same as associated field

Second - Same as associated field

Subfield Codes

$6 - Linkage (NR)

$a-z Same as associated field

$0-5 Same as associated field

$7-9 Same as associated field

Examples:

880 2#$6110-01/(2/r $aHeading in Hebrew script linked to associated field

880 ##$6530-00/(2/r $aAdditional physical form available information in Hebrew script

880 1#$6100-01/(N $aHeading in Cyrillic script

880 10$6245-02/$1 $a[Chinese characters]

880 ##$6260-02/(2/r $a[Tel Aviv] : $b[Hebrew characters] $c[1985]

886 - FOREIGN MARC INFORMATION FIELD (R)

This field is used when converting foreign MARC records into the MARC format. It contains data from a foreign MARC record for which there is no corresponding MARC field.

Indicators

First - Type of field

0 - Leader

1 - Variable control fields (002-009)

2 - Variable data fields (010-999)

Second - Undefined

- Undefined

Subfield Codes

$a - Tag of the foreign MARC field (NR)

$b - Content of the foreign MARC field (NR)

$2 - Source of data (NR)

$a-z - Foreign MARC subfield (R)

$0-9 - Foreign MARC subfield (R)

Examples:

886 0#$2intermrc $b00860nambb6200206###4500

886 2#$2ibermarc $a019 $b## $aVG 586-1992

886 2#$2unimrur $a709 $b1# $aNapalkov (Litvak). Vladimir Nikolaevich: sm.

886 2#$2ukmarc $a690 $b00 $a00030 $dGreat Britain $z11030 $abutterflies $z21030 $alife cycles

887 - NON-MARC INFORMATION FIELD (R)

Indicators

First - Undefined

- Undefined

Second - Undefined

- Undefined

Subfield Codes

$a - Content of non-MARC field (NR)

$2 - Source of data (NR)

8

MARC 21 FORMAT FOR HOLDINGS DATA

This document lists all valid and obsolete data elements that may appear in MARC 21 holdings records. It is intended to meet the need for a simple data element list to support MARC system development and online validation of MARC data elements. This listing does not include any descriptions or examples of MARC data elements. Descriptions and examples can be found in the MARC 21 Concise Holdings Format.

—Leader and Directory—

LEADER

Character Positions

00-04 - Record length

05 - Record status

c - Corrected or revised

d - Deleted

n - New

06 - Type of record

u - Unknown

v - Multipart item holdings

x - Single-part item holdings

y - Serial item holdings

07-08 - Undefined character positions

09 - Character coding scheme

- MARC-8

a - UCS/Unicode

10 - Indicator count

11 - Subfield code length

12-16 - Base address of data

17 - Encoding level

1 - Holdings level 1

2 - Holdings level 2

3 - Holdings level 3

4 - Holdings level 4

5 - Holdings level 4 with piece designation

m - Mixed level

u - Unknown

z - Other level

18 - Item information in record

i - Item information

n - No item information

19 - Undefined character position

20-23 - Entry map

20 - Length of the length-of-field portion

21 - Length of the starting-character-position portion

22 - Length of the implementation-defined portion

23 - Undefined

DIRECTORY

Character Positions

00-02 - Tag

03-06 - Field length

07-11 - Starting character position

—Control Fields (001-008)—

001 - CONTROL NUMBER (NR)

003 - CONTROL NUMBER IDENTIFIER (NR)

004 - CONTROL NUMBER FOR RELATED BIBLIOGRAPHIC RECORD (NR)

005 - DATE AND TIME OF LATEST TRANSACTION (NR)

007 - PHYSICAL DESCRIPTION FIXED FIELD (NR)

008 - FIXED-LENGTH DATA ELEMENTS (NR)

Character positions

00-05 - Date entered on file

06 - Receipt or acquisition status

0 - Unknown

1 - Other receipt or acquisition status

2 - Received and complete or ceased

3 - On order

4 - Currently received

5 - Not currently received

07 - Method of acquisition

c - Cooperative or consortial purchase

d - Deposit

e - Exchange

f - Free

g - Gift

m - Membership

n - Non-library purchase

p - Purchase

u - Unknown

z - Other method of acquisition

08-11 - Expected acquisition end date

[yymm] - Date of cancellation or last expected part

uuuu - Intent to cancel; effective date not known

- No intent to cancel or not applicable

12 - General retention policy

0 - Unknown

1 - Other general retention policy

2 - Retained except as replaced by updates

3 - Sample issue retained

4 - Retained until replaced by microform

5 - Retained until replaced by cumulation, replacement volume, or revision

6 - Retained for a limited period

7 - Not retained

8 - Permanently retained

13-15 - Specific retention policy

- No specific retention policy

13 - Policy Type

l - Latest

p - Previous

14 - Number of units

1-9 Number of units

15 - Unit type

16 - Completeness

0 - Other

1 - Complete

2 - Incomplete

3 - Scattered

4 - Not applicable

17-19 - Number of copies reported

20 - Lending policy

a - Will lend

b - Will not lend

c - Will lend hard copy only

l - Limited lending policy

u - Unknown

21 - Reproduction policy

a - Will reproduce

b - Will not reproduce

u - Unknown

22-24 - Language

- Blanks

und - Undetermined

25 - Separate or composite copy report

0 - Separate copy report

1 - Composite copy report

26-31 - Date of report

—Number and Code Fields (0XX)—

010 - LIBRARY OF CONGRESS CONTROL NUMBER (NR)

Indicators

First - Undefined

- Undefined

Second - Undefined

- Undefined

Subfield Codes

$a - LC control number (NR)

$b - NUCMC control number (R)

$z - Canceled or invalid LC control number (R)

$8 - Field link and sequence number (R)

014 - LINKAGE NUMBER (R)

Indicators

First - Type of linkage number

0 - Holdings record number

1 - Bibliographic record number

Second - Undefined

- Undefined

Subfield Codes

$a - Linkage number (NR)

$b - Source of number (NR)

$z - Canceled or invalid linkage number (R)

$6 - Linkage (NR)

016 - NATIONAL BIBLIOGRAPHIC AGENCY CONTROL NUMBER (R)

Indicators

First - National bibliographic agency

- National Library of Canada

7 - Agency identified in subfield $2

Second - Undefined

- Undefined

Subfield Codes

$a - Record control number (NR)

$z - Canceled or invalid control number (R)

$2 - Source (NR)

$8 - Field link and sequence number (R)

020 - INTERNATIONAL STANDARD BOOK NUMBER (R)

Indicators

First - Undefined

- Undefined

Second - Undefined

- Undefined

Subfield Codes

$a - International Standard Book Number (NR)

$c - Terms of availability (NR)

$z - Canceled/invalid ISBN (R)

$6 - Linkage (NR)

$8 - Field link and sequence number (R)

022 - INTERNATIONAL STANDARD SERIAL NUMBER (R)

Indicators

First - Level of international interest

- No level specified

0 - Serial of international interest

1 - Serial not of international interest

Second - Undefined

- Undefined

Subfield Codes

$a - International Standard Serial Number (NR)

$y - Incorrect ISSN (R)

$z - Canceled ISSN (R)

$6 - Linkage (NR)

$8 - Field link and sequence number (R)

023 - STANDARD FILM NUMBER (R) [DELETED]

024 - OTHER STANDARD IDENTIFIER (R)

Indicators

First - Type of standard number or code

0 - International Standard Recording Code (ISRC)

1 - Universal Product Code (UPC)

2 - International Standard Music Number (ISMN)

3 - International Article Number (EAN)

4 - Serial Item and Contribution Identifier (SICI)

7 - Source specified in subfield $2

8 - Unspecified type of standard number or code

Second - Difference indicator

- No information provided

0 - No difference

1 - Difference

Subfield Codes

$a - Standard number or code (NR)

$c - Terms of availability (NR)

$d - Additional codes following the standard number or code (NR)

$z - Canceled/invalid standard number or code (R)

$2 - Source of number or code (NR)

$6 - Linkage (NR)

$8 - Field link and sequence number (R)

027 - STANDARD TECHNICAL REPORT NUMBER (R)

Indicators

First - Undefined

- Undefined

Second - Undefined

- Undefined

Subfield Codes

$a - Standard Technical Report Number (NR)

$z - Canceled/invalid STRN (R)

$6 - Linkage (NR)

$8 - Field link and sequence number (R)

030 - CODEN DESIGNATION (NR)

Indicators

First - Undefined

- Undefined

Second - Undefined

- Undefined

Subfield Codes

$a - CODEN (NR)

$z - Canceled/invalid CODEN (R)

$6 - Linkage (NR)

$8 - Field link and sequence number (R)

035 - SYSTEM CONTROL NUMBER (R)

Indicators

First - Undefined

- Undefined

Second - Undefined

- Undefined

Subfield Codes

$a - System control number (NR)

$z - Canceled or invalid control number (R)

$6 - Linkage (NR)

$8 - Field link and sequence number (R)

040 - RECORD SOURCE (NR)

Indicators

First - Undefined

- Undefined

Second - Undefined

- Undefined

Subfield Codes

$a - Original cataloging agency (NR)

$b - Language of cataloging (NR)

$c - Transcribing agency (NR)

$d - Modifying agency (R)

$6 - Linkage (NR)

$8 - Field link and sequence number (R)

066 - CHARACTER SETS PRESENT (NR)

Indicators

First - Undefined

- Undefined

Second - Undefined

- Undefined

Subfield Codes

$a - Primary G0 character set (NR)

$b - Primary G1 character set (NR)

$c - Alternate G0 or G1 character set (R)

—Note Fields (5XX & 84X)—

541 - IMMEDIATE SOURCE OF ACQUISITION NOTE (R)

Indicators

First - Undefined

- Undefined

Second - Undefined

- Undefined

Subfield Codes

$a - Source of acquisition (NR)

$b - Address (NR)

$c - Method of acquisition (NR)

$d - Date of acquisition (NR)

$e - Accession number (NR)

$f - Owner (NR)

$h - Purchase price (NR)

$n - Extent (R)

$o - Type of unit (R)

$3 - Materials specified (NR)

$5 - Institution to which field applies (NR)

$6 - Linkage (NR)

$8 - Field link and sequence number (R)

561 - OWNERSHIP AND CUSTODIAL HISTORY (R)

Indicators

First - Undefined

- Undefined

Second - Undefined

- Undefined

Subfield Codes

$a - History (NR)

$b - Time of collation (NR) [OBSOLETE]

$3 - Materials specified (NR)

$5 - Institution to which field applies (NR)

$6 - Linkage (NR)

$8 - Field link and sequence number (R)

562 - COPY AND VERSION IDENTIFICATION NOTE (R)

Indicators

First - Undefined

- Undefined

Second - Undefined

- Undefined

Subfield Codes

$a - Identifying markings (R)

$b - Copy identification (R)

$c - Version identification (R)

$d - Presentation format (R)

$e - Number of copies (R)

$3 - Materials specified (NR)

$5 - Institution to which field applies (NR)

$6 - Linkage (NR)

$8 - Field link and sequence number (R)

563 - BINDING INFORMATION (R)

Indicators

First - Undefined

- Undefined

Second - Undefined

- Undefined

Subfield Codes

$a - Binding note (NR)

$u - Uniform Resource Identifier (R)

$3 - Materials specified (NR)

$5 - Institution to which field applies (NR)

$6 - Linkage (NR)

$8 - Field link and sequence number (R)

583 - ACTION NOTE (R)

Indicators

First - Undefined

- Undefined

Second - Undefined

- Undefined

Subfield Codes

$a - Action (NR)

$b - Action identification (R)

$c - Time/date of action (R)

$d - Action interval (R)

$e - Contingency for action (R)

$f - Authorization (R)

$h - Jurisdiction (R)

$i - Method of action (R)

$j - Site of action (R)

$k - Action agent (R)

$l - Status (R)

$n - Extent (R)

$o - Type of unit (R)

$u - Uniform Resource Identifier (R)

$x - Nonpublic note (R)

$z - Public note (R)

$2 - Source of term (NR)

$3 - Materials specified (NR)

$5 - Institution to which field applies (NR)

$6 - Linkage (NR)

$8 - Field link and sequence number (R)

841 - HOLDINGS CODED DATA VALUES (NR)

Indicators

First - Undefined

- Undefined

Second - Undefined

- Undefined

Subfield Codes

$a Type of record (NR)

0 - Type of record

1-2 - Undefined

3 - Character coding scheme

$b Fixed-length data elements (NR)

0-31 - Holdings 008 values

$e Encoding level (NR)

0 - Encoding level

842 - TEXTUAL PHYSICAL FORM DESIGNATOR (NR)

Indicators

First - Undefined

- Undefined

Second - Undefined

- Undefined

Subfield Code

$a Textual physical form designator (NR)

$6 - Linkage (NR)

$8 - Field link and sequence number (R)

843 - REPRODUCTION NOTE (R)

Indicators

First - Undefined

- Undefined

Second - Undefined

- Undefined

Subfield Codes

$a - Type of reproduction (NR)

$b - Place of reproduction (R)

$c - Agency responsible for reproduction (R)

$d - Date of reproduction (NR)

$e - Physical description of reproduction (NR)

$f - Series statement of reproduction (R)

$m - Dates of publication and/or sequential designation of issues reproduced (R)

$n - Note about reproduction (R)

$3 - Materials specified (NR)

$6 - Linkage (NR)

$7 - Fixed-length data elements of reproduction (NR)

0 - Type of date/Publication status

1-4 - Date 1

5-8 - Date 2

9-11 - Place of publication, production, or execution

12 - Frequency

13 - Regularity

14 - Form of item

$8 - Field link and sequence number (R)

844 - NAME OF UNIT (NR)

Indicators

First - Undefined

- Undefined

Second - Undefined

- Undefined

Subfield Code

$a - Name of unit (NR)

$6 - Linkage (NR)

$8 - Field link and sequence number (R)

845 - TERMS GOVERNING USE AND REPRODUCTION NOTE (R)

Indicators

First - Undefined

- Undefined

Second - Undefined

- Undefined

Subfield Codes

$a - Terms governing use and reproduction (NR)

$b - Jurisdiction (NR)

$c - Authorization (NR)

$d - Authorized users (NR)

$3 - Materials specified (NR)

$5 - Institution to which field applies (NR)

$6 - Linkage (NR)

$8 - Field link and sequence number (R)

—Location and Access Fields (852 & 856)—

Fields 852 and 856 contain information about where an item is physically located and how can be accessed physically or electronically (for digitized items). A description of the configuration required when other holdings information fields are associated with multiple 852 fields is given under the in the section Separate and Embedded Holdings Information in the Introduction to the MARC Concise Format for Holdings Data.

852 - Location (R)

856 - Electronic Location and Access (R)

852 - LOCATION (R)

Identifies the organization holding the item or from which it is available. May also contain detailed information about how to locate the item in a collection.

Indicators

First - Shelving scheme

- No information provided

0 - Library of Congress classification

1 - Dewey Decimal classification

2 - National Library of Medicine classification

3 - Superintendent of Documents classification

4 - Shelving control number

5 - Title

6 - Shelved separately

7 - Source specified in subfield $2

8 - Other scheme

Second - Shelving order

- No information provided

0 - Not enumeration

1 - Primary enumeration

2 - Alternative enumeration

Subfield Codes

$a - Location (NR)

$b - Sublocation or collection (R)

$c - Shelving location (R)

$e - Address (R)

$f - Coded location qualifier (R)

$g - Non-coded location qualifier (R)

$h - Classification part (NR)

$i - Item part (R)

$j - Shelving control number (NR)

$k - Call number prefix (R)

$l - Shelving form of title (NR)

$m - Call number suffix (R)

$n - Country code (NR)

$p - Piece designation (NR)

$q - Piece physical condition (NR)

$s - Copyright article-fee code (R)

$t - Copy number (NR)

$x - Nonpublic note (R)

$z - Public note (R)

$2 - Source of classification or shelving scheme (NR)

$3 - Materials specified (NR)

$6 - Linkage (NR)

$8 - Sequence number (NR)

Examples :

852 01$aCtY $bMain $hLB201 $i.M63

852 81$a[location identifier] $bMain $cmezzanine stacks

852 ##$aDLC $bManuscript Division $eJames Madison Memorial Building, 1st & Independence Ave., S.E., Washington, DC USA $j4016

852 00$a[location identifier] $bRef. $fle

852 81$a[location identifier] $bRef $gholographic issue

852 01$aNvLN $hZ67 $i.L7

852 4#$aDLC $bMicRR $jMicrofilm 82/528 MicRR

852 51$a[location identifier] $b0108 $lNYT MAG

852 ##$aDLC $hG3820 1687 $i.H62 $mVault

852 81$aFrPALP $bAnnex $ccenter shelves $e10, rue du General Camou $e75007 Paris $nfr

852 81$a[location identifier] $b0131 $p1100064014

852 ##$a[location identifier] $bMain $coversize shelving $qchild's graffiti on end papers

852 0#$a[location identifier] $bMain $t1 $hPZ7.D684 $iA1 1979

852 ##$3v. 1-6 $a[location identifier] $bScience Library $t1

852 ##$aMH $cCurrent issues in R.R. $x1-54 on order in Mfiche

852 01$aDLC $bSer Div $hA123 $i.B456 $zSigned by author

852 0#$82 $a[location identifier 2] $hcall no.

856 - ELECTRONIC LOCATION AND ACCESS (R)

The information required to locate an electronic resource. The information identifies the electronic location containing the resource or from which it is available. It also contains information needed to retrieve the resource by the access method identified in the first indicator position. The relationship of the electronic location and access information in field 856 to the resource identified by the record as a whole is identified by the second indicator. The information contained in this field is sufficient to allow for the electronic transfer of a file, subscription to an electronic journal, or logon to an electronic resource. In some cases, only unique data elements are recorded which allow the user to access a locator table on a remote host containing the remaining information needed to access the resource.

Field 856 is repeated when the location elements vary (subfields $a, $b, $c) and when more than one access method may be used. It is also repeated whenever the electronic filename varies (subfield $f) except when a single intellectual work is divided into different parts for online storage or retrieval.

Indicators

First - Access method

- No information provided

0 - Email

1 - FTP

2 - Remote login (Telnet)

3 - Dial-up

4 - HTTP

7 - Method specified in subfield $2

Second - Relationship

- No information provided

0 - Resource

1 - Version of resource

2 - Related resource

8 - No display constant generated

Subfield Codes

$a - Host name (R)

$b - Access number (R)

$c - Compression information (R)

$d - Path (R)

$f - Electronic name (R)

$g - Uniform Resource Name (R) [OBSOLETE]

$h - Processor of request (NR)

$i - Instruction (R)

$j - Bits per second (NR)

$k - Password (NR)

$l - Logon (NR)

$m - Contact for access assistance (R)

$n - Name of location of host (NR)

$o - Operating system (NR)

$p - Port (NR)

$q - Electronic format type (NR)

$r - Settings (NR)

$s - File size (R)

$t - Terminal emulation (R)

$u - Uniform Resource Identifier (R)

$v - Hours access method available (R)

$w - Record control number (R)

$x - Nonpublic note (R)

$y - Link text (R)

$z - Public note (R)

$2 - Access method (NR)

$3 - Materials specified (NR)

$6 - Linkage (NR)

$8 - Field link and sequence number (R)

Examples:

856 1#$uftp://harvada.harvard.edu $kguest

856 2#$aanthrax.micro.umn.edu $b128.101.95.23

856 1#$amaine.maine.edu $cMust be decompressed with PKUNZIP $fresource.zip

856 1#$uftp://wuarchive.wustl.edu/mirrors2/win3/games/atmoids.zip $cdecompress with PKUNZIP.exe $xcannot verify because of transfer difficulty

856 0#$akentvm.bitnet $facadlist file1 $facadlist file2 $facadlist file3

856 42$3Finding aid $uhttp://lcweb2.loc.gov/ammem/ead/jackson.sgm

856 0#$auicvm.bitnet $fAN2 $hListserv

856 2#$amadlab.sprl.umich.edu $nUniversity of Michigan Weather Underground $p3000

856 41$uhttp://www.jstor.org/journals/0277903x.html

856 40$uhttp://www.cdc.gov/ncidod/EID/eid.htm $qtext/html

856 42$3Essays from annual reports $uhttp://woodrow.mpls.frb.fed.us/pubs/ar/index.html

856 1#$uftp://wuarchive.wustl.edu/mirrors/info-mac/util/color-system-icon s.hqx $s16874 bytes

856 41$uhttp://purl.oclc.org/OCLC/OLUC/34907403/1 $xhttp://export.uswest.com/

856 40$uhttp://www.ref.oclc.org:2000 $zAddress for accessing the journal using authorization number and password through OCLC FirstSearch Electronic Collections Online. Subscription to online journal required for access to abstracts and full text

856 4#$zPart of the Ovid Mental Health Collection (MHC) Follow instructions on MedMenu page for Ovid login $uhttp://info.med.yale.edu/medmenu/info%5Fcbc html

856 42$3French version $uhttp://www.cgiar.org/ifpri/reports/0297rpt/0297-fr.htm

856 4#$uhttp://susdl.fcla.edu/cgi- bin/cgiwrap/~fdl fdlcgi?FA00000011%2Fjpg $yElectronic resource (JPEG)

856 ##$uhttp://susdl.fcla.edu/cgi- bin/cgiwrap/~fdl fdlcgi?FA00000011%2Fpdf $yElectronic resource (PDF)

—Caption and Pattern Fields (853-855)—

853 - Captions and Pattern—Basic Bibliographic Unit (R)

854 - Captions and Pattern—Supplementary Material (R)

855 - Captions and Pattern—Indexes (R)

CAPTION AND PATTERN FIELDS—GENERAL INFORMATION

853 - CAPTIONS AND PATTERN—BASIC BIBLIOGRAPHIC UNIT (R)

The caption that is appropriate for each level of enumeration and chronology that is present in a related 863 Enumeration and Chronology Basic Bibliographic Unit field and codes that define the publication pattern of the item. A display may be generated from the contents of field 853 and the related 863 field(s) to which it is linked by subfield $8 (Field link and sequence number).

Indicators

First - Compressibility and expandability

0 - Cannot compress or expand

1 - Can compress but not expand

2 - Can compress or expand

3 - Unknown

Second - Caption evaluation

0 - Captions verified; all levels present

1 - Captions verified; all levels may not be present

2 - Captions unverified; all levels present

3 - Captions unverified; all levels may not be present

Subfield Codes

$a-$h - Enumeration captions

$a - First level of enumeration (NR)

$b - Second level of enumeration (NR)

$c - Third level of enumeration (NR)

$d - Fourth level of enumeration (NR)

$e - Fifth level of enumeration (NR)

$f - Sixth level of enumeration (NR)

$g - Alternative numbering scheme, first

level of enumeration (NR)

$h - Alternative numbering scheme, second level of enumeration (NR)

$i-$m - Chronology captions

$i - First level of chronology (NR)

$j - Second level of chronology (NR)

$k - Third level of chronology (NR)

$l - Fourth level of chronology (NR)

$m - Alternative numbering scheme, chronology (NR)

$n - Pattern note (NR)

$p - Number of pieces per issuance (NR)

$t - Copy (NR)

$u - Bibliographic units per next higher level (R)

[n] - Number of parts

var - Varies

und - Undetermined

$v - Numbering continuity (R)

c - Number increments continuously

r - Numbering restarts at the completion of the unit

$w - Frequency (NR)

$x - Calendar change (NR)

$y - Regularity pattern (R)

$z - Numbering scheme (R)

$3 - Materials specified (NR)

$6 - Linkage (NR)

$8 - Field link and seque

Examples:

853 20$81 $av. $bno. $u6 $vr $i(year) $j(month) $wm $x01,07

853 20$81 $av. $bno. $u4 $vr $i(year) $j(season) $wq $x21

853 03$81 $av. $b[no.]

853 03$81 $a(year)

853 03$81 $a(unit)

853 01$82 $anew ser.:v.

853 03$81 $av. $bno.

853 00$81 $av. $bsect. $u12 $vr $cno. $u7 $vr $dpt. $uvar $vr $i(year) $j(month) $k(day) $l[week] $wd $x01

853 23$81 $av. $bno. $gno. $u12 $vr $x01 $i(year) $j(month)

853 20$81 $av. $i(year)

853 03$81 $av. $bno. $gno. $i(year) $j(season)

853 22$81 $av. $bno. $u12 $vr $i(year) $j(month) $k(day) $ww $x01

853 22$81 $av. $bno. $u04 $vr $i(year) $j(month) $wq $x12 $tc

853 20$81 $av $bno. $u12 $vr $i(year) $j(month) $wm $x11

853 03$81 $av. $bno. $ww $yow01,0699we,0700we,0801we,0802we,0803we, 0804we,98we, 99we

853 20$81 $av. $bno. $u26 $ur $ww $x0101 $yow05we nce number (NR)

854 - CAPTIONS AND PATTERN—SUPPLEMENTARY MATERIAL (R)

The caption that is appropriate for each level of enumeration and chronology that is present in a related 864 Enumeration and Chronology—Supplementary Material field and codes that define the publication pattern of the item. It is used only when the supplementary material is not separately cataloged. A display may be generated from the contents of field 854 and the related 864 fields(s) to which it is linked by subfield $8 (Field link and sequence number).

Guidelines for applying the content designators defined for field 854 are given in the Captions and Pattern—General Information section.

Indicators

First - Compressibility and expandability

0 - Cannot compress or expand

1 - Can compress but not expand

2 - Can compress or expand

3 - Unknown

Second - Caption evaluation

0 - Captions verified; all levels present

1 - Captions verified; all levels may not be present

2 - Captions unverified; all levels present

3 - Captions unverified; all levels may not be present

Subfield Codes

$a-$h - Enumeration captions

$a - First level of enumeration (NR)

$b - Second level of enumeration (NR)

$c - Third level of enumeration (NR)

$d - Fourth level of enumeration (NR)

$e - Fifth level of enumeration (NR)

$f - Sixth level of enumeration (NR)

$g - Alternative numbering scheme, first level of enumeration (NR)

$h - Alternative numbering scheme, second level of enumeration (NR)

$i-$m - Chronology captions

$i - First level of chronology (NR)

$j - Second level of chronology (NR)

$k - Third level of chronology (NR)

$l - Fourth level of chronology (NR)

$m - Alternative numbering scheme, chronology (NR)

$n - Pattern note (NR)

$o - Type of supplementary material (NR)

$p - Number of pieces per issuance (NR)

$t - Copy (NR)

$u - Bibliographic units per next higher level (R)

[n] - Number of parts

var - Varies

und - Undetermined

$v - Numbering continuity (R)

c - Number increments continuously

r - Numbering restarts at the completion of the unit

$w - Frequency (NR)

$x - Calendar change (NR)

$y - Regularity pattern (R)

$z - Numbering scheme (R)

$3 - Materials specified (NR)

$6 - Linkage (NR)

$8 - Field link and sequence number (NR)

Examples :

854 00$81 $av. $bsuppl. $i(year) $j(month $k(day)

854 00$81 $av. $bsuppl.

854 00$81 $a(year) $wa

854 03$81 $a(year) $b(month) $c(day) $wd $yodsa

854 02$81 $av. $bno. $u11 $vr $i(year) $j(month) $wm $x01 $ypm01,02,03,04,05, 06,07/08,09,10,11,12

854 03$81 $av. $bno. $u10 $vr $i(year) $j(month) $w10 $x09 $yom07,08

854 03$81 $av. $bno. $u4 $vr $i(year) $j(month) $w4 $x01 $yps21,22,23,24

854 00$81 $aSupplement to v. $i(year) $wa $x01

854 33$81 $a(year) $b(month)

854 00$81 $a(year) $omap supplement

855 - CAPTIONS AND PATTERN—INDEXES (R)

The caption that is appropriate for each level of enumeration and chronology that is present in a related 865 Enumeration and Chronology Indexes field and codes that define the publication pattern for the item. A display may be generated from the contents of field 855 and the related 865 field(s) to which it is linked by subfield $8 (Field link and sequence number).

Guidelines for applying the content designators defined for field 855 are given in the Captions and Pattern—General Information section.

Indicators

First - Undefined

- Undefined

Second - Undefined

- Undefined

Subfield Codes

$a-$h - Enumeration captions

$a - First level of enumeration (NR)

$b - Second level of enumeration (NR)

$c - Third level of enumeration (NR)

$d - Fourth level of enumeration (NR)

$e - Fifth level of enumeration (NR)

$f - Sixth level of enumeration (NR)

$g - Alternative numbering scheme, first level of enumeration (NR)

$h - Alternative numbering scheme, second level of enumeration (NR)

$i-$m - Chronology captions

$i - First level of chronology (NR)

$j - Second level of chronology (NR)

$k - Third level of chronology (NR)

$l - Fourth level of chronology (NR)

$m - Alternative numbering scheme, chronology (NR)

$n - Pattern note (NR)

$o - Type of index (NR)

$p - Number of pieces per issuance (NR)

$t - Copy (NR)

$u - Bibliographic units per next higher level (R)

[n] - Number of parts

var - Varies

und - Undetermined

$v - Numbering continuity (R)

c - Number increments continuously

r - Numbering restarts at the completion of the unit

$w - Frequency (NR)

$x - Calendar change (NR)

$y - Regularity pattern (R)

$z - Numbering scheme (R)

$3 - Materials specified (NR)

$6 - Linkage (NR)

$8 - Field link and sequence number (NR)

Examples :

855 ##$81 $av.

855 ##$81 $a(year) $oalphabetical index

855 ##$81 $a(year) $oten year cumulation

—Enumeration and Chronology Fields (863-865)—

ENUMERATION AND CHRONOLOGY FIELDS—GENERAL INFORMATION

863 - ENUMERATION AND CHRONOLOGY—BASIC BIBLIOGRAPHIC UNIT (R)

This field contains the enumeration and chronology of a basic bibliographic unit in the holdings of the reporting organization. A display may be generated from the contents of field 863 and the related field 853 (Captions and Pattern—Basic Bibliographic Unit) to which it is linked by subfield $8 (Link and sequence number).

Indicators

First - Field encoding level

- No information provided

3 - Holdings level 3

4 - Holdings level 4

5 - Holdings level 4 with piece designation

Second - Form of holdings

- No information provided

0 - Compressed

1 - Uncompressed

2 - Compressed, use textual display

3 - Uncompressed, use textual display

4 - Item(s) not published

Subfield Codes

$a-$h - Enumeration

$a - First level of enumeration (NR)

$b - Second level of enumeration (NR)

$c - Third level of enumeration (NR)

$d - Fourth level of enumeration (NR)

$e - Fifth level of enumeration (NR)

$f - Sixth level of enumeration (NR)

$g - Alternative numbering scheme, first level of enumeration (NR)

$h - Alternative numbering scheme, second level of enumeration (NR)

$i-$m - Chronology

$i - First level of chronology (NR)

$j - Second level of chronology (NR)

$k - Third level of chronology (NR)

$l - Fourth level of chronology (NR)

$m - Alternative numbering scheme, chronology (NR)

$n - Converted Gregorian year (NR)

$p - Piece designation (NR)

$q - Piece physical condition (NR)

$s - Copyright article-fee code (R)

$t - Copy number (NR)

$w - Break indicator (NR)

g - Gap break

n - Nongap break

$x - Nonpublic note (R)

$z - Public note (R)

$6 - Linkage(NR)

$8 - Field link and sequence number (NR)

Examples :

863 #0$81.1 $a5-12 $i1884-1892 $zv.9, Jan. 1889 damaged.

863 30$81.1 $a113-123 $i1923-1928 $j01- 06

863 41$81.1 $a3 $b1 $i1944 $j22

863 51$81.1 $a1 $b5 $i1976 $j01 $k16 $p1100026004

863 30$81.1 $a1-10 $i1943-1952 $zbound

863 41$81.1 $a3 $b2 $i1974 $j05

863 42$81.1 $a1- 29

863 42$81.2 $a30- 40

864 - ENUMERATION AND CHRONOLOGY—SUPPLEMENTARY MATERIAL (R)

The field contains the enumeration and chronology of supplementary material that are not separately cataloged in the holdings of the reporting organization. A display may be generated from the contents of field 864 and the related field 854 (Captions and Pattern—Supplementary Material) to which it is linked by subfield $8 (Link and sequence number).

Additional information about some data elements in this field are given in the Enumeration and Chronology Fields—General Information section.

Indicators

First - Field encoding level

- No information provided

3 - Holdings level 3

4 - Holdings level 4

5 - Holdings level 4 with piece designation

Second - Form of holdings

- No information provided

0 - Compressed

1 - Uncompressed

2 - Compressed, use textual display

3 - Uncompressed, use textual display

4 - Item(s) not published

Subfield Codes

$a-$h - Enumeration

$a - First level of enumeration (NR)

$b - Second level of enumeration (NR)

$c - Third level of enumeration (NR)

$d - Fourth level of enumeration (NR)

$e - Fifth level of enumeration (NR)

$f - Sixth level of enumeration (NR)

$g - Alternative numbering scheme, first level of enumeration (NR)

$h - Alternative numbering scheme, second level of enumeration (NR)

$i-$m - Chronology

$i - First level of chronology (NR)

$j - Second level of chronology (NR)

$k - Third level of chronology (NR)

$l - Fourth level of chronology (NR)

$m - Alternative numbering scheme, chronology (NR)

$n - Converted Gregorian year (NR)

$o - Title of supplementary material (NR) [864]

$p - Piece designation (NR)

$q - Piece physical condition (NR)

$s - Copyright article-fee code (R)

$t - Copy number (NR)

$w - Break indicator (NR)

g - Gap break

n - Nongap break

$x - Nonpublic note (R)

$z - Public note (R)

$6 - Linkage(NR)

$8 - Field link and sequence number (NR)

Examples :

864 30$83.1 $a1-3 $i1983-1985 $xbind in 1 v. when next issue arrives

864 30$81.1 $a1910- 1988

864 40$81.1 $a1-3 $i1983-1985

865 - ENUMERATION AND CHRONOLOGY—INDEXES (R)

This field contains the enumeration and chronology of indexes that are not separately cataloged in the holdings of the reporting organization. A display may be generated from the contents of field 865 and the related field 855 (Captions and Pattern—Indexes) to which it is linked by subfield $8 (Link and sequence number).

Additional information about some data elements in this field are given in the Enumeration and Chronology Fields—General Information section.

Indicators

First - Field encoding level

- No information provided

3 - Holdings level 3

4 - Holdings level 4

5 - Holdings level 4 with piece designation

Second - Form of holdings

- No information provided

0 - Compressed

1 - Uncompressed

2 - Compressed, use textual display

3 - Uncompressed, use textual display

4 - Item(s) not published

Subfield Codes

$a-$h - Enumeration

$a - First level of enumeration (NR)

$b - Second level of enumeration (NR)

$c - Third level of enumeration (NR)

$d - Fourth level of enumeration (NR)

$e - Fifth level of enumeration (NR)

$f - Sixth level of enumeration (NR)

$g - Alternative numbering scheme, first level of enumeration (NR)

$h - Alternative numbering scheme, second level of enumeration (NR)

$i-$m - Chronology

$i - First level of chronology (NR)

$j - Second level of chronology (NR)

$k - Third level of chronology (NR)

$l - Fourth level of chronology (NR)

$m - Alternative numbering scheme, chronology (NR)

$n - Converted Gregorian year (NR)

$o - Title of index (NR) [865]

$p - Piece designation (NR)

$q - Piece physical condition (NR)

$s - Copyright article-fee code (R)

$t - Copy number (NR)

$w - Break indicator (NR)

g - Gap break

n - Nongap break

$x - Nonpublic note (R)

$z - Public note (R)

$6 - Linkage(NR)

$8 - Field link and sequence number (NR)

Examples :

865 4#$81.1 $a1918-1921 $oIndex $zbound at end of volume to which it applies

865 4#$81.1 $a1969-1978 $oTen-year cumulative index

865 4#$81.1 $a1969-1978 $oTen-year cumulative index

865 4#$81.1 $a1918-1921 $oIndex $zbound at end of volume to which it applies

—Textual Holdings Statement Fields (866-868)—

TEXTUAL HOLDINGS STATEMENT FIELDS—GENERAL INFORMATION

866 - TEXTUAL HOLDINGS—BASIC BIBLIOGRAPHIC UNIT (R)

Indicators

First - Field encoding level

- No information provided

3 - Holdings level 3

4 - Holdings level 4

5 - Holdings level 4 with piece designation

Second - Type of notation

0 - Non-standard

1 - ANSI/NISO Z39.71 or ISO 10324

2 - ANSI Z39.42

Subfield Codes

$a - Textual string (NR)

$x - Nonpublic note (R)

$z - Public note (R)

$6 - Linkage(NR)

$8 - Field link and sequence number (R)

867 - TEXTUAL HOLDINGS—SUPPLEMENTARY MATERIAL (R)

Indicators

First - Field encoding level

- No information provided

3 - Holdings level 3

4 - Holdings level 4

5 - Holdings level 4 with piece designation

Second - Type of notation

0 - Non-standard

1 - ANSI/NISO Z39.71 or ISO 10324

2 - ANSI Z39.42

Subfield Codes

$a - Textual string (NR)

$x - Nonpublic note (R)

$z - Public note (R)

$6 - Linkage(NR)

$8 - Field link and sequence number (R)

868 - TEXTUAL HOLDINGS—INDEXES (R)

Indicators

First - Field encoding level

- No information provided

3 - Holdings level 3

4 - Holdings level 4

5 - Holdings level 4 with piece designation

Second - Type of notation

0 - Non-standard

1 - ANSI/NISO Z39.71 or ISO 10324

2 - ANSI Z39.42

Subfield Codes

$a - Textual string (NR)

$x - Nonpublic note (R)

$z - Public note (R)

$6 - Linkage(NR)

$8 - Field link and sequence number (R)

—Item Information Fields (876-878)—

ITEM INFORMATION FIELDS—GENERAL INFORMATION

Indicators

First - Undefined

- Undefined

Second - Undefined

- Undefined

Subfield Codes

$a - Internal item number (NR)

$b - Invalid or canceled internal item number (R)

$c - Cost (R)

$d - Date acquired (R)

$e - Source of acquisition (R)

$h - Use restrictions (R)

$j - Item status (R)

$l - Temporary location (R)

$p - Piece designation (R)

$r - Invalid or canceled piece designation (R)

$t - Copy number (NR)

$x - Nonpublic note (R)

$z - Public note (R)

$3 - Materials specified (NR)

$6 - Linkage (NR)

$8 - Field link and sequence number (NR)

876 - ITEM INFORMATION—BASIC BIBLIOGRAPHIC UNIT (R)

Indicators

First - Undefined

- Undefined

Second - Undefined

- Undefined

Subfield Codes

$a - Internal item number (NR)

$b - Invalid or canceled internal item number (R)

$c - Cost (R)

$d - Date acquired (R)

$e - Source of acquisition (R)

$h - Use restrictions (R)

$j - Item status (R)

$l - Temporary location (R)

$p - Piece designation (R)

$r - Invalid or canceled piece designation (R)

$t - Copy number (NR)

$x - Nonpublic note (R)

$z - Public note (R)

$3 - Materials specified (NR)

$6 - Linkage (NR)

$8 - Field link and sequence number (NR)

877 - ITEM INFORMATION—SUPPLEMENTARY MATERIAL (R)

Indicators

First - Undefined

- Undefined

Second - Undefined

- Undefined

Subfield Codes

$a - Internal item number (NR)

$b - Invalid or canceled internal item number (R)

$c - Cost (R)

$d - Date acquired (R)

$e - Source of acquisition (R)

$h - Use restrictions (R)

$j - Item status (R)

$l - Temporary location (R)

$p - Piece designation (R)

$r - Invalid or canceled piece designation (R)

$t - Copy number (NR)

$x - Nonpublic note (R)

$z - Public note (R)

$3 - Materials specified (NR)

$6 - Linkage (NR)

$8 - Field link and sequence number (NR)

878 - ITEM INFORMATION—INDEXES (R)

Indicators

First - Undefined

- Undefined

Second - Undefined

- Undefined

Subfield Codes

$a - Internal item number (NR)

$b - Invalid or canceled internal item number (R)

$c - Cost (R)

$d - Date acquired (R)

$e - Source of acquisition (R)

$h - Use restrictions (R)

$j - Item status (R)

$l - Temporary location (R)

$p - Piece designation (R)

$r - Invalid or canceled piece designation (R)

$t - Copy number (NR)

$x - Nonpublic note (R)

$z - Public note (R)

$3 - Materials specified (NR)

$6 - Linkage (NR)

$8 - Field link and sequence number (NR)

—Other Variable Fields (88X)—

880 - ALTERNATE GRAPHIC REPRESENTATION (R)

Indicators

First - Same as associated field

Second - Same as associated field

Subfield Codes

$6 - Linkage (NR)

$a-z - Same as associated field

$0-5 - Same as associated field

$7-9 - Same as associated field

MARC Acronyms

AACR	Anglo American Cataloguing Rules, esp. the original (1968) ed.
AACR2	Anglo American Cataloguing Rules, 2nd ed. (1978); rev. 1988 (AACR2R) and 1998
ACOC	Australian Committee on Cataloguing
A-G MARCit	see MARCit
ALA	American Library Association
AusMARC	Australian MARC; largely replaced by MARC21
Autocat	An electronic forum for the discussion of all questions relating to cataloguing and authority control in libraries
BDRB	see DCRB
BIBCO	Cooperative monographic cataloging program, a component of the Program for Cooperative Cataloging (LC), through which participants create cataloging records using mutually agreed upon standards
Big Red Books	LCSH (Library of Congress Subject Headings) in printed form
BL	British Library
BNB	British National Bibliography
CanMARC	see MARC
Catss	See MARCit
CCC	Canadian Committee on Cataloguing

CC:DA	Committee on Cataloging : Descriptive & Access of ALA, which develops proposals to JSC
CDS	Cataloging Distribution Service (LC)
CIP	Catalog(u)ing in Publication; data provided by national cataloguing agencies for printing on the verso of title pages; also incomplete MARC record based on that data; pronounced "sip" or "see eye pea"
CLA	Canadian Library Association
CONSER	An international cooperative serials cataloging program, now a component of Program for Cooperative Cataloging (LC); also used to refer to their manual.
CORC	Cooperative Online Resource Catalog, a metadata creation systems for websites (OCLC)
CPSO	Cataloging Policy and Support Office (LC)
CSB	Cataloging Service Bulletin (LC). ISSN 0160-8029.
DC	Dewey Classification or Dublin Core (the latter a minimum standard for bibliographic records); better to use DDC for Dewey Classification
DCRB	Descriptive Cataloging of Rare Books (LC manual); formerly BDRB (Bibliographic Description of Rare Books); both given in lower case
DDC	Dewey Decimal Classification
DLC	Code (NUC/OCLC/MARC) for the Library of Congress, according to the MARC Code List for Organizations, found in the 040 (cataloging source) field of MARC authority and bibliographic records created or updated by staff at the Library of Congress; "D" represents District of Columbia, where LC is located.
EAD	Encoded Archive Description
ESTC	English Short-Title Catalogue, database hosted by RLG; English-language publications and all

publications in Great Britain 1473-1800

FRBR — Functional Requirements of Bibliographic Records. an IFLA report

FTP — File transfer protocol: method of data transmission via the Internet

Green Book — Rules for Description Cataloging in the Library of Congress (1949)

GSAFD — Guidelines on subject access to individual works of fiction, drama, etc. (ALA). The code "gsafd" is used in the subfield 2 of MARC field 655 to indicate that the genre term used in that field comes from the list of genre headings included in GSAFD When genre term from the list is used in 655. these initials appear in $2

IFLA — International Federation of Library Associations and Institutions.

ISBD — International Standard for Bibliographic Description, from which the AACR punctuation marks come; initials following in parentheses indicate format for which intended. e.g. (G) general. (M) monographs

ISBN — International Standard Bibliographic Number (MARC 020)

Bowker's Frequently Asked Questions about the ISBN :

ISSN — International Standard Serials Number (MARC 022)

Library of Congress pamplet *ISSN is for Serials* :

JSC — Joint Steering Committee for AACR

LA — Library Association (British)

LC or LOC — Library of Congress. LC's Online Catalog

LCC — Library of Congress Classification

LCCN — Library of Congress Control Number (formerly Library of Congress Card Number). carried in MARC field 001 in records distributed by

Cataloging Distribution Service and in MARC field 010 also Library of Congress Cataloging Newsline, the electronic journal of the Cataloging Directorate

LCNA Library of Congress Name Authorities; originally LC's own name authority file, now maintained jointly with NACO

LCRI Library of Congress Rule Interpretations. The British Library and the National Library of Canada also have rule interpretations, which have been combined in AACR2 Decisions & Rule Interpretations published by ALA and CLA

LCSH Library of Congress Subject Headings

Mansell see NUC

MARBI Machine Readable Bibliographic Information committee; "the body within the American Library Association responsible for developing official ALA positions on standards for the representation in machine-readable form of bibliographic information. MARBI focuses its attention on the development of the MARC format."

MARC Machine Readable Cataloguing, coding for bibliographic information; MARC 21 ("21" for 21st century) currently harmonizes USMARC and CANMARC.

MARCit Bibliograhic utility featuring authority control owned by Auto-Graphics replacing Canada's Catss (formerly Utlas); unrelated software for creating MARC records from websites

MCD Music Cataloging Decisions; published by the Library of Congress, these are the music equivalent of the LCRIs

MeSH Medical Subject Headings (NLM).

NACO Cooperative name authority program, a component of PCC (LC) and responsible for the NAF"

NAF	Name Authority File or National Authority File (also known as LCNA)
NLC	National Library of Canada
NLM	National Library of Medicine or National Library of Medicine Classification (substitutes "W" for LCC's "R" for medicine; also adds "QS" through "QZ" for the pre-clinical sciences—biochemistry, anatomy, microbiology, pathology, etc.)
NUC	National Union Catalog (printed volumes, microfiche only from 1983); pre-1956 imprints also called Mansell for its publisher.
OCLC	OCLC Online Computer Library Center, Inc., international bibliographic service, based in Dublin, Ohio; proprietor of WorldCat. Began as Ohio College Library Center.
PCC	Program for Cooperative Cataloging (LC), its components are BIBCO, CONSER, NACO and SACO
Red Book	ALA Cataloguing Rules for Author and Title Entries (1949)
RI	see LCRI
RLG	Research Libraries Group
RLIN	Bibliographic database of RLG
RSN	Record sequence number; 001 and 010 at LC, 001 and 016 at NLC, 001 in other systems; other system numbers sometimes moved to 035
SACO	Subject Authority Cooperative Program, a component of PCC (LC), a conduit for submitting additions and changes to LCSH
SCM	Subject Cataloging Manual (LC) In three sections
SCM:C	Subject Cataloging Manual Classification
SCM:S	Subject Cataloging Manual. Shelflisting
SCM:SH	Subject Cataloging Manual. Subject Headings

SUDOC	Superintendent of Documents (U.S.) classification MARC 086 0
UBCIM	Universal Bibliographic Control and International MARC Core Programme at the International Federation of Library Associations and Institutions (IFLA). Its purpose is "to coordinate activities aimed at the development of systems and standards for bibliographic control at the national level and the international exchange of bibliographic data...."
UDC	Universal Decimal Classification, an European scheme which allows number building to express relationships between subjects
UKMARC	U.K. MARC format; likely to be superseded by MARC 21
UniMARC	International MARC format (IFLA); less used than MARC 21
USMARC	The United States MARC format, now MARC 21; previously LCMARC
Utlas	see MARCit
WLN	Washington/Western Library Network; former bibliographic utility featuring quality and authority control purchased by OCLC
WorldCat	